THE NEW REALITY OF WALL STREET

THE NEW REALITY OF WALL STREET

An Investor's Survival Guide to Triple
Waterfalls and Other Stock Market Perils

Donald G. M. Coxe

McGraw-Hill
New York   Chicago   San Francisco
Lisbon   London   Madrid   Mexico City   Milan
New Delhi   San Juan   Seoul   Singapore
Sydney   Toronto

3 4 5 6 7 8 9 0 DOC/DOC 0 9 8 7 6 5 4 3

ISBN 0-07-141753-2

This publication is designed to provide accurate and authoritative information in regard to the subject matter covered. It is sold with the understanding that neither the author nor the publisher is engaged in rendering legal, accounting, or other professional service. If legal advice or other expert assistance is required, the services of a competent professional person should be sought.

> *—From a Declaration of Principles jointly adopted*
> *by a Committee of the American Bar*
> *Association and a Committee of Publishers*

McGraw-Hill books are available at special quantity discounts to use as premiums and sales promotions, or for use in corporate training programs. For more information, please write to the Director of Special Sales, Professional Publishing, McGraw-Hill, Two Penn Plaza, New York, NY 10121-2298. Or contact your local bookstore.

Library of Congress Cataloging-in-Publication Data

Coxe, Donald.
   The new reality of Wall Street : an investor's survival guide to triple waterfalls and other stock market perils / by Donald Coxe.
       p. cm.
     ISBN 0-07-141753-2 (hc : perm paper)
     1. Stocks.   2. Investments.   I. Title.
     HG4661.C68 2003
     332—dc21

                                                        2002154983

The publisher and the author gratefully acknowledge permission from Dymocks Book Arcade, Ltd and Schocken Books, a division of Random House, Inc., to print excerpts from Richard H. Graves, *Bushcraft*, copyright Dymock's Book Arcade, Ltd and from HarperCollins Publishers, Inc. to print the excerpt from Jane Sneddon Little, *Eurodollars: The Money Market Gypsies*, copyright © 1975 Harper & Row.

This book is printed on recycled, acid-free paper containing a minimum of 50% recycled de-inked fiber.

For Judy

Contents

Preface

Woodcraft may be defined as the art of finding one's way in the wilderness and getting along well by utilizing Nature's storehouse. . . . As for book learning in such an art, it is useful only to those who do not expect too much of it. No book can teach a man how to swing an axe or follow a faint trail. . . . Yet a good book is the best stepping-stone for a beginner. . . . It gives a clear idea of general principles. It can show, at least, how not to do a thing—and there is a good deal in that—half of woodcraft, as of any other art, is in knowing what to avoid.

—Horace Kephart

So, YOU LOST BIG ON TECHNOLOGY STOCKS, and the same Wall Street people who told you to buy them and never told you to sell them now tell you they're about to come back strong, "when the economy comes back."

How 20th century of them.

The 1990s aren't coming back.

Neither is Nasdaq. The stock market that enriched corporate insiders beyond their wildest dreams and impoverished retail investors beyond their worst nightmares is no longer rewriting the rules on investing.

Three years of this century have produced three shocks: Technology and telecom stocks have experienced a crash of 1929 proportions; the United States fell into a brief recession followed by a problematic recovery, and a War on Terror began on 9/11. Those three shocks combined to produce a major global bear market.

And Baby Boomers are three years closer to retirement.

So what should you do now?

Unlike the successful investment books of the 1990s, this is a Survival Guide. It's modeled on two splendid wilderness books: Horace Kephart's classic *Camping & Woodcraft* (Macmillan, 1949), and Richard Graves's *Bushcraft* (Warner Books, 1974). Both those guides were for urban dwellers prepared to assume nature's risks in order to reap the rewards of living in the outdoors. They were based on the conviction that wilderness survival depended on knowing—and using—wisdom accumulated over generations.

This book is written on the same premise: Investors who knew—and used—investment wisdom accumulated over generations have come through the stock market collapse quite comfortably. Those who invested based on the new rules of the 1990s have been mauled by bears.

As you will learn, the Nasdaq crash is a precise—almost eerie—replay of six other crashes, including the Great Crash of 1929 and the Nikkei crash that began 60 years later. Its outcome was totally predictable to students of market lore. Those big-name strategists and pundits who failed to warn investors about the coming collapse chose to ignore history.

Because of those past crashes, we know a lot about the financial landscape ahead. It bears scant resemblance to the world of the 1990s. It's rocky out there, not verdant, but that means reduced cover for bears and other predators. There are opportunities for prudent foragers, but rewards won't come easily.

Wall Street and Silicon Valley got together in an undeclared partnership to wire the world, enrich themselves, and convince a whole new class of investors into trusting the partners with much of their life savings. It was a great deal for the partners, but a terrible deal for the investors. Never in the history of major stock markets were the rewards so skewed to insiders at the expense of outsiders.

This book will tell you how it happened, why it happened, and what you need to do to rebuild your savings.

As drab as the investment landscape may appear, it's safer for investors than it has been for five years. You didn't know how risky it was then, and you probably don't know how safe it is now. There are no lush and easy pickings like the crops of the 1990s, but there are fewer poisonous mushrooms and fewer bears around the blueberries.

You have learned that good times in the stock market don't last forever.
You will learn that bad times don't either.

Acknowledgments

THIS BOOK SUMS UP what I've learned in three decades of institutional investing. Much of what I picked up came from others—colleagues, clients, and competitors. I am grateful to them.

I am particularly appreciative of the encouragement and counsel of my colleagues within the BMO Financial Group. They are too numerous to mention, but I especially thank Gilles Ouellette, Bill Downe, Bill Leszinske, Gord Lackanbauer, Brian Steck, Sherry Cooper, Eric Tripp, Mike Miller, Randy Johnson, Thalia Kingsford, Cindy Holmes, Peter McNitt, Peter Morris, and Tom Wright.

Those who undertook the arduous task of evaluating the manuscript deserve special thanks, and I appreciate the comments and suggestions I received from Margaret Wente, Robert Klemkowsky, Chaviva Hosek, and Robert Helman. My editor, Kelli Christiansen, not only commissioned the book but was a great help with her analysis of the material as the book unfolded.

Writing a book of this scope while continuing work as portfolio strategist and fund manager meant reliance on extensive technical and editorial support. Angela Trudeau as researcher and editorial assistant, Patricia Treble as fact-checker, and Sandra Naccarato as chartist were wonderful. Any errors that remain are mine alone.

I have been writing about markets for as long as I've been managing money. That habit comes from the journalism training I got in my first job—as an Associate Editor at *National Review,* under the expert supervision of the Managing Editor, the patient Priscilla Buckley.

Above all, I am thankful for the unstinting support and wise editorial critiquing throughout this undertaking from my wife, Judy.

Donald G. M. Coxe
Chicago, Illinois
January 2003

Prologue

THE THIRD MILLENNIUM ARRIVED amid optimism and ecstasy, as leaders in politics, the academy, and business predicted a glorious new era.

But then, so had the Second Millennium.

The medieval enthusiasts who got themselves into trouble by predicting the onset of a New Age gave us a new word. They are known to historians as *chiliasts,* derived from the Greek word for 1000—the term for those who believed that the arrival of a special date meant special wonders.

There were various kinds of cults back then, but all involved an assumption that Heaven was headed for Earth—for good or ill. Many people divested themselves of their possessions in preparation for the Second Coming.

Those earlier ecstatics were in trouble when the year 1000 came and went. Those who'd sold out cheaply and had given to the less fortunate were understandably upset with the mystics who'd misled them. They tended to express their resentment in strong terms.

It's different this time—in two ways.

First, although this time millions of people also divested themselves of all or a substantial portion of their possessions, they didn't give their wealth to the poor. They gave it to a new class of new rich. The beneficiaries, with exquisite timing, exercised stock options on companies they managed whose period of earnings gains was about to turn into a period of earnings collapse.

Second, most of today's chiliasts have not been subject to serious abuse—physically, financially, or legally. Most retain their jobs, which means they are receiving a new round of stock options at today's depressed share prices, so they stand to win big all over again if stocks recover even modestly. If there is a justification for this process, it comes from words uttered in the 1st century: "That unto everyone which hath shall be given; and from him that hath not, even that he hath shall be taken away from him."

It took only a few weeks of the new century before the New Era fantasies collided with reality.

Since then, the stock market and economy have been badly beaten up. Those injuries came from the collective attempt of the stock markets and economies of the 1990s to defy one law.

Gravity.

At its peak (March 10, 2000), Nasdaq had a stated price-earnings ratio of 351 (though when the income statements of companies losing money were included, with stock option costs, its real level was more than 500 times earnings).

It was bound to fall of its own weight. The question was never *if* but *when*. By any measurement, it was—by far—the most absurdly overvalued stock index in the history of finance. Compare that stratospheric multiple with three other crashes: U.S. stocks in 1929 and 1987 and Japanese stocks in 1989. The price/earnings (p/e) ratio on the Dow Jones Industrials at the onset of the Great Depression was in the high 20s, as it was on October 19, 1987, the day the market fell 22.6 percent; at its peak, the ratio on the Tokyo Nikkei Index was 92.

Gravity finally took charge. Nasdaq's Moon shot had carried it so far from Earth's pull that when it rolled over and began its descent, it moved slowly at first. Then, like a space capsule, it accelerated as it reentered the atmosphere in its plunge toward terra firma.

Those with a respect for history found Nasdaq's costly meeting with gravity ironic.

Why?

Because the first recorded crash since the birth of stock markets inflicted big losses on the man who formulated the law of gravity, Sir Isaac Newton. What happened to England and to the scientist Einstein called the greatest mind of all time is instructive.

The South Sea Bubble (1720) was a scheme so preposterous that most historians still find it hard to explain how so many people could fall for the idea that a private company—one of the first "joint stock companies"—

could make its investors rich by assuming the national debt. Sir Isaac's experience tells us what we need to know to understand market manias.

As president of the Royal Society, Newton was at the epicenter of science, technology, and London society. As the South Sea enthusiasm spread, he joined his friends in "taking a flutter" on South Sea shares.

When those shares rose rapidly in value, Newton decided to take a handsome profit. He had analyzed the scheme and concluded it was, at the very least, highly risky.

But South Sea shares kept going up, and the conversations in the coffeehouses and at Royal Society gatherings were all about the huge profits his friends and associates were earning from this new phenomenon of joint stock companies. When Newton admitted he had sold, his friends and fellow scientists smirked, bragging of their own huge gains.

He could finally stand the peer pressure no longer, and so he bought back in as the shares were nearing the magic level of £1000 each. Peer pressure proved to be the irresistible force against what should have been the immovable object of the world's most massive intellect.

Newton was among the nation's biggest losers as the shares crashed to £135. As he mourned to friends thereafter, he found he could understand the movement of heavenly bodies but not of markets on Earth.

There was a parliamentary investigation, and the chancellor of the exchequer (finance minister) and some of the company's board of directors were sent to the Tower of London for their parts in what was declared to be a scheme of fraud.

It was convenient for the bruised egos of those who had lost heavily to define the whole game as fraud. But it is doubtful that fraud was the key to the South Sea fiasco. The real cause was the build-up of a critical mass of optimism, faith, and fanaticism that swept the land, seducing the wise and foolish alike.

That remains the pattern. In all the great crashes that have succeeded the South Sea, outright fraud has been a relatively minor component. In each case, the cry was, "Hang the crooks!" and there were show trials and punishments.

But in no case, including Nasdaq's collapse, have most of those involved been willing to admit that human frailty, not criminality, was the primary driving force. That these manias recur through history illustrates Santayana's dictum that those who will not learn from history are destined to repeat it.

Which elements of the South Sea Bubble and subsequent crashes reasserted themselves in Nasdaq?

- *A new kind of financial instrument. In 1720 it was shares in publicly traded "joint stock companies" whose prices were widely quoted, allowing investors to measure the growth in their own wealth—or how much they were missing out on by not being in.*

  In the 1990s it was technology stocks; yes, there had been tech stocks before, but not so many, and not since technology had become a part of everyday living. They were what they claimed to be: the Next New Thing. Among the most enthusiastic investors in tech stocks were those who were the most enthusiastic about technology, biotechnology, and the Internet.

- *A sense of a New Era being born. In 1720, England had a new king, and its stature in Europe after the Treaty of Utrecht promised a sustained age of peace, at a time of exciting scientific progress.*

  In the 1990s, America as victor in the Cold War would preside over an era of global peace. The new president was no mere Cold War retread but a forward-looking Baby Boomer, who shared the enthusiasm, optimism, priorities, and fun-loving style of the Sixties Generation.

- *In 1720 investors had never experienced a crash, and had the money to back their bets on a bright future.*

  The 1990s soon forgot about the Crash of 1987, which had been a brief flap that did not derail the economy, in part because the general public was not deeply involved in the stock market. The previous crash was in 1973–1974, but that was the Nixon crash, and the Boomers had, at the time, little political power and very little invested in the stock market.

- *In 1720 the magic appeal was a concept of wealth creation that, though hard to explain, seemed easy to understand. Its essence was an entirely new approach, and people wanted to believe that what was new was automatically good.*

  In the 1990s what was new was obviously good, even if you didn't understand how it worked. Many people who bought shares of, say, JDS Uniphase or Cisco would have had trouble explaining what the company actually did; even those who understood their hot products had only the vaguest idea how technology companies could make large, sustainable long-term profits in product lines in which there were few real barriers to entry. As Andy Grove, co-founder of Intel had written in *Only the Paranoid Survive,* every night he worried about some guy in a garage who would come up with the killer invention. Intel had survived several tech boom/bust cycles. Paranoia was almost nonexistent in the rest of Silicon Valley in this cycle: Euphoria had crowded it out.

- *In 1720 there was momentum, excitement, and wealth beyond dreams of avarice. South Sea shares were going up so fast that they swept doubt before them, and everybody who was anybody was in the game.*

  In the 1990s tech billionaires were greater heroes than rock stars or professional athletes; tech billionaires were cool. Young people labored long hours for tech start-ups, each hoping to be the next centimillionaire or even billionaire. Nor were these dreams mere fantasies: For a while, more new billionaires were being minted in months than had been created in all previous American history. Nasdaq's upward momentum blew away doubt and skepticism.

- *In 1720 there was a virtual unanimity of opinion among the elites that nothing could go wrong. Although dissent was not banned by law, peer group pressure among the wealthy commercial class and the aristocracy was so powerful that almost no prominent people stood up to ask whether the emperor really had clothes.*

  In the 1990s, when Warren Buffett, the most successful American portfolio investor in history, rejected the entire technology industry as an investment concept, he was derided as old and out-of-date; ditto for self-made billionaire Sam Zell. Only a handful of academics challenged the prevailing ethos. Endowment funds of leading universities switched major percentages of their portfolios into venture capital investing in start-up companies, and faculties were universally supportive. If one was with it, one was in it.

- *After the crash, a parliamentary investigation, criminal charges, and an epidemic of finger-pointing.*

  And the bleat goes on.

  A little more than 280 years after Newton learned that financial gravity was as powerful a force as natural gravity, the process was repeated on a grander, global scale.

  It had reappeared from time to time during the intervening centuries. In the 19th century there were booms and busts tied to overbuilding of canals and railways. In each case, optimism led to intoxication, leading to a massive hangover.

Rule I. Gravity always asserts itself. That its assertion produces such
    widespread financial ruin comes from investors' refusal to follow
    a rule enunciated by another great scientist. . . .
Rule II. Einstein said that compound interest is the greatest force in
    the universe. Compound interest is at the root of successful
    wealth building, whether one invests in stocks or bonds. But it
    only works as a wealth-builder within reasonable numeric limits.
    For example, when the S&P rose more than 20 percent for five
    straight years, a feat never before achieved, it raised near-insuper-
    able challenges for the next and succeeding years. Nasdaq's 88
    percent leap in 1999 could not be compounded higher, and there-
    fore the outcome was reverse compounding—a force as potent as
    compounding.

In each of history's boom-bust cycles, the capital assets built during the
boom fell to values that a new generation of entrepreneurs could use profitably, and a new cycle began.

The Russian economist Nikolai Kondratieff, working in the 1920s,
observed these cycles and constructed an historical pattern of long waves.
He correctly forecast the Great Depression, for which Stalin praised him.
But he then predicted that based on the long waves, capitalism would come
back. Since Stalin had assured his followers that the Depression's onset signaled the death throes of capitalism, Kondratieff's forecast was anathema.
He sent the economist to death in Siberia. Kondratieff remains, as far as I
know, the only economist murdered for making an accurate forecast. It is
said (by cynics) that his successors have learned from his example. That
explains why the economic consensus has never predicted the coming of a
recession and why economists have trouble agreeing on when it came and
when it ended. Bearers of bad news used to be beheaded. Now they are just
denied tenure—or attentive audiences.

These major crashes are economically and financially transforming
events, and, as such, are structurally different from the normal bull/bear
blow-offs tied to economic cycles and the normal excesses of fear and
greed.

Each modern replication of this collective rush into the abyss had
enormous effects on the economy and on capital markets. In particular,
each pointed the way to the investment strategies that would be most successful . . . not just for ensuing years, but for ensuing decades.

As Churchill said, "The farther backwards you can look, the farther
forward you are likely to see." This book is meant to be a practical

Investor's Survival Guide, which means its extensive discussion of past folly is not just history for the curious to savor. It is market lore every investor can use, like the lore accumulated over centuries that sustains users of the wilderness.

It will be a long time before the next Triple Waterfall hits the capital markets. It may be a long time before the next big stock market plunge. In the meantime, the investment landscape will be littered with both the carcasses and the opportunities created by Nasdaq's collapse.

CHAPTER 1

A Taxonomy of Bears

The signs animals leave on the ground can be more revealing than any book written by man, but unfortunately few people are able to see these signs and even fewer still can read them.

—R. GRAVES

MOST INVESTORS LOSE MONEY—and many are wiped out—in bear markets. This chapter, which could as well have been called the Investor's Basic Survival Guide for Bear Encounters, describes the different kinds of bears.

It can be a matter of life and death for hikers to know which species of bears' territory they are invading. Similarly, investors should learn to distinguish the kind of bear attacks the market faces.

If you're in the Rockies, you watch out for black bears and, most important of all, grizzlies; in Alaska, you look for kodiaks and polar bears; in Churchill, Manitoba, you know when the polar bears are coming—by the hundreds—and you prepare accordingly.

For investors, there are four basic breeds of bears, but one of them has two subgroups, making five classifications of Furry Financial Furies altogether.

One reason so many investors get mauled by bears is that Wall Street not only fails to warn of bear attacks, but even resists labeling a falling market as a bear market until investor losses have already reached painful levels.

The Street is like lodge operator who avoids frightening customers by talking of bear risk. The Street has euphemisms for falling markets: They begin as "pauses," then become "pullbacks," then "corrections." The Street forbears saying "bear."

When Nasdaq was plunging in April 2000, the Street was virtually unanimous that this was merely a "correction." I wrote at the time: "The term 'correction' is itself interesting. It implies a change from doing something wrong to doing something right. . . . Was the stock market wrong when it went up and right when it went down?"

Maybe so.

The bear groups:

Teddy Bears
Baby Bears
Papa Bears
Mama Bears (Mini and Big)

Despite their seeming playfulness, these are deadly serious classifications. They can be as crucial for investors' wealth as the differences in size, gender, and breed of bear can be for hikers who come upon actual bears.

Why try to classify market slumps into such bear categories?

Because most of the literature on bear markets lumps all downturns together, and this makes it difficult for novices to understand the nature of bear risks at any given time.

Know your bear.

TEDDY BEARS

Teddy Bear markets are childishly explosive tantrums. The financial outbursts cause temporary fear and pain and look, in retrospect, absurdly overdone. *The stock market may change leadership, but it does not change direction,* because nothing fundamental is involved, and the outburst is not the culmination of years of speculative excess. Teddy Bears are no picnic; they resemble playground fights, not gang wars.

The centennial of teddy bears was observed last year. (Ever alert for a quick buck, The U.S. Postal Service issued four commemorative stamps.) According to the *Chicago Tribune,* these toys were named for Teddy Roosevelt, who, on a bear hunting trip to Mississippi in 1902, failed to bag a bear. The trip sponsors found a bear, lassoed it, and tied it to a tree, inviting him to shoot it. Teddy shouted "Spare the bear!" and freed it. A cartoonist drew the scene, depicting a frightened cub. Thus was born the teddy bear industry, which produces one of the four most popular collectibles.

Many park rangers see teddies differently. They are appalled that so many city dwellers raised on furry toys expect bears to be cute. Worse, there have been cases of tenderfeet finding cubs and trying to pet them, with horrific consequences.

Since teddy bears are named after a president, it is fitting that this history of stock market bears begin with accounts of two outbursts tied to presidents.

The Ike Teddy: September 24, 1955
The Ike Teddy (see Chart 1-1) came when President Eisenhower suffered a heart attack while vacationing in Colorado bear country. He was sequestered for seven weeks in Fitzsimmons Army Medical Center. When he returned to Washington, he reassured the nation that he was in good health.

CHART 1-1   S&P 500 (January 1, 1955 to December 31, 1955)

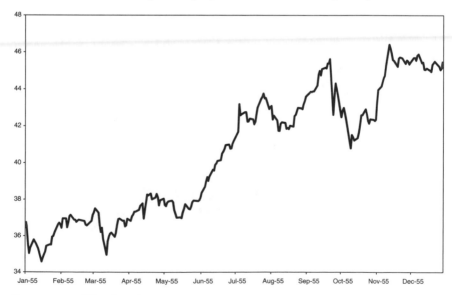

Data courtesy of Bloomberg Associates.

The market's brief bout of panic produced the biggest stock market trading volume since 1933. The "reasoning" behind this emotional outburst was the fear that if Ike died, Vice President Nixon would become president and would be defeated by a Democrat in the 1956 election. At that time, Wall Street was dominated by a Wasp, white-shoe, country-club Republican elite. Basically, their fear of Adlai Stevenson, former governor of Illinois (who had run in 1952 and would run again in 1956), was irrational.

The U.S. economy was on a baby-boom roll, and a Democrat in the White House would not have derailed it.

The JFK Teddy: March 1962

Another onset of Wall Street Demophobia produced the JFK Teddy (see Chart 1-2).

In March 1962, President Kennedy intervened in the steel industry contract negotiations. He pressured the United Steelworkers to accept what he called a noninflationary agreement, which would not only hold back steel price increases but would be a guide to other big pending labor agreements. (Yes, back then the steel industry was *that* big and *that* important to the national economy.)

CHART 1-2   S&P 500 (January 1, 1962 to December 31, 1962)

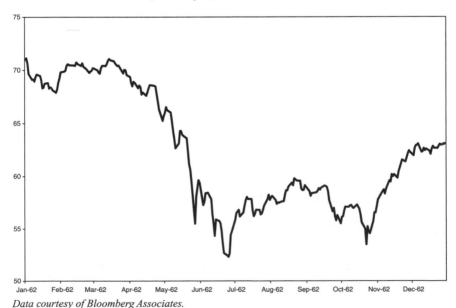

Data courtesy of Bloomberg Associates.

Within days, U.S. Steel boosted steel prices 3.5 percent, which was swiftly matched by most other steel companies. Kennedy's response was to unleash the FBI on the industry, sending agents to the homes of steel company executives, threatening antitrust prosecutions and announcing that the Pentagon would switch its procurement from companies who raised prices to those who held the line.

Most important for a jittery market, he let the press know of a supposedly off-the-record comment he uttered in the heat of the "crisis": "My father always told me that all businessmen were sons of bitches, but I never believed it till now." (Joe Kennedy's fortune, it is worth noting, was built on bootlegging during Prohibition, so he might have had a jaundiced view of business ethics.)

That "quotation" proved to have more emotional impact than the lofty parallel Sorensenisms in JFK's inaugural address ("Ask not what your country can do . . . etc."). It shocked the stock market into paranoia that the Democrats were going to launch a war on the business community.

In reality, Mr. Kennedy was much more sophisticated—and had a greater understanding of the workings of the economy—than most members of the Wall Street old-money elite. He was the author of the tax cut that got the economy moving, and his intellectual rationale for it would be later used by Ronald Reagan in gaining congressional approval for his more ambitious tax cuts, the key component of the "Reagan Revolution."

Although leading Wall Street voices warned of a major new bear market, it was, of course, a splendid buying opportunity. The ingredients of a true bear market did not exist. Wall Street was just being childish.

The Jimmy Teddy: September 1967

The hot new idea of the mid-1960s was conglomerates—companies that grew fast by gobbling up other companies, without regard for what industry they were in. The theory was that you achieved "synergy" by putting together seemingly unrelated companies and industries, so that, in terms of company earnings, $2 + 2 = 5$.

The conglomerate fad produced substantial overvaluation within one group of equities, and a stock market correction *that was a true correction.* (See Chart 1-3.) It was not a major bear market, because it was (1) localized, and (2) not part of any broader economic and financial deterioration. It was a warning that the market was getting frothy and that "concept" stocks were becoming all too voguish, but it was not the Beginning of Something Big.

CHART 1-3   Ling-Temco-Vought (June 1964 to September 30, 1969)

Data courtesy of Bloomberg Associates.

That conglomerates could have threatened the American business establishment and become the glamour stocks of Wall Street would seem absurd to today's generation of investors, accustomed to believing that glamour means technology.

Companies such as Ling-Temco-Vought and ITT built themselves a cachet in the go-go stock market of that era—the first in which mutual funds were significant players. Bernie Cornfeld, a great mountebank, was wowing investors with his pitch, "Do you sincerely want to be rich?"

Slick operators like Jimmy Ling understood that as long as their own company's stock had a higher price-earnings ratio (p/es) than the broad market, it could grow seemingly endlessly by buying up companies with much lower earnings multiples. Each new acquisition was "accretive to earnings." They told the gullible that they weren't just acquisitors: The head office supervised capital spending budgets and provided legal and accounting services to all parts of the empire. These last-listed services, seemingly innocent, were crucial, because they needed to ensure that per-share earnings rose every quarter to merit the label "growth stock," even though their diverse collection of companies was deeply exposed to cyclical organizations. That was why they had such low p/es that they were vulnerable to takeovers by the conglomerators. A packing plant whose stock had never sold at more than nine times earnings could be bought by a conglomerate whose p/es was 22, and it gave the conglomerate an immediate gain in earnings per share.

Ling kept expanding LTV with buyouts. At the peak, his company included a major airline, a huge sporting goods company, a major defense contractor, the third biggest meat packer, and many smaller corporations. He finally blew it by bidding to acquire aging, adipose, polluting Jones & Laughlin Steel at a price that suggested the company was really an alchemical marvel that could turn iron ore into gold. The bubble burst. The Teddy Bear's stuffing was exposed, and soon the floor was littered with the detritus of a market promotion gone bad.

As painful as the conglomerate collapse was to the stock market, however, it did not create a true bear market, because the pain was localized. Furthermore, there were so many serious market analysts and investors who had ridiculed the conglomerators' claims of synergy that they enjoyed the humiliation of the "fast-buck boys" and saw this as the stock market punishing miscreants—precisely what healthy markets should do.

Teddy Bears are vexing, but there's no need to give up on stocks because of them. They'll eventually scuttle off and leave you to picnic in peace and prosperity.

BABY BEARS: THE EUROBEARS

A Baby Bear is a vicious mauler. He gets very angry ("Who's been eating my porridge?") and inflicts real wounds before he's driven from the scene. He gets that way because he is a *Bank Bear* who emerges when the banking system is in trouble, and he is out to wound or kill. His attack is a *financial*, not an *economic* event.

The Greenspan Baby Bear: October 19, 1987

The classic Baby Bear was the 1987 crash. The Dow Jones Industrials fell 508 points—22.6 percent—in one terrifying day—compared to 12.8 percent on the worst day in 1929 (see Chart 1-4). Stock markets across the world crumbled as panic went global. To put the scale of that plunge into perspective, a 20 percent decline over any period of time is generally used as the threshold for calling a sell-off a true bear market. That the market could fall more than the requisite amount to be labeled a bear in one day was unthinkable. It had never happened before, nor has it happened since.

Had central bankers not rallied resources, the global financial system might have collapsed. At the time, I was a portfolio strategist for Wertheim, a leading Wall Street research shop. (I recall the anguish of that day vividly,

CHART 1-4   S&P 500 (July 1, 1987 to December 31, 1987)

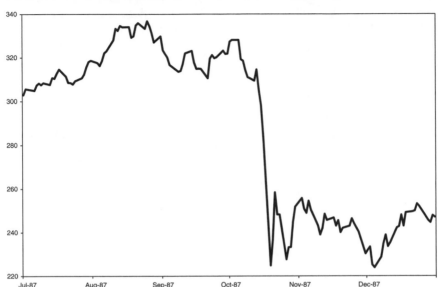

Data courtesy of Bloomberg Associates.

and I'll come back to it in Chapter 7, in the section "Eurodollars and the Crash of 1987").

The market opened under the weight of an unprecedented volume of sell orders driven from the overnight collapse in the S&P 500 Futures and Options contracts traded in Chicago and Europe. The so-called cash market—the New York Stock Exchange—could not handle such a torrent. This was the first time that the market most investors thought of as "the real stock market" was overwhelmed by the violent activity in synthetic contracts traded in an exchange (the Chicago Mercantile Exchange) that had previously been known as the home of contracts in pork bellies and cattle.

The market plunged 200 points, then rallied so that it was down just 128 points at noon. An hour later it was down 185, and the rout was on. By day's end, more than $500 billion had been wiped from stock market capitalizations. Some leading brokerage houses were in serious financial difficulties.

President Reagan was called to the cameras to calm the markets, but the Great Communicator was, for once, not up to the job. He seemed befuddled, and said he understood that many investors were "taking profits."

During and immediately after the debacle, the media were awash in doomsayers who spoke of "another '29" and other such auguries of despair. Few analyzed what had really happened.

Indeed, little has been written about that collapse that explained how it happened and why it could happen again. A commission headed by Nicholas Brady pinned the blame on the large volume of trading arising from so-called portfolio insurance arrangements in which active trading firms used the futures and options contracts to back or hedge their stock positions. Some Pied Pipers at that time had claimed that you could achieve 100 percent protection of your stock portfolio against loss by skillfully balancing those positions.

As long as you didn't have much company.

If too many people buy heavy insurance, and the risk they're insured against turns out to be bigger than the insurers imagined, the system implodes. Portfolio insurance had developed rapidly during the early years of what would be the biggest bull market of all time, and nobody involved in using or issuing anticipated anything like October 1987.

This naïvely perilous concept made a bad condition much worse that day, but the real problem was a crisis in the dollar itself, as foreign holders rushed to exit from the greenback by unloading their holding of eurodollars. That, in effect, was the iceberg hitting the *Titanic,* and the much-publicized portfolio insurance problems simply exposed the inadequacy of the lifeboats.

Baby Bear crashes are financial crises born in the baby of money markets—the eurodollar market. Crises develop because of the gigantic scale of that market, which is virtually unregulated. The big institutions that use it develop great faith in its functioning, and sometimes that faith turns out to be misplaced.

In particular, major players develop great faith in synthetic financial instruments called "derivatives." Derivatives are artificial financial products tied to the performance of "real" financial products, such as stocks, bonds, and currencies. They come in many forms, such as options, futures, and swaps. They're useful tools for spreading and controlling financial risk. But like everything else created by humans, they can break down. They become perilous precisely when too many major players have acquired too much faith in them and are betting too much on their invulnerability.

That misplaced confidence in the stability of financial derivatives recalls the prescient observations of John Kenneth Galbraith, in *The Atlantic Monthly* of January 1987:

History may not repeat itself, but some of its lessons are inescapable. One is that in the world of high and confident finance little is ever really new. The controlling fact is not the tendency to brilliant invention; the controlling fact is the shortness of public memory, especially when it contends with a euphoric desire to forget.

Little has changed in 2000 years. According to some authors, Cicero's last words, just before Mark Antony's hired assassins cut his throat, were: *"Memoria populi parva est."* The people's memory is short.

The Russian Bear: Summer and Autumn 1998
The Russian Bear was the most recent Baby Bear. (See Chart 1-5.) The Russian default during the summer was followed by the collapse of a major hedge fund that arrogantly called itself Long Term Capital Management. (It was a short-term player that was destined to be in business for only a short time because it relied on a short history of finance and proved to be an incompetent manager of capital.)

This was a true eurodollar-driven financial crisis (discussed in "Monetarism, 1975–1989" in Chapter 6) that savaged the stock market briefly. It

Chart 1-5   S&P 500 (January 31, 1998 to December 1, 1998)

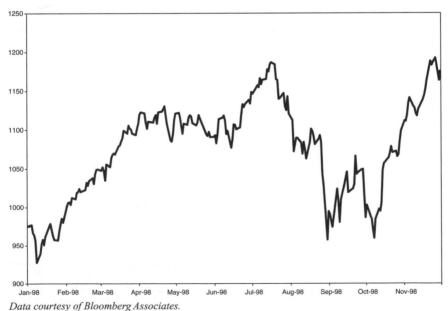

Data courtesy of Bloomberg Associates.

did not mean the end of the bull market. Indeed, the people most frightened in October were a few insiders on Wall Street and the top people at the Federal Reserve. In fact, this was a case of a few overvalued and overpaid elitists in Greenwich, Connecticut, who had great connections, caused a near panic, and got bailed out. Financial historians would probably have called it one of the most unseemly episodes in American finance had the next four years not supplied enough outrageous stories to scandalize the most cynical reporter.

The winning investment strategy in a Baby Bear market is to watch the TED spread (see "The TED Spread: Global Finance's Thermometer" in Chapter 7) on a day-to-day basis. Because it measures risk in the financial system—by showing the spread in yields between eurodollar deposits and Treasury bills—the TED has an unfailing record for showing when the system is in trouble and for registering an "All Clear" after the crisis has passed. As long as the TED is widening—going up—equity investors should be cautious, and should be reducing exposure to long-duration stocks (see "Duration and Risk in Bonds and Stocks" in Chapter 10). Only after the TED has fallen back sharply is it safe to increase equity exposure.

The Baby Bear is a TED Spread Bear—but definitely not a Teddy Bear.

PAPA BEARS

The Papa Bear is the end-of-economic-cycle bear, and he never fails to appear when a recession is coming (see Chart 1-6). He's stuffed with salmon and blueberries and ready to hibernate. He only appears in advance of a recession and goes back into hibernation a few months before a *sustained* economic recovery begins.

Paul Samuelson's most famous observation was his sneer that "Wall Street indexes predicted all nine out of the last five recessions." What the Nobel economist was alleging was that all bear markets are driven by fears of impending recession: In our terms, they would all be Papas. His epigram is enshrined in the economists' pantheon, because it was so self-serving; the economic consensus had never predicted a recession in advance, and that futility continues to this day, more than three decades after Samuelson's utterance.

The typical postwar economic cycle comes in stages:

1. The existence of the recession becomes apparent.
2. The Fed slashes interest rates and expands the money supply.

Chart 1-6   S&P 500 (January 1, 1979 to September 1, 1982)

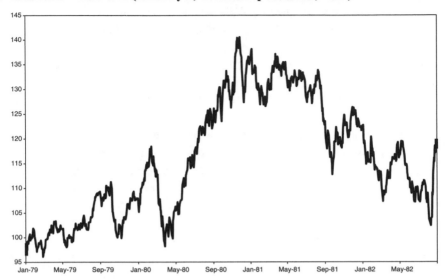

Data courtesy of Bloomberg Associates.

3. Remaining excess levels of inventory get worked off amid rising demand, but new factory production continues to shrink, producing more layoffs.

4. Final demand from consumers becomes so strong that retail, wholesale, and, ultimately, factory inventories shrink.

5. Factories expand production to meet soaring demand, creating new jobs.

6. Factory and office-building vacancies are absorbed and new construction booms.

7. Prices of products rise, starting with raw materials, then semifinished goods, then finished goods.

8. Credit demand becomes intense.

9. It is now time for the Fed "to take away the punch bowl," in the classic formulation of Fed chairman McChesney Martin.

The Papa Bear is drawn from hibernation by the whiff of rising interest rates and rising inflation, mixing with the background scent of still-rising stock prices. He emerges, feeds heartily, and then disappears from the scene until the cycle has ended.

The most recent Papa Bear appeared in 2000. The Mini-Mama collapse of technology stocks exposed vast overinvestment in technology gear. Business demand collapsed, and the tech stock plunge took some of the edge off consumer optimism. The entire stock market began to follow Nasdaq's lead down—roughly 10 months ahead of the onset of a recession that wouldn't be certified as such until July 2002. Papa knew better.

Papa appeared to go back into hibernation after 9/11, but it turned out to be a rarity—a mere Papa pause. He reemerged in February 2002, amid fears of a renewed global economic slowdown and talk of a U.S. "double dip" recession.

MAMA BEARS

The female of the Bear species is far deadlier than the male. In particular, a Grizzly Mama with cubs is the most dangerous large mammal in the Lower 48 States. Campers and investors should walk, not run, from her. Better still, they should try to confine their activities to times and places where Mamas are unlikely to appear.

The most vicious stock market bears are Mamas. There are two kinds: Mini-Mamas and Big Mamas.

Mini-Mamas

They only appear at the advent of Triple Waterfall collapses, which we'll discuss in the next chapter. They are the avenging bears who keep killing and devouring until an entire belief system has been destroyed. They can produce recessions or depressions. They are Mini-Mamas, despite their ferocity, because they confine their hunting to one industry or stock group, but they are major bears because their appearance means that a belief system and ethos will be wiped out.

There have been four clearly defined Mini-Mamas in the past century: the Triple Waterfall plunges of gold, silver, and oil stocks, and Nasdaq's collapse.

When gold, silver, and oil stocks collapsed, it meant that the inflation phobia of the 1970s had been vanquished. That was the sea change in belief that was needed for the unfolding of the 18-year disinflationary bull market in equities and the 20-year disinflationary bull market in bonds.

When Nasdaq lost more than three-quarters of its value, it was convincing evidence that the New Era euphoria of the 1990s had been crushed, taking with it the equity bull market. The next bull market will be built on a new belief system. Like the making of fine wine, building such a system out of the wreckage of smashed illusions is a process that cannot be hurried.

Big Mamas
There have been three Big Mama Bears since World War I: the Triple Waterfall of 1929–1933, which led to the Great Depression; the Triple Waterfall of 1972–1975, which was a major cause of what proved to be the worst recession since the Depression; and the Japanese Triple Waterfalls of 1989 to the present. Each of these Big Mama attacks produced financial and economic catastrophe.

Mama Bears are the ursine equivalent of Dresden-style bombing. They kill the guilty and the innocent alike, and continue to ravage until the core beliefs that allowed the Triple Waterfall to move beyond the Optimism stage (as discussed in "Optimism" in Chapter 2) have been totally eradicated.

STRUCTURAL, NOT URSINE BEARS?

What about "structural bear markets," a term heard frequently since Nasdaq rolled over and commenced its death plunge?

The esteemed Ned Davis uses this term to describe long sweeps of stock market history in which the market essentially went nowhere. The most recent was January 1966 to August 1982. At the beginning of that period, the Dow Jones Industrials were at 970, and at the end they were at 776. (According to some calculations, at that point the venerable index, adjusted for inflation, was back roughly to where it had been at its peak in 1929. In 16 years it went to the 1000 range 25 times and swiftly retreated.)

Davis and other market mavens believe we entered a period of structural bear markets in 1998, when the Advance/Decline line on the New York Stock Exchange broke down. (That Advance/Decline line is the scorecard of trading on an index or exchange; it compares the number of stocks going up in a given day or week with the number going down, and expresses that number in a chart. In a true bull market, the line keeps going up, because more stocks are rising than falling. When the reverse occurs, the market is narrowing, and is preparing to enter a bear phase. It is a truly democratic market index, because it lumps together all stocks on the exchange, big and small. A rise in General Electric on a day can be more than offset on the Advance/Decline line by the fall of two little companies.)

Thereafter, although most market indices—led by the levitating Nasdaq—went to new highs, most stocks did not. This failure of the broad market to "confirm" the indices was the sign that the market's underpinnings were beginning to erode.

"Structural bear market" is a useful term for this phenomenon, but within such long market periods, there are intervening bullish and bearish periods—of differing types. As such, the term isn't particularly helpful to any investor except a major institution that will be around for centuries to characterize the whole period as a bear market. Market historians can use such sweeping terminology, but ordinary mortals need more precision.

Although, all told, the 1970s were not a good period to be investing in most U.S. stocks, there were some splendid rallies. From the low of 577 in 1974, the Dow leaped to 1014 in 1976—nearly a three-quarters jump. It also rose more than 30 percent from its 1978 low, to fail again at the 1000 level in 1981. These were more than brief short-covering rallies, they were powerful *failing* rallies, offering investors great opportunities.

Moreover, as I can attest, the period after 1974 was a splendid time to be investing in most Canadian and Australian stocks, and in such U.S. stock groups as oils, gold, chemicals, agribusiness, and forest products. A broad-brush dismissal of the period as a structural bear market would have blinded the investor to great opportunities. I was a money manager in Canada during that period, and our clients were happy campers, regularly earning double-digit returns.

The ursine categories cover the ways to lose serious money. A structural bear market covers a long period in which it is more difficult—but by no means impossible—to make serious money. *We are probably in such a period now, but there are lots of investment opportunities.*

2

Triple Waterfalls

In thick fog or fast-falling snow, the best of men may go astray for the lack of a faithful needle. Make it a rule, then, an iron rule, of wilderness life, never to leave your bed in the morning without compass, jackknife and waterproof matchbox filled.

—H. KEPHART

WATERFALLS ARE FOR WATCHING, not navigating.

Canoeists exit from rivers when the water flow accelerates alarmingly, signaling a coming waterfall, or a series of waterfalls. They portage around the cataracts and resume paddling where the river is navigable.

We are living downstream from a financial Triple Waterfall.

The defining event of our economy and our capital markets was the spectacular rise and fall of technology and telecom shares. With Nasdaq down as much as 79 percent from its high in March 2000, most investment commentary—and most of Wall Street's sales materials—talks of a "burst bubble." Now that the bursting is over, the thinking goes, so is the problem. All that's needed now is an economic recovery to get Nasdaq at least modestly healthy, providing leadership for a new bull market.

Not so.

Triple Waterfalls aren't mere bubbles. *They are financial pandemics that take not months, not years, but decades to run their course.* An understanding of Triple Waterfall behavior is the most useful basis for sound investment policy formulation for the early decades of the Third Millennium.

Triple Waterfall is the term used by some technical analysts to describe the chart pattern of a very special kind of boom/bust event. Most analysts call it "bubble-bursting," because the collapse ends a bubble era.

But bursting is not what happens in financial markets when a major market excess is expunged. The process is a long drama in the form of a three-act tragedy on the Greek model, as described by Aristotle in his *Poetics:*

> A tragedy is the imitation of an action that is serious, and complete in itself . . . with incidents arousing pity and terror, with which to accomplish its purgation of these emotions. . . .
>
> Tragedy is an imitation of a whole and complete action of some amplitude . . . which has a beginning, a middle, and an end.

The beginning of Triple Waterfalls is "New Era" ebullience, which is swiftly corrupted into *hubris,* the overweening pride that corrupts the process of analysis and reasoning that operates as a restraint on misconduct. The middle stage is the beginning of the punishment for hubris: two deep stock market plunges, each followed by a rally that fizzles before it can reverse the market drop. The end is a long, remorseless period of punishment and pain. (Forgiveness was not a significant component of Greek religious beliefs. If you enraged Olympians, you had to endure terrible punishment.)

The buildup and plunge that make Triple Waterfalls such panoramic market events are driven by the spread of *Shared Mistake,* an overarching belief system that gradually coalesces among intellectual, business, and political elites. Shared Mistake is one of those blessedly infrequent mass illusions when near unanimity about the market's current and longer-range bullish prospects engulfs Wall Street, industry, the media, and the intellectual elites.

The participation of the intellectual elites—who ordinarily take scant notice of Wall Street—is what distinguishes Shared Mistake from ordinary market froth and folly. When the elites join in, then government is also drawn in as supporter, cheerleader, and even enforcer, and the counterbalancing forces within democracy that promote stability and moderation are eroded. The coziness of Big Business with the Republican administrations of the 1920s was a big factor in the powerful bull market of that time. The coziness of Silicon Valley with the Clinton administration was a big factor in the powerful bull market of our own time. So strong was that relationship that it had a big influence upon changing American policies toward China.

Each plunge takes the market to a new low, and the last, killing drop takes years—usually decades—to complete.

Note the three separate cascades of the Nasdaq decline in Chart 2-1, and the two strong, failing rallies.

CHART 2-1   Nasdaq (October 1, 1997 to December 31, 2002)

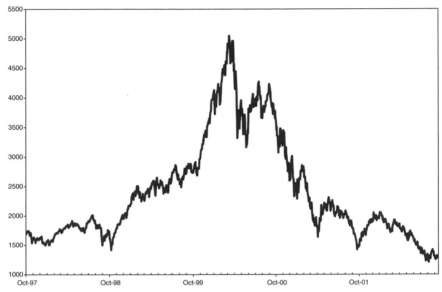

Data courtesy of Bloomberg Associates.

It is a cascading collapse in three stages, and marks the end of an entire era. It's good there have been so few, because they are so catastrophic. What makes them so lethal is their three-part performance—three plunges, interrupted by two rallies. Those rallies are really forms of torture: They tantalize wounded investors, who still hold on to the belief system that must ultimately be smashed to smithereens. During those rallies, investors return to the market and "average down," in the vain hope that the good days are about to return and they will be able to recoup. The Triple Waterfall continues until nearly all those who once believed have given up, or moved on, or died.

There are six stages to a Triple Waterfall, as Chart 2-2 shows, with typical timelines:

1.   Optimism: 2 years
2.   Faith: 2 years
3.   Fanaticism: 1 to 2 years
4.   Sudden Shock: First Cascade, 6 to 12 months
5.   Last Chance: Second Cascade, 2 to 10 months
6.   Long-Term Collapse: Third Cascade, 12 to 20 years

CHART 2-2   The Six Stages of the Triple Waterfall

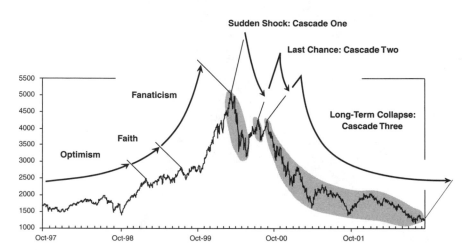

Data courtesy of Bloomberg Associates.

Using Aristotle's formula, Act One is composed of the first three stages, Act Two is Stages Four and Five, and Act Three is Stage Six.

Note the asymmetry between the length of time of joy and the length of time of agony. Capitalism is Calvinism in action, with the punishment delivered while the sinner yet lives. Its relationship to the religious aspect is that the punishment one faces after death for one's sins covers a much greater time period than the sinning time on Earth. Buying and holding a tech stock for a time period beginning in 1999 and continuing through this decade is a good way to prepare oneself for the pain of Purgatory (which is not a Calvinist concept), if not the torture of Hell (which is). One can end the punishment, of course, by repenting of the sin, selling out, and moving on.

What could be called the seven capital *C* crashes of the past 74 years have collectively had enormous importance in shaping our capital markets and our economy. Politicians, central bankers, and business leaders may claim they shape our economic destinies, but major financial convulsions overwhelm these players.

The basic ingredients of these seven events are so similar that investors who understood the earlier manias came unscathed through the later ones. Those who understand all seven will be most likely to prosper in coming years. As Mark Twain observed, "History doesn't repeat itself. But it does rhyme." That similarity explains why no strategist who failed to predict Nasdaq's collapse deserves to be taken seriously today.

Despite their differences in timing and in asset classes, the tripartite waterfall stock chart patterns are virtually identical:

- The Great Crash: 1926–1933

- Nifty Fifty Crash: 1972–1982

- Three Inflation Hedge Crashes: 1977–1999

    - Gold

    - Silver

    - Oil Stocks

- Nikkei Crash: 1985–?

- Nasdaq Crash: 1997–?

Moreover, the economic impact of these manias lives on for decades. Since 1929, the U.S. economy has lived most of its time in the shadows of previous crashes—as we do today. It may well be that only World War II and the Baby Boom were greater influences on capital markets than these financial events.

OPTIMISM

All markets rise and fall in response to swings in optimism and pessimism. What distinguishes a nascent Triple Waterfall is a sustained growth in optimism about an *asset class*—growth that continues to build even as the stock market takes its ordinary ups and downs. Investors gradually begin to discern an underlying pattern of consistency and rising prices that differs from the ordinary bullish/bearish price swings. It is the Start of Something Big.

For optimism to take charge in financial markets on a sustained basis, there must first be "an era of good feeling." People must feel good about the nation's position in the world, about its growth prospects, and about their own economic circumstances.

For example, the Roaring Twenties was an era of unprecedented U.S. prosperity. Everyone agreed that World War I was "the war to end all wars." The United States had emerged from the war as global industrial leader and creditor to the world. The dollar had supplanted the British pound as the international nongold store of value. Hollywood movies and American pop and jazz music were gaining fans worldwide. U.S. technology was the wonder of the world. Stocks of the leading technology companies—radio, telephone, and automobile—were in vogue.

Some of that same sense of American superiority animated the late 1960s buildup of enthusiasm for growth stocks—the belief that the sales and earnings of many leading American companies would grow regardless of the economy. That led in the 1970s to the Nifty Fifty craze, in which a few dozen large-capitalization companies outperformed the stock market month after month, with their price-earnings ratios moving further and further above the earnings multiple for the broad stock market. A new class system had emerged, and companies in the upper class could look with snobbish disdain on the vast number of companies in the lower classes.

It was Japan's swing from the insecurity and vulnerability of the postwar era to the "Japan Inc." arrogance of the 1980s that provided the emotional and intellectual basis for that Triple Waterfall—a collapse that continues to this day.

In the 1990s the United States, as winner of the Cold War, was the sole global superpower and could provide the umbrella that would mean sustained global peace—*Pax Americana*. The Gulf War showed how a quickly formed global military coalition under U.S. leadership and direction could win against an entrenched enemy in a matter of hours, based on the superior technology available to U.S. troops. It was almost a body-bag-less victory, and therefore had the antiseptic bloodlessness of a Luke Skywalker skirmish in *Star Wars*. President George Bush (the First) exulted in "the 100-Hour War," which inaugurated the "New World Order," and basked briefly in an 89 percent approval rating.

Concurrently, the Internet was the newest global pathway for the export of U.S. pop culture, craved by young people from Moscow to Tehran to Beijing. Inflation had been crushed. The booming economy was generating millions of cool jobs—from tech and telecom software and hardware design and marketing, to paid activism with a fast-multiplying group of tax-exempt NGOs, to flextime jobs at Starbucks. (That the manufacturing jobs that had been the basis of the U.S. labor movement were melting away was no big deal, because those industries were big polluters, and they were headquartered in declining Midwest cities, not in Silicon Valley, Austin, Raleigh-Durham, Phoenix, Albuquerque, Hollywood, New York, or Boston. Their stocks were considered as uncool as their locations.)

Amid such ebullience, the upward slope of the Triple Waterfall pattern begins to form. The stock market rises, led by a group or groups that encapsulate this new optimism. People who bought these stocks early become missionaries for them. Wall Street picks up on the stories and begins hiring more staff to peddle and trade stocks.

As pullbacks and profit taking occur, New Era thinking emerges to supply theoretical and intellectual rationales to ratify, stimulate, and legitimate investors' gut feelings, unleashing rising levels of optimism and greed. Dissenters challenge these assumptions and justifications, scoffing at valuations and urging investors to take profits in the winning group and to move funds into safer investments. Many take the cautionary advice. They will follow the ensuing run-up with anguish, and most of them will come to regret their cowardice and jump back in at much higher prices. This is the point at which the market moves from mere optimism to something much more powerful. . . .

FAITH

Prior to trusting your life to a bush-made rope, always test it.
—R. GRAVES

"Faith moves mountains," as the cheerful old Christian maxim says.

Whether or not you believe that statement, you should certainly believe that Faith moves markets. There is a mountain of evidence to support *that* assertion.

All bullish moves come from the intersection of optimism and greed. Triple Waterfalls are special, because they come from profound changes in the nation's belief system. They transcend the capital markets.

It was Faith that the American economy was so strong and so special, driven by the world's mightiest corporations, that fueled the stock market in 1927 and 1928; that same faith looked at weakening economies abroad not as something to worry about, but as a sign that the United States was especially blessed.

It was a new Faith in the 1960s that some major American companies had found the formula for sustained growth under any and all circumstances that fueled the run-up in what would be known as the Nifty Fifty stocks in the early 1970s.

Faith can be a belief in a negative: The 1970s conviction that inflation was an incurable component of modern democratic societies triggered a retreat from conventional investments—such as bonds and bank term deposits—into inflation hedges, which included gold, silver, oil, real estate (particularly farmland), art, and collectibles. That faith reshaped the collective bargaining process, as unions and management assumed that inflation would remain out of control, making the relatively new Cost of Living Adjustments (COLAs) a component of many contract negotiations, and one that was often bitterly contested.

If Faith is the driving force of what becomes a new secular religion, financial liquidity is its collection plate. Unless real money supplies (adjusted for inflation) rise, and unless credit becomes successively easier to obtain, investor enthusiasm and quasi-intellectual New Era arguments will not reach the critical mass of a self-sustaining speculative blow-off. This liquidity flow originates with aggressive monetary creation by central banks.

A particularly egregious example was the global reflation of 1973–1974, after the Arab oil boycott and a major Russian crop failure triggered a trebling of prices for oil and grains. Western central bankers tried to insulate their populations from soaring prices of foods and fuels, but ended up, as Milton Friedman predicted, spawning sustained inflation.

Liquidity surges can also develop from cross-border investment flows as one economy, currency, and stock market acquire particular allure, and global investors rush to get in on the great opportunity. The huge surge in Japanese stocks after the 1987 stock market crash came about because the Bank of Japan succumbed to pressure, particularly from the United States, to refloat the global system. Japan was running a monstrous Current Account surplus with the industrial world, and that success was at risk if a renewed stock market plunge triggered a recession and an upsurge in protectionism. That monetary cornucopia had come at a time when ordinary Japanese people were discovering the stock market as a savings vehicle. They felt supremely confident about the outlook for the shares of the companies in Japan Inc. (as did investors in the rest of the world, who rushed to buy shares in the companies that looked ready to take over the whole world).

As more and more people come to share the same belief system, there is rapid growth in corporate mergers, takeovers, and capital investment, spurred by a continuing torrent of investment funds supplied by the investing public. (That rapid growth will become a fevered epidemic in the next—and final—stage of the buildup toward the Triple Waterfall's peak.) Since the outlook appears so wonderful, companies believe they just have to invest all available funds to increase their profits even faster.

This is the stage at which the coalescence of enthusiasms and Faith produces a dangerous unanimity called *Shared Mistake*.

At its root, Shared Mistake is honest illusion, not fraud. But it is fostered by a slick horde of Shills & Mountebanks (hereinafter sometimes called simply S&Ms) who gain sudden prominence by promoting the investment concept heavily to the general public. In most cycles, these promoters came from Wall Street; in the Nasdaq boom, many came from the media. They predicted endless profit growth, giving corporate management cover to issue forecasts that might otherwise have been widely regarded as optimistic in the extreme. Prominent academics become S&Ms, writing books about gigantic stock market profits, and speaking—for large fees—to packed seminars of greedy investors.

These differing groups reinforce one another's enthusiasms and greed, providing endless fodder for retail investors' conversion to the secular religion. Major wealth-management organizations begin buying aggressively into the concept, partly under pressure from wealthy old-money clients who are horrified at the rapid multiplication of *nouveaux riches*.

Shared Mistake doesn't just drive the stock market. When the leading elites of Wall Street, business, the academy, and government agree with the leading elites of the media that a New Era has dawned, a new capital investment boom occurs. This becomes an accelerating process, as companies buy up other companies to acquire productive assets more cheaply and quickly than they could build them themselves. This in turn drives up asset values, stimulating more capital investment to deal with the shortage psyche that has begun to engulf society. It will create the seeds of its own destruction through massive overinvestment.

FANATICISM

This is the stage at which Shared Mistake becomes a near-universal force. It becomes so powerful an influence, and such a ramifying force within society, that it can best be understood by comparison with cults, superstitions, and religious manias.

What makes this story resemble a Greek tragedy is the hubris that so permeates society's power structures, creating massive excesses that provoke terrible and prolonged punishment. "Whom the gods would destroy, they first make mad." It is hubris to the point of madness that characterizes the Fanaticism stage of Triple Waterfalls, thereby justifying the horrendous punishments that lie ahead.

Veteran hikers, campers, and sailors have learned to be wary of long-range weather forecasts. They carry with them foul-weather gear, and they pull ashore and into campsites if telltale cloud and wind changes signal that the official forecasts might be in error.

That kind of survival instinct, which most investors have in varying degrees, virtually vanishes in the final up leg of the Triple Waterfall, when Shared Mistake acquires awesome power.

This is the stage when all that high-powered central bank money, and all that high-powered Street promotion, and all that high-powered media excitement, and all that high-powered intellectual justification combine to create an unstoppable juggernaut.

The Nasdaq Triple Waterfall, being the biggest and worst of them all, supplies many examples of the Fanaticism stage.

Dissent is suppressed along Wall Street—largely through market forces, but sometimes through overt action. Analysts and portfolio strategists who question the prevailing belief system lose out in prestige—and even jobs—to those who peddle the New Religion. In one now-famous example, Merrill Lynch recruited Henry Blodget, a youthful Oppenheimer technology analyst who had gained sudden fame by predicting that Amazon would go to $400 a share. He replaced a more cautious analyst.

Jeff Bezos, CEO of Amazon.com, was named "Person of the Year" by *Time*. Bob Woodward published *Maestro*, a best-selling book on Alan Greenspan that gave him credit for managing the economy of endless growth fueled by continuous productivity gains from the "New Economy."

That kind of Fanaticism arising from a monoculture of Shared Mistake characterizes the earlier crashes.

In October 1929, Irving Fisher, a prominent academic, published a brilliantly reasoned paper that proved that stocks were not selling at risky prices, because the stock market had many years of strong growth ahead of it. It was greeted with widespread praise and was widely cited by Wall Street Shills & Mountebanks in the weeks after the Great Crash, encouraging shocked investors to believe that this was nothing more than a correction.

During the three inflation-hedge Triple Waterfalls (gold, silver, and oil), belief in hard assets at times migrated from the secular to the mystic. Numerous investment advisers predicted prices for gold in the thousands of dollars per ounce range. The falling value of the dollar was talked of in the same breath with accounts of the Weimar hyperinflation.

The intellectual roots for the Faith in inflation that moved to Fanaticism about endless inflation came from the Club of Rome, a collection of distinguished leftist intellectual-politicians who began meeting in 1968. These neo-Malthusians were wined and dined on Lucullan scale, after which they would emerge to issue forecasts of global starvation and devastation because of inadequate supplies of food and fuels for a population that would in the future grow even more rapidly than it had since 1950.

In fact, the Baby Boom was already over; population growth in the industrial world had begun to decelerate and would turn negative in the next millennium; education of women would lead to declines in fertility rates across much of the Third World. Meanwhile, the Green Revolution, which improved pesticides and fertilizers and advanced farm equipment, would soon create a new kind of permanent food problem: how to control the production gluts, and how to control the endless increases in farm subsidies. Sharp rises in oil prices would inevitably trigger large new production from high-cost areas such as the North Sea. But Shared Mistake ruled out consideration of those realities for many years. Indeed, until the Triple Waterfall collapses in the inflation hedges, the prevailing intellectual climate was of endless shortages and nightmarish disasters. Of such were the nearly unanimous forecasts of oil at $100 a barrel that led to drilling in the Arctic Ocean, billions wasted on shale deposits, overbuilding in refineries, and overconstruction of oil drilling and servicing equipment.

Late in the decade, the Hunt brothers tried to corner the world silver market, with the assistance of Saudi investors. According to stories that circulated after the crash, their argument that silver was deeply undervalued after it had already run up from $1 an ounce to $20 was based on an interpretation of a passage in the Old Testament about the relative values of silver and gold. They managed to drive silver to $54 an ounce in 1980, the greatest price gain by far of any of the inflation hedges, before the metal entered its three-stage collapse.

Some of the talk was dreamy, some was apocalyptic, but all the talk during the late 1970s was of commodity inflation. The Shah of Iran proclaimed that oil was too valuable a resource to be burned as fuel. The publicity given to the 1973 El Niño that led to widespread crop failures made the new discipline of climatology chic. Among the opportunists who gained large followings were climatologists who predicted the coming of an era of global cooling that would unleash a new Ice Age, which would mean further, exponential increases in oil prices. (Some of these Ice Age experts switched to warning of global warming in the 1980s, when oil stocks were in their Triple Waterfall crash phase.)

The Nifty Fifty version of Shared Mistake was in place by late 1972. By then, growth stock investing had gained the status of the only style for truly sophisticated institutional investors. These were the investment management firms who ran mutual funds or who served the fastest-growing market—pension funds. What made this market so appealing was the switch in funding style. Until the 1960s, many corporations funded their defined benefit pension plans with annuity contracts and/or bond portfolios. By the 1970s, nearly all sizable plans were self-managed, with heavy equity orientation.

In that culture, the traditional "Graham & Dodd" value investing made famous by the published writings of Wall Street icon Benjamin Graham was passé. In particular, looking for low price-earnings ratios was old hat. As one of the stars of that era told adoring audiences, "The higher the p/e the more money you make on the stock. A company that grows earnings at 20 percent that trades at 50 times earnings makes you more money than a company with the same growth rate at 20 times."

The essence of the Nifty Fifty mania was the belief that some companies—such as IBM, Xerox, and Avon—were so strong that they could ride out any downturn and gain market share and earnings. "Buy and hold" was the investment strategy. At the Fanaticism stage, cyclical stocks—those tied more closely to the ups and downs of the economy—went far out of favor, creating historic investment opportunities for Warren Buffett and Sir John Templeton—investors who had drunk deeply of the wisdom of Graham & Dodd.

The Japanese version of Fanatical Shared Mistake was, in retrospect, almost inevitable in an ethnocentric nation that had made such astonishing strides after World War II because of internal cohesion, hard work, and high savings. Their remarkable success, and their strong ethnocentrism, ultimately led to the level of pride that is the stuff of great crashes.

When the Nikkei was trading at an 80 multiple, I visited Japan and talked to many businessmen. When I asked how their bank stocks could be selling at four times the multiples of stocks in other countries, they pointed out the sustained earnings growth of their banks. "But," I objected, "at the rate they charge for loans, they barely cover their borrowing costs, and make no provision for loan charges, as will be required under the new Basel Capital Accord. They aren't really making money."

My hosts demurred, pointing out that the banks were making huge gains from their holdings of stocks and real estate.

> "But," I said, "what happens when prices of real estate and stocks go into long bear markets."
>
> "That cannot happen here, because of price maintenance," they replied.
>
> "But bear markets come, you'd admit," I argued.
>
> "Never here," they insisted.

And indeed, there had not been a sustained bear market in Japan for decades. The Japanese, who had been so cautious since the MacArthur era, became collectively afflicted with hubris after the U.S. stock market crash in 1987. They began buying up trophy U.S. properties, such as Pebble Beach golf course and Rockefeller Center.

(Had they thought through the implications of Hubris, as spelled out in Greek tragedy, they'd have known it would have been followed by Nemesis, then Catharsis. But Sophocles wasn't required reading at the Japanese banks.)

At the Fanaticism stage, stockbrokers who do not produce "buy stories" on the red-hot (or absolutely cool, depending on your temperature alignment) equity group lose their clients to those with reputations for "aggressive" investing. And investment managers who apply rules of prudence to clients' accounts lose business to managers who show fabulous performance numbers to prospects. I recall, in January 2000, a full-page advertisement for a mutual fund organization showing the results of their Technology Fund, which had more than doubled in 1999. As the law requires, there was a small-print disclaimer saying that "past performance is not a guide to future results," yet the entire purpose of this ad was to scream otherwise.

Our organization has a reputation for value investing, and in 1999 I was getting insulting phone calls from people who owned the Relative Value Fund I managed, ridiculing me for not knowing where the money was to be made.

Although "New Era" belief seems universal, there are always a few quiet dissenters. They are moving to the exits at this stage, but they choose not to publicize their disagreement with the market. Joe Kennedy and Bernard Baruch were among the wealthy who were even wealthier in 1932 than they had been in 1929. As J. K. Galbraith said in a speech in 1998: "If you forget everything else tonight, remember this, that when you hear someone say, 'We have entered a new era of permanent prosperity,' then you should immediately take cover, because that shows that financial idiocy has really taken hold and that history, all history, is being rejected."

Those seminars in 1998 and 1999 at which leading Shills & Mountebanks dazzled retail investors were powerful emotional experiences. As they flashed up slick PowerPoint presentations showing how ordinary small investors had become millionaires, it was like Billy Graham on a great night in the 1960s, with new converts joining the ecstatically converted. Only this was about Mammon, not God—Greed, not Gratitude. One could feel and smell the lust for sudden riches in those packed halls. As one who was forced to attend some of those lust-ins, I came away scared and appalled.

I knew how the next acts of this play went, and I felt sorry for almost everyone in the room except the Mountebank who had drawn the crowd, seduced them, then departed with a large paycheck.

He would not be around to help them when the inevitable tragedy began to unfold. The investors' hubris, which he had so skillfully stroked to tumescence, was bound to evoke the wrath of the gods of market forces. Nemesis was out there, somewhere, getting ready to inflict fearsome punishment on those who had defied the laws of wealth building.

SUDDEN SHOCK: FIRST CASCADE

The first sell-off comes without warning. Although it shocks market participants, the news continues to be good, and the players had learned from the Shills & Mountebanks that they profit by "buying the dip." (This expression became an article of faith in the Nasdaq Triple Waterfall. Each time the technology stocks succumbed to profit taking or bad news, the media were alive with Shills & Mountebanks who told investors, "Buy the dip!" They never once said, "Sell the top!")

So the individual investors buy the dip. That means the corporate insiders with millions of cheap stock options, sensing that the game is over, have someone to sell to as they start cashing in big. (The scale of their profits and sales is discussed in "Stock Options and Nasdaq's Triple Waterfall" in Chapter 5.)

Only this time it is no mere dip, to be followed by another strong rally to another wondrous new high. It is the beginning of a Triple Waterfall crash that will wipe out more than three-quarters of the value of Nasdaq— or of the stock market in 1929, or of many of the Nifty Fifty stocks, or of the gold, silver, and oil stocks, or of the value of Japanese stocks in 1989. If a long journey does indeed begin with a single step, then a multiyear journey to financial collapse begins with one failed rally.

That first sell-off usually comes at a time central bankers have begun tightening, fearful of the growth of an asset bubble. The Fed kept the spigots open too long in 1929, then tightened forcefully, precipitating the crash.

It made the same mistake in October 1998, panicking because of the Russian default and the collapse of Long Term Capital Management, a huge hedge fund whose investors included leading Wall Street insiders; it followed up that brief experience in crony capitalism by unleashing a torrent of liquidity in 1999 because of fear of a banking crisis with Y2K. It then tried to drain the excess liquidity from the system, but found—as had its predecessors—that all that liquidity had created serious problems of its own, which a sudden drought could not cure. (Mr. Greenspan gave a speech at the Jackson Hole conference in 2002 defending his policies of 1998–1999 but denying that a central bank could ever be sure of the existence of a bubble. Nasdaq's p/e ratio was above 70 when he turned on the hose in 1998, and above 100 when he turned it on again in 1999. And he had trouble seeing a bubble? He was given an honorary knighthood by Queen Elizabeth II in 2002. A writer in the *Financial Times* suggested he be admitted to the Order of the Bubble.)

As the pace of liquidation slows, the Shills & Mountebanks reemerge, proclaiming the appearance of once-in-a-lifetime bargains. They use the sharp drops as buy stories, thereby deflecting the growth of doubt among the true believers: "Look! Cisco's at 60 bucks! You won't see Cisco at 60 again!"

That oft-pitched line made me recall Wall Street's single most honest sales pitch. When the U.S. Treasury issued its first-ever 6 percent 20-year bonds in 1968, Wall Street enthusiastically peddled what it immediately called "the Magic Sixes" with the following promo: "You won't see 6 percent Long Treasurys again!"

Right.

Inflation was already beginning its rise to what would be double-digit levels in the 1970s, and those Long Treasury Bonds never traded above issue price (par). In September 1981 long Treasury yields reached the unheard-of level of 15.75 percent, so the pain of those 1968 buyers was still intense, 13 years after a purchase they had regretted every month since.

But Wall Street was right. You didn't see 6 percent Long Treasurys again (until the 1990s, long after the Magic Sixes had matured).

And yes, the S&Ms were right about Cisco: You didn't see Cisco at 60 for long, but you did see it at 9.

LAST CHANCE: SECOND CASCADE

In three of the last century's Triple Waterfalls, investors had a chance to sell into the rally at the end of the First Cascade at relatively modest cost. Indeed, in 1930 the stock market rallied so strongly that it briefly touched 1929 levels before entering the Second Cascade. Similarly, the Nikkei rallied to 34,000 from 29,000 in 1990, and Nasdaq rallied to 4200 from 3480 in 2001.

The Second Cascade is the stage at which the first signs of the major flaws underlying Shared Mistake are revealed:

- *1930*. Stocks cannot go up when there's a depression on.

- *1974*. Many of the Nifty Fifty stocks have entered terminal declines:
  They are not growth stocks immune to the economic cycle, they're
  overpriced cyclical stocks with serious competitive problems.

- *1983*. For inflation hedge assets, the plunge gains speed as Paul Volcker
  shows adamantine determination to crush inflation, even at the cost
  of record-high interest rates and a deep recession: Monetarism is
  proving to be, in fact, the right medicine for the disease of inflation.

- *1990*. The Nikkei enters a terrifying decline as it slowly registers on
  all but the most solipsistic Japanese theorists that Japan is not an
  island that can set its own valuations forever. For many of the biggest
  stocks in Tokyo, including many of the biggest banks, what has
  begun is hari-kari in slow motion.

- *2001*. Investor sticker shock: The truth in techs, as in so many of the
  Nifty Fifty stocks, is that they are falsely labeled growth stocks. In
  fact they're actually capital goods cyclical stocks, and as such, they
  can have big losses, and they certainly are not worth big multiples.
  Moreover, the boom in private equity and IPO financing has created
  huge overcapacity among suppliers. It turns out those telecom companies do not have unlimited deep pockets. Who will buy all this gear?

The S&Ms are less in evidence, but they keep reassuring the dwindling
ranks of the faithful that stocks are coming back "once the economy recov-
ers" or "when the next El Niño causes another crop failure" or "when
another Arab-Israeli war produces another boycott" or "when Volcker is
forced to resign," or whatever. But their pronouncements no longer carry
much weight, and they are now being openly attacked by skeptics who had
been lying low during the Fanaticism period. Conflicts of interest about
their performance begin to emerge.

The stage is being set for catastrophe.

LONG-TERM COLLAPSE: THIRD CASCADE

This is the long, grinding collapse that finishes the process. It takes more
than a decade before the asset class reaches its final bottom (or final resting place, if you will).

Stocks didn't trade at lower yields than bonds until the mid-1950s. The
Nifty Fifty stocks as a group underperformed the stock market throughout

the 1980s. Japan's stock indices keep hitting new lows 13 years after their market peaked.

Gold and silver trade for small fractions of their prices of two decades ago. Oil stocks only bottomed out in their percentage weighting in the S&P at 3.4 percent 17 years after they peaked at nearly 30 percent.

RECOGNIZING A TRIPLE WATERFALL
IN TIME TO PROTECT YOURSELF

Since Triple Waterfalls are the most dangerous of market phenomena, investors need to know when they are in a Triple Waterfall situation, as compared with one of the less ferocious bears.

Triple Waterfalls have their own defining characteristics. That so many have been stunned by the extent of the collapse in technology and telecom stocks shows how few have made any serious study of market history.

It's not as if there's a shortage of investment professionals: The number of graduating Chartered Financial Analysts breaks records each year (with growth particularly strong among foreign students).

It's not that readable books on previous crashes do not exist. To name a few: *A Short History of Financial Euphoria,* by John Kenneth Galbraith; *Extraordinary Popular Delusions* and the *Madness of Crowds,* by Charles Mackay; and *Manias, Panics, and Crashes: A History of Financial Crises,* by Charles Kindleberger.

It's not as if the chart patterns aren't attention-getters.

Sir John Templeton, one of the wisest of investors, observed: "The four most dangerous words in investing are 'It's different this time.'" He had retired from active investing to devote himself to his foundation, but reemerged during the late stages of the Nasdaq mania to proclaim that it was the "biggest financial insanity" of all time. Given such an astounding opportunity, he felt honor-bound to get reinvolved. He shorted dot-com stocks, making an additional $90 million for the foundation.

The lesson is that each generation must make its own mistakes, as if nothing in previous history were relevant.

But you need not share in the worst financial experiences of your own generation. Opt out.

Triple Waterfalls are different from other kinds of market enthusiasms, because, by involving and infecting society at large, they transcend the stock market. The Baby Bear collapse in 1987 was a correction within the financial community and financial system. The public at large was only vaguely aware that the stock market was getting expensive and the dollar was in trouble. The economy was not derailed by the crash, although global stock market leadership did shift from the United States to Japan—a shift that would prove disastrous for the Japanese, because it set the stage for their Triple Waterfall—which would never have occurred had the Bank of Japan not been forced into massive reflation after the crash.

Two factors differentiate Triple Waterfalls from ordinary bull market excesses.

The Ideological Superstructure of a Market

The first distinguishing characteristic of Triple Waterfalls is the active involvement of the intellectual elites—known as the clerisy—in the building of an ideological superstructure over the market's value system—a sand castle destined to be washed away. The clerisy are those within the academic, media, and political communities who are interested in ideas and trends, and eager to communicate their views to others.

The presence of the clerisy gives the financial community even greater confidence that its viewpoint is right—because all those really smart and really distinguished people who have spent their lives looking down their noses at us as grubby capitalist traders are now saying we are where it's at.

What the Street denizens are not considering—so great is their delight in being respected and envied by the chattering classes—is George Orwell's observation about the clerisy: "No idea is so crazy and ill-founded that it cannot be believed by an intellectual."

The Spirit of a Market

Because Triple Waterfalls are collective financial suicides, they are rooted more deeply in human nature than in the ordinary give and take, bull and bear, of financial markets. To a Freudian psychologist, they would have to be manifestations of *Thanatos*—the love or preoccupation with death, which is generally called the "death wish." *Thanatos* is the opposing emotional force to *Eros*—love of life, as manifested in the sexual urge—the libido, which is part of the "animal spirits" of bull markets. Thrill seekers love to take extreme personal risks—such as parachute jumps, high dives, or using cocaine, heroin, or Ecstasy.

What happens in Triple Waterfalls is that a process driven by a form of *Eros* in the Optimism stage and in the early months of the Faith stage swiftly becomes overlaid with *Thanatos,* signaling the onset of the Fanaticism stage.

In its entry on Eros, the *Oxford English Dictionary* quotes W. Empson's Gathering Storm: "The Freudians regard the death-wish as fundamental, though 'the clamour of life' proceeds from its rival '*Eros*.'" (Empson's book was published in 1940; Churchill would later title the first volume of his history of World War II *The Gathering Storm*. His portrayal of the behavior of the allies in the years leading up to the war makes them look as if they had a collective death wish. Since I know of no evidence that Churchill was a Freudian, I assume this was coincidental.)

In its entry on *Thanatos,* the OED quotes a 1935 article in the *British Journal of Psychology:* "Freud's final duality was the division of the mind into two sets of instincts which he termed life instincts and death instincts respectively—or, if one prefers the Greek names, *Eros* and *Thanatos*." Another citation is from Germaine Greer (1970) in the *Female Eunuch:* "Our life-style contains more *Thanatos* than *Eros*." (The Nifty Fifty Triple Waterfall was in its Faith stage when her book came out, but I doubt she was making a market forecast.) As Cole Porter wrote of the late stages of the Jazz Age:

> The world has gone mad today
> And good's bad today. . . .
> Anything goes.

In the Fanaticism stage, the financially erotic keep showing their love by investing more, but they are joined by formerly skeptical market players, whose willingness to bet their futures by buying in at that stage is probably a form of financial death wish. Instinctively they know that they stand to lose their money, but they willingly bet their financial lives in order to be part of a financial form of Felliniesque bacchanalia.

Perhaps you're uncomfortable with the notion that Freudian psychology has anything useful to tell us about stock market behavior. Think again. Last year's winners of the Nobel Prize in Economics were economic behaviorists, whose work rejects the rational *Homo economicus* of classical economic theory. Their experiments showed that most people can—and do—behave in economically irrational fashion when offered clear-cut choices. (Investment managers who use computer analytics to forecast stock market performance, such as our organization, believe that the stock market can and does behave irrationally; this is contrary to believers in the "Efficient Market Hypothesis," who think that it is a waste of time to try to analyze the market because it is, at all times, efficiently priced based on publicly available information. We would argue that anyone who thought Nasdaq at 5000 was an efficient price-setting medium should not be allowed to manage other people's money.)

Perhaps you want to believe that the market is simply driven by the shifting tides of Fear and Greed. But in Triple Waterfalls, Fear becomes an endangered emotional species, and Greed is glorified. How do *Eros* and *Thanatos* relate to Fear and Greed? Answer: Their relationships shift as the mania unfolds.

As the life-affirming emotion, *Eros* drives the "animal spirits" of the entrepreneurs and risk takers in the early and middle stages of the New Era. But in its climactic phase, it is joined by the dark side of the force of human nature, which comes to join a party that is about to morph into the Dance of Death. Since Death is the end of everything, it announces its arrival on the scene by inducing market players to throw away their rule books and guidebooks and throw themselves into the embrace of the New Economy. The market cannot make that last, orgasmic rush to the top as long as a substantial body of opinion within the marketplace retains a stubborn attachment to the principles of the past. As those belief systems die off, a vacuum is created, and in rushes *Thanatos,* who will remain in charge for more than a decade.

C H A P T E R

How Triple Waterfalls Reshape the Landscape

There is a bush saying about cooking fires—"The bigger the fire, the bigger the fool."

—R. GRAVES

CHICAGO'S GREAT FIRE OF 1871, which burned most of the downtown and adjacent areas, did not derail the plans of its leading businessmen and visionaries. The city went on to achieve greatness beyond what even its most enthusiastic boosters would have expected in the days before the disaster struck.

The catastrophe changed the city for the better, because a cadre of local geniuses looked on the burning ruins as the opportunity to lay out a model city that would be able to handle growth much better than the ramshackle and chaotic large/small town it had been before the fire.

Triple Waterfalls create new opportunities—for the economy and for investors. They wipe out the previous financial landscape, destroying the vestiges of yesterday's bad ideas. They cleanse the economic environment.

Because Romans loved to gorge themselves to excess for hours, they invented the vomitorium. One repaired to this chamber from time to time during a 15-course meal, to make space for new culinary delights.

The Triple Waterfall is a grand financial vomitorium. It disgorges unneeded or obsolete assets and prepares the way for new production and consumption. (Lest the reader think the analogy breaks down because the retching Roman elites went to the vomitorium voluntarily, note that nobody had to buy technology and telecom stocks.)

THE GREAT CRASH: 1926–1933

The Great Crash could have been the basis of a major new era of U.S. and global growth had (1) the Fed understood its role as central banker to the world, and (2) Congress passed a trade liberalization act, rather than the trade stultification of the Smoot-Hawley Tariff.

This was a deflationary Papa Bear Crash, and what was needed—immediately and for years thereafter—was reflationary and liberalizing policymaking. Churchill, who was in the wrong job as Britain's Chancellor of the Exchequer, had kept Britain on the gold standard in 1926 (which he himself had restored the year before) when the overstressed nation should have devalued. Britain hung grimly on, devaluing only after the crash. The global banking situation was in serious trouble. Collapses began, culminating in May 1931 with the collapse of Credit-Anstallt. Although it was an Austrian bank that few Americans had ever heard of, its demise signaled a renewed intensification of the global crisis. It had the longer-range effect of weakening Austria relative to Germany, a weakness that would be exploited by Hitler in the *Anschluss*.

Europe, which together with the United States was just about all of the industrial world at the time, was in debt (mostly to the United States) because of World War I. The American dollar was now the global standard, and what was needed to restore stability was a U.S. Current Account deficit, liquefying the debtor countries with dollars.

Instead the world got the Smoot-Hawley Tariff. It had been introduced in Congress just before the Black Monday Crash in 1929 and helped trigger it, and was signed into law by President Herbert Hoover in 1930. Smoot-Hawley closed the U.S. market to imports from those debtor nations, forcing them into default and the world into depression.

During the 1930s there were intervening equity rallies, but gold, gold mining shares, and long Treasury bonds were the winning investments in the deflationary decline that engulfed the world.

What most Americans learned from this horror was the riskiness of equities. Thereafter, until the mid-1950s, stocks were valued on the basis of their dividends, and the attractive shares were those whose dividends were higher than Treasury yields.

In other words, the Third Cascade of that Triple Waterfall lasted for roughly two decades. Stocks as an asset class underperformed bonds, gold, and real estate throughout the 1930s and did not begin trading as equities again for more than 25 years after the onset of the First Cascade of the crash.

THE NIFTY FIFTY CRASH: 1972–1982

In contrast to 1929, the Crash of 1973–1974 was an inflationary Papa Bear event, driven by double-digit inflation and soaring commodity prices. (See Chart 3-1.) Monetary policy was disastrously expansive.

The bubble that burst was the idea that stocks were good inflation hedges, and that a group of high-priced stocks could continue to earn lofty profits regardless of inflation or the state of the economy.

That stocks are good hedges against modest, *anticipated* inflation is certainly true. If the CPI is going up 2 to 3 percent every year, companies can manage their pricing and their union contracts to stay ahead of infla-

CHART 3-1   S&P 500 (January 2, 1968 to August 12, 1982)

Data courtesy of Bloomberg Associates.

tion. Indeed, it is this aspect of corporate performance that makes equities cornerstones in the portfolio of retirees: Their portfolio's value and their dividend income are expected to stay ahead of inflation.

Unanticipated inflation is another matter. Among economists, Milton Friedman was virtually alone in expecting double-digit inflation; the populace was in shock, and many—if not most—U.S. corporations were hurt. To make matters much worse, that extreme inflation produced a deep recession; at that time, nearly all the experts except Friedman believed that inflation and recessions could not go together.

So U.S. stocks were simultaneously hit with unanticipated inflation and unanticipated recession. The Nifty Fifty stocks were "priced for perfection." Their price-earnings ratios were extremely high, because expectations of future earnings growth were extremely high. They had reached what analysts call the "North Pole position," where your next step had to be down. When those "glamour" stocks went down, they pulled the entire stock market with them. They had sucked most of the air out of the stock market in the months before they entered their Triple Waterfall Crash, and there were few investors—other than the then relatively unknown Warren Buffett—to buy the overlooked stocks.

At the bottom, in December 1974, the p/e ratio on the Dow Industrials briefly registered below six. Investors had given up on stocks because the supposedly invulnerable stocks turned out to be the sickest in the whole market, and it was unclear who their successors would be. The thought was: better to put money into hard assets.

That crash helped develop the inflation psyche that would be the defining characteristic of the 1970s. It triggered a rush into inflation-hedge assets—farmland, coins, collectibles—and the three that together crashed during the Triple Waterfalls in the 1980s—gold, silver, and oil.

Inflation is partly monetary, partly driven by shortages of foods and fuels, and partly psychological. Short-term shocks like the oil boycott or the El Niño crop failures produce commodity price leaps, but only an excess of money and a generalized psychological acceptance of inflation's inevitability make those shock effects permanent.

The crash of the Nifty Fifty stocks came when exogenous forces—those that come from outside the market, rather than the endogenous forces, which are problems and excesses within the market itself—showed that the nature of that generation's Shared Mistake was a culture that accepted fallacious arguments for these stocks' high valuations.

When IBM and Xerox were plunging and Homestake (a big gold mine) and Kerr-McGee (a big oil producer) were rising, the investment argument had been turned on its head.

Although it was runaway inflation that ultimately destroyed the Nifty Fifty bull market, the bear market began with a noneconomic event. Mighty IBM lost at trial in an antitrust suit brought by a tiny competitor called Telex.

Telex vs. IBM

I recall that landmark lawsuit well. I was working as a rookie investment officer at the time, and was lucky—or cheeky—enough to challenge the prevailing consensus.

My employer was a major Canadian life insurer, which owned a remarkably large position in IBM. The company had owned these shares since the Depression. It had bought and held them because of their high dividend yield. The imbedded capital gains were, of course, enormous, and each time the company had lightened up in the past, it regretted the sale, since IBM just kept reaching new peaks.

I looked at the issues in IBM's antitrust suits with the Justice Department and with Telex. I had written my law journal article on an aspect of U.S. antitrust law. I went back and dug out the article and reviewed the landmark cases, then wrote a long memo to the finance committee, suggesting that IBM's chances of winning were no better than 60–40, and if it lost either suit, its shares would plunge.

My boss liked the memo, but he expressed concern that the board would be upset unless I researched the matter much further. I was sent to Wall Street to interview the analysts who covered IBM at the leading firms who covered us.

It took a week. Not one analyst thought there was a chance IBM could ever lose any lawsuit. They kept pointing out the odds: IBM had more than 200 top antitrust counsel on its side, whereas Telex had six or seven.

I returned to report that the pricing of IBM shares allowed no chance for legal defeat. As a former trial lawyer, I also observed that having 200 lawyers might be a huge disadvantage.

My employer agreed to sell one-third of its position. A week later Telex won round one of its case with IBM. There was a delayed opening of stocks that morning on the New York Stock Exchange, and IBM opened down heavily. The biggest bear market since 1929 had begun.

Since luck is a big factor in almost all trials, that outcome was, for nearly everybody, a major piece of luck. Bad luck for IBM stockholders, bad luck for stock investors, but good luck for a wannabe senior investment officer.

The Shared Mistake

IBM's upset defeat was a textbook example of Shared Mistake. To assign 100 percent probability to the belief that IBM could keep winning every skirmish was a reflection of the awe in which it was held. Weeks before that demarche, *The New Yorker* ran a full-page cartoon that showed an old man on his huge deathbed, surrounded by evidences of wealth and by his family. He was gasping, "Don't let them sell my IBM!"

(Earlier it had run another full-page cartoon that expressed the ethos of the giddy growth stock era. A man is shouting at his broker from a telephone booth. Across the road, a huge factory, labeled AMALGAMATED CHEMICAL is in flames. The caption reads, "I don't care about its long-term growth prospects! Sell my Amalgamated Chemical!")

So majestic and mighty was IBM that some investment counselors recommended that retired persons hold more than 50 percent of their savings in IBM shares. Their argument: Capital gains taxes are roughly half the rate of taxes on interest and dividends. IBM grows its earnings predictably 15 to 20 percent a year, and the stock price rises at least that fast, because the p/e ratio doesn't shrink. Therefore, just sell off part of your IBM holdings annually for current income and you'll never outlive your savings.

In reality, IBM's era of the magnificent mainframe was soon to come to an end. Apple Computer would change the game. IBM's share price today is below its 1973 peak (adjusted for inflation).

There would never be another IBM, I thought. No company would ever acquire that mystique again. Fortunately for my clients and me, there was Microsoft.

In 1999, I got another chance to dust off my law school notes. I advised clients that Microsoft had a good chance of losing its antitrust suit. Many clients rejected the advice. In essence their argument was, "Microsoft is bigger than the government"—a sure sign of Shared Mistake. As with IBM a generation earlier, Microsoft's defeat months later coincided with the First Cascade of the most recent Triple Waterfall Crash (discussed in "The Nasdaq Crash: 1997 to ?" below).

Avon was another example of the power of a Nifty Fifty Shared Mistake. At its peak, Avon stock had a p/e ratio of 90. Avon's unique business plan was personalized selling of cosmetics and personal care items through salespeople to women in their homes. Its signature of the ringing doorbell and "Avon calling" made it the very best kind of "household word." It really worked superbly.

If the "lady of the house" were at home.

All those male portfolio managers who bid up Avon shares in 1970–1972 didn't think about the implications for the company's sales strategy when a large percentage of women reentered the work force after having their children.

"Avon calling" became "Avon falling" as its shares plunged during the next 15 years. Then the company restructured itself and once again became a superb investment.

The Nifty Fifty Triple Waterfall created investment opportunities in (1) the kinds of solid free-cash generators prized by Warren Buffett, such as Coca-Cola and Gillette, and (2) inflation-hedge companies, such as oil and gas producers, gold mines, agribusiness companies, base metals, and forest products.

Meanwhile, an investor who had bought and held the shares of the Nifty Fifty in 1972 would have underperformed the stock market until the 1990s. Inflation hedges beat that portfolio in the 1970s, and the disinflation stocks (consumer growth and financial) beat it in the 1980s.

So much for "Buy and Hold."

If you're holding a portfolio constructed on Triple Waterfall Fanaticism, you lose. Big.

THE THREE INFLATION-HEDGE CRASHES: 1977–1999

The period from 1972 to 1983 was a time in which the Western world was beset with a seemingly endless sea of economic and political troubles:

1. The major Russian crop failure of 1972 led to the "Great Grain Robbery" in 1972–1973 in which Russia secretly bought nearly all available supplies of U.S. wheat at a government-subsidized price of $1.65 a bushel; prices thereupon skyrocketed to more than $5 a bushel, setting off food price inflation.

2. The Yom Kippur War and the oil boycott of 1973 led to a trebling of oil prices.

3. Watergate destroyed the Nixon presidency in 1973–1974 in a long, agonizing process that seared the national consciousness; the sense that the presidency had lost its legitimacy caused moderates and conservatives to lose heart, liberals to lose their optimism about the inevitability of progress, and radicals to believe that the time for revolution was at hand.

4. U.S. defeat in Vietnam in 1975 launched a long era of national self-flagellation and finger-pointing, and a seeming breakdown in law and order.

5. Britain's long decline accelerated in a decade of collapsing productivity and labor chaos, leading to the 1979 election of a tough,

principled conservative, Margaret Thatcher. She confidently predicted she would be joined in power by fellow conservative Ronald
Reagan, whose optimistic new right-wing populism would transform America's economy and whose strategic vision would make
America a great power again. (She told me in a private conversa-
tion in 1978 that she expected to win three elections, and that Reagan would win two. She said that between them they would
restructure their economies, rebuild their defenses, and, "Who
knows? By the time we leave public life, we may have won the
Cold War." She was, among other things, one great forecaster.)

6. Inflation became entrenched globally in 1971; more and more cen-
    tral bankers blamed the falling U.S. dollar for the problem; Paul
    Volcker, newly installed chairman of the Federal Reserve, met with
    them at the Belgrade IMF Conference in October 1979 and was
    told a new global collapse loomed unless the U.S. dollar was stabi-
    lized. Volcker proclaimed the imposition of transparent mone-
    tarism—in which money supply targets would be announced in
    advance, and the Fed would enforce them, regardless of the impact
    on interest rates, the economy, or the dollar. That was the policy
    long favored by Milton Friedman. Interest rates skyrocketed, and
    the United States entered the first phase of a double-dip recession.

7. Reagan defeated Carter in 1980. His tax cuts and deregulation
    backed up the anti-inflationary monetary policies being pursued
    by Paul Volcker.

8. By 1981, Japan emerged as the virtually unchallenged industrial
    leader of the world, supplanting long-established companies in the
    United States, Canada, and Europe. Japan's might reinforced a
    growing pessimism that the decline of the West, as predicted by
    Oswald Spengler in the book of that name in 1918, had now begun
    and would continue inexorably.

It was against this tumultuous background that a trio of hard assets—
gold, silver, and oil—and the shares of the companies that produced them
took over leadership in global stock indices. Not all that glittered was gold,
which shared the stage with silver and oil.

In the 1970s some of the best of people went astray. The markers and
guideposts that had worked most of the time since World War II seemed to
have been lost in a fog—or to have lost their ability to give reliable information. Investor survival could not be found in bank accounts, leading
stocks, or bonds. A whole new collection of Pied Pipers and Shills &

Mountebanks appeared, warning of the collapse of the financial world and urging investors to profit from it with inflation hedges.

The culmination of Club of Rome gloom, the failure of equities to recover strongly from the Nifty Fifty Crash, political and economic dysfunction, and the failure of central banks to protect currency values gave the world a new challenge: stagflation.

Stagflation was an ugly new word to define an ugly new problem: rising inflation at the time of stagnating economies.

In the 1970s, investors began to retreat from financial assets to hard assets. That process eventually would become a new form of mania. What began as reasoned hedging against *unanticipated* inflation became a mania to get rich from the coming collapse of currencies, banks, and financial systems.

Polls showed that most Americans thought the nation had lost its way.

Wall Street was a shrunken, frightened place, in part because the Nifty Fifty Crash had destroyed the investments it had peddled hardest, but also because of the SEC's imposition of fully negotiated brokerage commissions. On May 1, 1975—Mayday, as it was swiftly termed by terrified brokers—Wall Street was forced to slash all institutional commissions (by as much as 90 percent) and reduce most retail commissions. Not only had the stock market then endured a Papa Bear horror, but in the ensuing recovery, trading volumes were too light to make up for the collapse in institutional commission rates.

The inflation hedge crashes were different than the other Triple Waterfalls of the 20th century: Wall Street was only modestly culpable. The hype, distortions, and misinformation that led to the spectacular run-ups in the inflation hedge assets were not, in large measure, hatched on Wall Street. Indeed, the arguments used by the extreme doomsayers (who urged people to load up on guns and gold) were that the "Old Economy" investments would not work anymore; the financial world was facing a new kind of inflation challenge caused by a massive rise in oil costs, which had led to a massive buildup of dollar deposits by oil sheikhs in leading banks, which had been massively loaned to Third World dictatorships and kleptocracies, leading to massive defaults that would trigger a massive global financial collapse. They shrilled that collapse would make paper money—whose value was plunging because of double-digit inflation, anyway—virtually worthless.

Gold (1975–1999)

As the classic inflation hedge, gold became both symbol and star actor in the inflation hedge mania that produced three Triple Waterfalls. Because the motivations that drove them skyward and then sent them plunging were virtually the same, and because these Triple Waterfalls were virtually contemporaneous, it makes sense to consider them together. Their dramatic rises smashed investors' beliefs in conventional financial assets, and their dramatic collapses smashed inflation psyches, restoring belief in conventional financial assets, thereby marking the end of the inflation/stagflation era.

Gold's price was frozen at $35 an ounce after the Bretton Woods Agreement in 1944 established the American dollar as the new global store of value. The United States held most of the world's known supplies of gold, and it agreed to sell gold from its hoard to other central banks at $35. U.S. citizens were barred from holding gold bullion, and U.S. gold mines had to sell their output to the government at the fixed price.

In August 1971, President Nixon "closed the gold window," which meant the United States would no longer sell its dwindling gold reserves to other central banks. That meant the dollar was no longer gold-backed, even in theory, and it was the signal for an outbreak of inflation that the administration sought to halt with wage and price controls. They failed, disastrously.

Gold's price worked higher during the 1970s (see Chart 3-2), but when the U.S. dollar's plunge against key global currencies seemed out of control, gold took off and a mania spread worldwide.

CHART 3-2   Gold (January 1, 1968 to December 31, 1982)

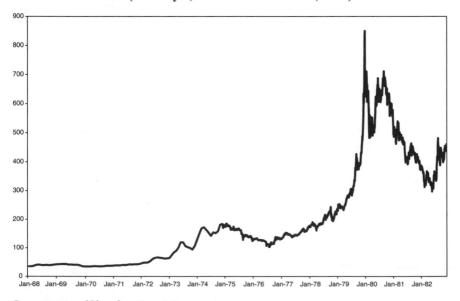

Data courtesy of Bloomberg Associates.

Silver (1975–1999)

Silver followed gold's rise (see Chart 3-3), and then surged ahead of it when the Hunts, one of America's wealthiest families, with a fortune built on oil, made a deal with Saudi partners to corner the world silver market. This was the only Triple Waterfall that was not driven primarily by Shared Mistake. Apart from the co-conspirators and some serious inflation fanatics, few economists, strategists, or institutional investors believed silver was worth anything approaching $50 an ounce. It could be said that the Shared Mistake that inflation could never be tamed fueled the whole bizarre run-up, but silver would not have been a preferred hedge against inflation without the short-lived Hunt-Saudi cabal.

A personal anecdote recalls the excitement at the time of the peak of that Triple Waterfall.

When my son Stuart was born in 1967, a friend (of leftist persuasion) gave him a piggybank "for a young capitalist." I thought it was a fine idea, and began putting silver coins into it each day. I was a firm believer that silver prices were headed much higher, because the hoard of monetary silver in the United States was melting rapidly.

CHART 3-3   Silver (January 1, 1968 to December 31, 1982)

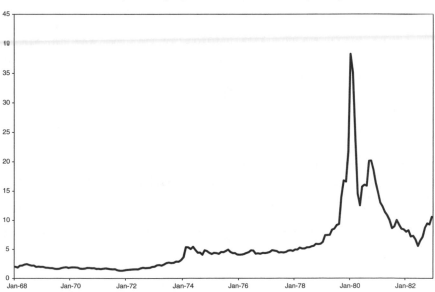

Data courtesy of Bloomberg Associates.

By the time Stuart was four, the piggybank was heavy with dimes, quarters, and half-dollars. I explained to him that it was his bank, but he was not to touch it, because it would eventually pay his way to college. We established a ritual on his birthday, pouring out the coins and counting his wealth.

By the time he was seven, there were no new-minted silver coins for his bank, but I had become adept at sorting out silver from dross and was able to add more coins—at a fast-dwindling rate—until 1980. On his fourteenth birthday, in January 1981, when we counted out his savings, he had just over $100 face value, but with silver now selling at $51 an ounce, they were worth more than $2000. I recommended he sell. He said, "Give me a day to think about it, Dad."

The next day he authorized me to sell half his position.

I took the bag of coins with me to a dealer in Toronto. I stood in a long line. People were cashing in everything silver they had. It was weighed by the storekeeper, who then paid cash. The man ahead of me in line had antique candlesticks. He knew they would be melted down within hours, but he'd have his money.

I got Stuart's $1000 and set off to a sales meeting in Toronto. I was trying to win the investment management of a union pension fund for our firm. Our investment performance compared very favorably to other Canadian investment managers during the 1980s, because we were great believers in endless inflation.

In my presentation to the all-male union committee, I said I'd changed my views on inflation because of what Paul Volcker was doing. I told them interest rates were about to peak, and long-term bonds were going to become the next winning asset class. For me, and for the consultant who had arranged for my appearance, this was a sea change. I had achieved notoriety in investment circles during the 1970s by telling audiences, "The proper holding period for a long-term bond is the same as for a hand grenade after you've pulled the pin."

They appeared uninterested in my presentation, so I decided to try a new tack, and told them about my son's piggybank and how he was cashing in his bet on inflation.

That got their attention. They began peppering me with questions.

The consultant called me a week later. "Don, I don't know if you made up that story, but it got you half the business. When you told a committee of Italian fathers about your son's piggybank, they were sold."

Postscript: The store on Queen Street went bankrupt days later. The silver bubble was about to burst. Although the price of silver on the commodity exchange would stay strong until March, that bankruptcy showed the flaw in the reasoning of the Hunts and their fellow speculators who thought they could corner the market. They reasoned that the amount of newly mined silver was grossly inadequate for the demand. Furthermore, there were only a few pure silver mines in the whole world. Most silver is found—in relatively small amounts per ton of ore mined—mixed in with ore bodies mined primarily for lead and zinc, and some is also found associated with gold mines. Because even a 900 percent increase in silver prices would not mean great new production of lead and zinc to get that silver, silver had to keep going higher. The ultimate collapse in silver prices came because the Hunts grossly underestimated the amount of the potential meltdown of "aboveground silver."

Although the supply of new silver was scanty, the supply of old silver worldwide was huge. It wasn't in bars of bullion. It was in other forms, where melting and/or refining became profitable once silver prices rose above $15 an ounce—let alone $40. First to respond to this bonanza were hospitals. They began refining their old x-rays for their silver content, and, to coin a phrase, found they had a gold mine.

Next came coin dealers, who started paying premiums for bagged silver coins—the ones minted before the U.S. Mint's supply of silver ran out. They were melted down into bars of bullion and sold into the commodity market. Then came hundreds of small furnace operators (like the store where I sold Stuart's cache for cash) who would buy anything silver, paying cash on the nail. They also produced bullion bars, which ended up in the commodity exchanges.

The Hunts had virtually cornered the world market for bars of bullion and had also virtually cornered the world futures market for delivery of bullion. They owned all the silver there was, except for all the old silver out there that could be melted down—and then everything old was new again.

Afterward, two of the Hunt brothers—who had been members of the small league of the truly rich Big League—were bankrupt. The financial survivor was Lamar, who had invested some of his share of the inheritance from their father in his football club, the Kansas City Chiefs. He was the only rich Hunt brother left standing amid the wreckage of the silver Triple Waterfall collapse.

Oil Stocks

Oil was a different investment story, because, apart from stories we heard from time to time of fully laden tankers resting for years in Norwegian fjords, investors did not load up on physical oil. They did buy futures, but the real story of this Triple Waterfall was in the prices of shares in the oil companies.

At its peak in 1981, Dome Petroleum (the Nortel of its time) was roughly one-quarter of the weight of the Toronto Stock Exchange. It would be virtually bankrupt within three years.

At their peak in 1982 (see Chart 3-4), oil stocks—a group that includes integrated oil companies, refiners, exploration and production companies, and drilling and oil service companies—formed 29.5 percent of the weight of all stocks in the S&P 500. At their bottom in 1999, their weight was under 3.5 percent. Once again, a Buy and Hold strategy would prove disastrous.

There were two components in the Shared Mistake that led to oil stocks' Triple Waterfall:

1. The conviction that, with the possible exception of gold or silver, oil was the best and safest hedge against inflation, which would never be controlled.

2. The conviction that oil would remain in short supply forever; periods of weakness would mean modest price pullbacks, but they would be followed by periods of sustained shortage, which would

CHART 3-4   Toronto Stock Exchange Oil & Gas Index (January 7, 1977 to August 31, 2000)

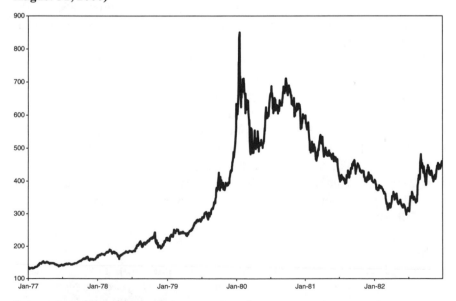

Data courtesy of Bloomberg Associates.

drive prices to new peaks in each cycle, with $50-a-barrel prices likely to be the average. Moreover, near-permanent instability in the Middle East meant that oil prices would at times hit $100 a barrel. The two oil shocks of the 1970s had shown the power of OPEC and the willingness of the Middle Eastern oil producers to combine in political-driven strategies against the West.

From the mid-1970s on, oil company shares became a special kind of growth stock. They were the glamour stocks of what came to be called "the New Economy" (a term that would help create the seventh and greatest Triple Waterfall two decades later). The futurists coined that term to describe companies that produced "scarce" commodities and thus benefited from a world of scarcity: not enough fuel, not enough food, not enough metals, and not enough forests. These were the "New Economy companies."

As oil stocks became glamour stocks, Shills & Mountebanks (yes, they had S&Ms in that New Economy, too) and Pied Pipers emerged to pitch the monstrous rewards of investing in the Arctic Ocean, drilling for geopressurized methane deep under the Louisiana crust, and shale deposits in the Rockies, let alone the projects in new African nations amid endless civil wars.

After the collapse of the regime of the Shah of Iran, oil prices skyrocketed anew. A new sense of permanent crisis became ingrained in the thinking of oil companies, investment bankers, investors, academics, politicians in democracies, and among the dictators in the oil-exporting nations. Jimmy Carter, sweater-clad because the White House heat had been turned down, spoke to Americans of a "new crisis of confidence," which became known as the "malaise" of America.

With that kind of unanimity of opinion, companies in any aspect of the exploration, production, and refining of hydrocarbons found themselves showered with investment capital at a time when cashflows were rising rapidly. Although it would be a splendid ride for investors holding oil stocks, it would not create hordes of new billionaires, as would the next "New Economy" mania. Stock options were seldom seen and rarely heard of, so the executives and other insiders of the oil companies did not become billionaires during this boom.

What they could—and did—do was invest in their own businesses. They poured money into every aspect of hydrocarbon exploration, production, refining, and marketing. Skyrocketing costs of drilling rigs and skyrocketing labor rates for oil service personnel were no deterrent to drilling in remote locations. Oil was king, and his courtiers showered him with their wealth. This would prove to be one of history's greatest examples of Shared Mistake.

To quote P. J. O'Rourke (in another context): If you shower company executives with virtually free money in amounts beyond their wildest dreams, it is the equivalent of giving a party of teenage boys whiskey and car keys.

During the late 1970s, oil companies built refineries and pipelines far beyond what the market could absorb, and technology improvement in the decades since then has meant that output from the refineries has continued to expand. They drilled for oil and gas in locations that, even if great discoveries had been made, only astronomic product prices could justify.

In other words, they provided the world of the 1980s—and for most of the 1990s—with energy security and cheap energy.

The disinflationary world of the 1980s and the quasideflationary world of the 1990s were driven, in significant measure, by the collapses of the inflation hedges, and in particular by the overinvestment in hydrocarbon production and refining from oil's Triple Waterfall.

Investors during those decades who invested in the former darlings of the 1970s were losers.

Investors during those decades who invested in the disinflation-driven sectors of the market—such as technology, financials, consumer staples, and consumer cyclicals—were big winners from what proved to be the greatest bull market of all time.

THE NIKKEI CRASH: 1985 TO ?

Japan's experience with a Triple Waterfall (see Chart 3-5) reflects the unique qualities of that society. As a conquered nation that had democracy imposed on it by General MacArthur, Japan had a special sense of vulnerability. This led to large-scale protectionism, particularly in food production. The nation has had the most autarkic agricultural policies on Earth.

A recent OECD Report compares government support payments to farmers per agricultural hectare. Australian farmers receive $2, Canadians $53, American farmers $117—a sum that will rise sharply because of the 2002 Farm Bill—and European Union farmers $676 per hectare. Japanese farmers receive $9709 per hectare.

Because of the thriftiness that insecurity promotes, the formidable engineering and export prowess of Japan Inc., and because Japan never experienced a true postwar baby boom, the nation was an excess cash generator by the mid-1970s. (The United States never experienced the thriftiness of insecurity, and its Baby Boom meant that most of its internally generated capital was needed for housing, schools, superhighways, etc.)

CHART 3-5 Nikkei (January 1, 1985 to September 26, 2002)

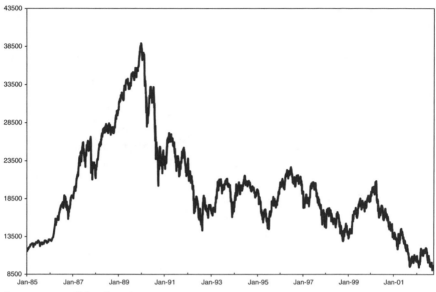

Data courtesy of Bloomberg Associates.

Since it was national policy to keep the yen's value low to protect local manufacturers and farmers, Japan used its swelling exchange and private capital reserves to invest abroad. It swiftly became the United States' greatest creditor, a factor that Japanese prime ministers sometimes used to advantage in hardball negotiating between the two countries.

Japan's cheap yen policy ultimately foundered on the rocks of a dangerously overvalued dollar as the Twin Deficits of the Reagan era—fiscal and Current Account—undermined global confidence in the reserve currency, despite the prudent monetary management of Paul Volcker.

On September 21, 1985, at a meeting at the Plaza Hotel in New York, Treasury Secretary James Baker got the finance ministers of the other four leading industrial nations to agree to a managed devaluation of the dollar. Baker assured them that this would prevent the protectionists in Congress from imposing massive trade barriers on imports of foreign goods, thereby threatening the global recovery. They agreed.

But the dollar fell so far and fast that by 1987 it was threatening to once again become an engine of global inflation. Meeting at the storied Louvre in Paris (see "Monetarism, 1975–1989," in Chapter 6), the finance ministers agreed on a new joint policy of dollar support, conditioned upon control of U.S. budget deficits. The erosion of the dollar under that support agreement triggered the stock market crash of October 19, 1987, when stocks fell 22.6 percent.

That pattern of global cooperation pulled Japan from its bystander role of the 1970s, and it became a key actor by the mid-1980s. So when the stock market plunged, the world called on Japan to reflate prodigiously to avert a global economic collapse.

The Bank of Japan vigorously resisted the pressures imposed on it by the government and by the Ministry of Finance. However, it was forced to yield. It launched a sustained, massive monetary expansion that did indeed save the global economy and capital markets, but to the horror of the Bank of Japan, it sent Japanese stocks and real estate into orbit. The stock and real estate booms fed off each other as they soared.

Struggling to export capital to prevent the domestic bubble from reaching the bursting point, Japan bought properties abroad. (Earlier, Japanese companies had bought U.S. and European companies, stirring massive protest, so the nation switched to buying assets.) Japanese companies set records for prices of Old Masters and Impressionists at global art auctions. Another useful feature of those trophy acquisitions was that they counted in the trade statistics as imports from the nations where the art auctions were held. American and European manufacturers were having tough times making anything that the Japanese would be willing to buy, so sell them a Rubens, Cézanne, or Monet. Pebble Beach and Rockefeller Center became Japanese territory.

I was told back then that five or six golf courses had been opened between Vancouver and Whistler, British Columbia, where only Japanese businessmen could play. It was cheaper to buy the land, build the courses, and fly them there to play than to buy land at home or buy memberships in local clubs, which were selling for the price of apartment buildings in the United States. Those were the days when entire Japanese wedding parties were being flown to Vancouver, because it was cost-effective to hold the weddings in Vancouver hotels, compared to Tokyo establishments.

As astonishing as the rise in price of Japanese stocks was the Sinobubble in real estate. It was estimated in 1989 that if the Imperial Gardens in Tokyo were to come on the market, they would sell for more than the value of all the real estate in California.

At least one American capitalized on this bubble. A leveraged buyout operator named Al Cecchi bought Northwest Airlines, then sold its Tokyo office building for nearly the entire value of the airline prior to his takeover bid.

You might wonder: How could Japanese people buy real estate at those prices? This was not a society peopled with billionaires or even a large supply of centimillionaires. CEOs of companies such as Toyota earned roughly 20 times what their factory employees took home, apart from perks like golf club memberships.

Answer: Almost anyone with a friendly banker could afford it. Japanese banks were awash in cash because of the monetary explosion and the endless buildup of bank deposits—given Japanese habits of thrift—that they were eager to lend money out on any asset-based loans they could find.

By the time the Bank of Japan got the freedom to tighten, the Nikkei had reached such towering levels that Japanese stocks had become the biggest weight in global indices, far outstripping the United States, which had an economy roughly twice the size of Japan's. Nine of the ten biggest banks in the world were Japanese, and their loans were perilously tied to stocks and real estate. Japanese corporate profits peaked in the first half of 1989, but stock prices kept rising until the bank started tightening.

The Bank of Japan started tightening in December, raising the Overnight Discount Rate from 4.25 to 6 percent over the next eight months. The Nikkei fell by about one-third, and the first deflationary Triple Waterfall since 1929 had completed the First Cascade.

By the time the bank had begun easing, a self-reinforcing deflationary crash and recession process was established. As asset prices fell, Japanese banks were hollowed out. Without a dynamic banking system, the economy lost its vibrancy. The worse the problems for the banks, the more stock and real estate prices fell, and the greater the financial problems of the banks. The only speed in this downward spiral was the acceleration as segments of the economy chased their own tails.

A key component of the Shared Mistake that destroyed Japanese financial and economic global leadership was an inability among the elites to distinguish asset inflation from economic inflation.

The asset inflation that drove stock and real estate prices to incredible levels was rooted in the national desire to build domestic inflation hedges in a global economy in which inflation would always and forever be the primary challenge to the price system. Since Japan did not produce oil, gold, or silver, it lacked the domestic inflation hedges enjoyed by North Americans and Arabs.

But what the Japanese consensus ignored—and in Japan a consensus can be as stiff and unyielding as concrete—were three important aspects of the inflation question:

First, despite the monetary torrent and soaring asset prices, actual inflation was low, held down by productivity gains and by the determination of Japan Inc. to remain globally competitive.

Second, the nation was already entering demographic deflation, a condition that was almost unknown to demographers, and therefore a special case requiring unusual caution. Not only were the Japanese living longer in retirement—the Japanese live longer than anyone except the ruling clique in Beijing—but the collapse in birthrates meant the nation was not even replacing itself, let alone growing. That meant the real estate bubble was an even greater menace to the nation's longer-run financial stability than it would be if the next generation were more populous than the current generation. To whom will one sell the small homes being built at prices of roughly $1000 (U.S.) per square foot of floor space?

Third, the Japanese banking system never really complied with the Basel Accord because it never faced up to the implications of grossly inflated asset prices for its asset-based lending. Nor did it use reasonable valuations for much of its lending to *keiretsus*—business alliances in which each company owned stock in other members of "the group"—which included suppliers and customers. Once those asset prices began to shrink to realistic levels, and once global competition began to challenge the weaker members of the *keiretsus,* these houses of cards would collapse.

Finally, the end of the Cold War removed one of the few remaining contributors to global inflation (as discussed in "The Costs of War," in Chapter 4).

Japan's Triple Waterfall smashed the image of Japan Inc. as global economic shogun who could pick and choose his conquests at will. In 1989, for example, American CEOs representing industries as disparate as automobiles, office equipment, and banking openly talked of the real possibility that their industries would be totally dominated by Japanese companies within five years. (Bankers were particularly worried because Japanese banks were gradually taking over corporate lending in the United States based on their willingness to make loans at rates so low that no U.S. bank could compete.)

Then, rather suddenly, the Triple Waterfall washed away that seeming invincibility forever, substituting a gnawing, cancerous deflation.

That deflation, born in the Triple Waterfall of Japan's sense of endless superiority and uniqueness, was too powerful a force to contain within those islands. Like the wind, it spreads across the Pacific, changing pricing structures everywhere it touches down. Since 1997 it has been joined by an even stronger wind that started in China, a wind that is a new threat to the reeling power of Japan Inc.

THE NASDAQ CRASH: 1997 TO ?

Why was anyone surprised?

In retrospect, what is most astonishing about this display of folly, foolishness, and fraud on a scale that would awe Cecil B. DeMille or James Cameron is that it was such an accurate replay of previous Triple Waterfalls that anyone with knowledge of stock market history could not possibly have been astonished at the outcome.

This one went through each of the three stages in the run-up exactly according to script. It reached a peak that was equivalent to silver at $54 and gold at $875, and then began a collapse that has been a near-perfect three-stage plunge to oblivion. In the final stages of that 1999–2000 orgiastic rush, the Fanaticism stage had such power that it exceeded any previous mania. Tech stock buyers in January and February 2000 were so out of touch with reality that they had more in common with the Kool-Aid drinkers in Jonestown than with the Jazz Age bathtub-gin slurpers who were buying stocks in September 1929.

That Wall Street's best and brightest were urging investors on to this mass financial suicide is the greatest indictment of the ethics and competency of the Street in its long and colorful history. *There was no—repeat no—intellectual justification for tech and telecom stocks at those levels.* At the peak, Nasdaq's multiple was 351 times earnings (when the earnings of money-losing companies were included). Two and a half years later, after a 75 percent collapse, Nasdaq's multiple was infinite, because collectively its member companies were losing money. Even with a 75 percent plunge, the index had not pushed the great mass of tech and telecom stocks into a range that investors using conventional stock market valuation techniques could find acceptable (see Charts 2-1 and 3-6 through 3-8).

As the collapse unfolded, some people whose voices could not be heard above the shouting during the Fanaticism stage emerged. Some of them compared this mania to Dutch Tulipmania (1634–1637), and Wall Street's Shills & Mountebanks were shocked—*shocked!*—at the comparison. Tulip bulbs were mere trinkets, but these were real companies!

That comparison is easy, and amusing, but as a few revisionist historians have observed, it's unfair.

They argue that sheer survival might have explained why the famously phlegmatic Dutch seemed to go crazy for unique or rare tulip bulbs. Comparing Nasdaq at 5000 to Dutch tulips at the peak is unfair *to the Dutch*. The "mania" occurred during a phase in the Thirty Years War when Spanish Catholic troops were making progress toward a reconquest of the

CHART 3-6   Cisco (January 1, 1997 to December 31, 2002)

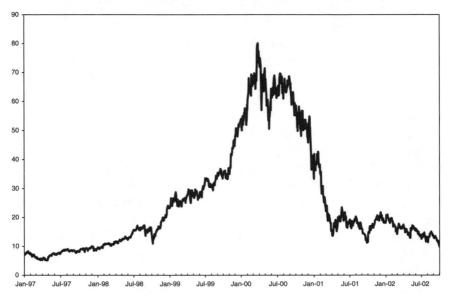

Data courtesy of Bloomberg Associates.

CHART 3-7   JDS Uniphase (January 1, 1997 to December 31, 2002)

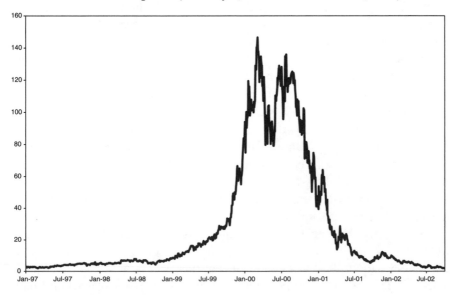

Data courtesy of Bloomberg Associates.

CHART 3-8   WorldCom (January 1, 1997 to October 3, 2002)

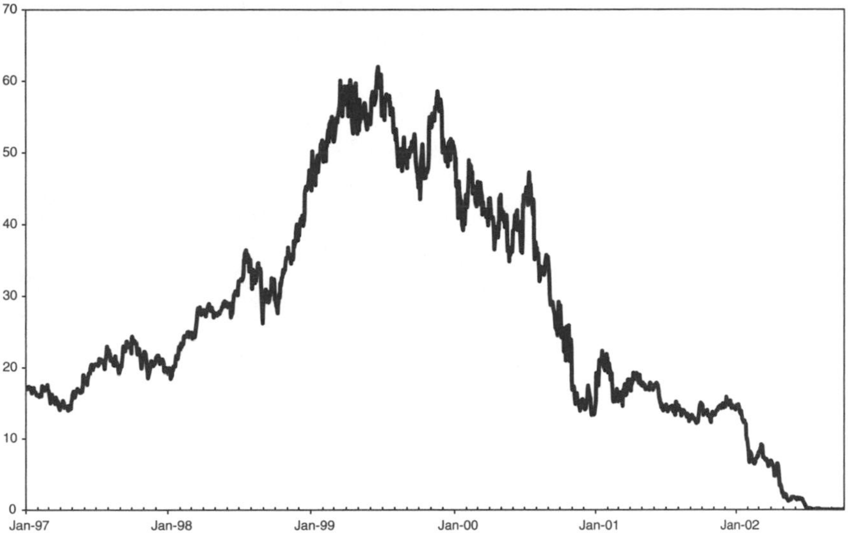

Data courtesy of Bloomberg Associates.

Netherlands. Since the Reformation, Spanish generals had been known in the Netherlands for applying the practices of the Spanish Inquisition to Dutch Calvinists. That meant red-hot grills, burning at the stake, and other Spanish enthusiasms.

The Dutch army under Frederick Henry, Prince of Orange, was in trouble when tulips took off. Why? Some market historians argue that it was, in part, a matter of survival. The Dutch bourgeois included many of the world's best horticulturists, and, goes the argument, they could escape to Protestant Germany or Britain and set up business again if the Spanish conquered Holland. Unique (not, if you'll pardon the pun, garden variety) bulbs could be for skilled horticulturists—at least in theory—what diamonds would be for German Jews three centuries later.

There was *no* such justification for tech stock buyers in 1999–2000. They were in the grip of the greatest collective idiocy in the history of finance, fueled by the most shameless sales pitches in the history of finance. At the core of this sordid sales phenomenon was the endless repetition of a seductive trade-off: between "New Economy" and "Old Economy" stocks. By labeling everything tied to computers, telecom, and the Internet as "New Economy," and the companies that collectively delivered more than 90 percent of GDP as the "Old Economy," the Shills & Mounte-banks were able to justify price-earnings ratios that made Japanese bank stocks at their 1989 peak look like deep-value stocks in comparison.

Some years ago, William F. Buckley, Jr. wrote a column about a news story of a high school boy who objected to a music class that included some exposure to the music of J. S. Bach, rather than entirely rock music. "Who cares about Bach?" this youth griped. "He's just some dead white guy." Buckley lamented the sterility in this young man's consciousness.

The anti-Bach boy could have been a symbol of the Nasdaq-driven stock mania. This was a market that loudly proclaimed that none of the old rules applied: earnings according to previous rules—obsolete; price-earn-ings ratios—obsolete; tangible asset ratios on the balance sheet—obsolete.

In place of these antiquated concepts of equity (and bond) valuation, we were told of "new metrics" (which meant totally new rules for valuing stocks). None of that "old dead Bach" stuff. Among these metrics were the number of patents issued to companies, and the number of hits on their Web site.

In *The Closing of the American Mind,* Allan Bloom described the cumulative degradation of an education system that occurred when teach-ers and students alike disdained the best of the past in favor of whatever was cool and new. That melancholy treatise came out in 1987, long before the tech Waterfall. But the mind set he described was the perfect breeding ground for the prejudices and inanities that would coalesce and metastasize into the New Economy, a construct that would devastate financial markets, impoverish many, wound millions, impose a recession on America and the rest of the industrial world, spring China from the margin of that industrial world to the most formidable competitive force within it—at the expense of millions of jobs in the West—and spawn more centimillionaires and bil-lionaires than all the economic progress of history.

How low will these stocks go during the long Third Stage of collapse? Many (particularly the dot coms, whose lifespan was the financial equiva-lent of the mayfly) have already paid the full price, having gone bankrupt (but not before enriching their insiders and Wall Street). Some of those, such as WorldCom—or World*Con*, as it became known—have joined the ranks of the undead, living in the dark world of Chapter 11. Many others will go to the cemetery or to WorldCom's world. Others will survive, and will ultimately prosper as being the last left standing.

Like other Triple Waterfalls, this one unleashed an excess of capital spending that leaves a huge hangover of excess capacity. Unlike, say, the oil Triple Waterfall, there were hundreds of firms with multi-billion-dollar market caps functioning in this mania, which meant the overspending was on a previously unimaginable scale. As of the summer of 2002, only 4 percent of all optical fiber cable was "lit"—which means the overcapacity was 25 to 1. Nor will this cable rust: It is glass, heavily enrobed in protective coverings. It will lie, intact, at the bottom of the sea like the *Titanic*. Unlike the *Titanic*, however, whose demise created opportunities for less sumptuous steamships, those cables will live on as near-zero cost competitors for the living—companies living dangerously as they burn through the money left in their treasuries from their heavy financings made when people really believed that demand for fiber would continue to grow forever at 60 percent a year.

As the mania took hold, the wise Paul Volcker sounded a warning: "The fate of the world economy is now totally dependent on the growth of the U.S. economy, which is dependent on the stock market, whose growth is dependent on about 50 stocks, half of which have never reported any earnings."

C H A P T E R

How Wars Shape Economies and Markets

Charles F. Lummis, having fractured his right arm so badly that the bone protruded, and being alone in the desert, gave his canteen strap two flat turns about the wrist, buckled it around a cedar tree, mounted a nearby rock, set his heels upon the edge, and threw himself backward. He fainted; but the bone was set.

—H. Kephart

"War is hell."

General Sherman's dictum applies to those who actually fight in it and to those unfortunate civilians whose losses are reported as "collateral damage." Mere survival became the overarching objective for millions of people in the last century, known as the "Century of Total War."

For investors, war is Purgatory. It can include the sudden shock to asset values that comes from the sudden shock of war. The three most recent examples have been the three Arab surprise attacks: the Yom Kippur War of 1973, Saddam Hussein's invasion of Kuwait in 1990, and al Qaeda's attacks on 9/11. Stock prices were part of the collateral damage from those shocks.

But *by themselves,* those assaults did not inflict lasting damage to stock prices. It was not the 1973 war that savaged the global economy and stock prices, it was the oil boycott and the trebled prices of oil. Saddam's invasion hit stock prices hard and oil soared to $40 per barrel, but the sudden victory of Desert Storm unleashed a spectacular stock market rally and drove oil prices to lower levels than they had been prior to the attack. Stock prices collapsed after 9/11, but then rallied when it became apparent that the economy was going to bounce back.

These short, sharp shocks are not the most important challenge to investor survival in wars. "War is regarded as nothing but the continuation of state policies with other means," said von Clausewitz, and when politics sucks much of the air out of the economy, there is little breathing room for equities. Capitalism is a system of risk taking, investment, research, and opportunism; it flourishes best when government creates a healthy environment based on the rule of law that offers the widest range of choice for businesses and consumers. That means peace, not war.

Hikers and campers may fear a sudden attack from a bear or cougar, but few fatalities occur. A surprise bite, however small, from a rabid raccoon or bat is to be feared: Unless inoculated promptly, the victim will die an agonizing death, and yet such outcomes are almost unknown in our time because the vaccines are so readily available and so effective. More insidious, and therefore more dangerous, is the bite of a mosquito carrying West Nile virus, malaria, yellow fever, or encephalitis. The immediate pain is trivial and short-lived. In many cases the victim may not even notice it. The real damage comes later, and can be prolonged and debilitating, if not fatal.

For equity investors who don't serve in the military or whose property is not damaged in fighting, the effect of modern wars is prolonged debilitation of portfolio valuations—for which there is no known cure except peace.

PEACE AT REASONABLE PRICE

In general, stocks are worth much less in wartime than in peacetime. That should be obvious, but there is a (to me, at least) surprising amount of conviction that war is great news for capitalists. The source of this conspiracy theory of history is, of course, Marx and Lenin, and the dwindling band of self-styled intellectuals who consider their analyses relevant.

Wars are double trouble for equity investors: They reduce corporate profits and they reduce the price-earnings ratios paid by the market on those profits.

First is the twofold effect on corporate profits: Wars may force governments to raise taxes, and "excess profits" are ripe fund-raising targets; and war-driven strains imposed on the economy (as discussed below) reduce pretax profits.

As for price-earnings ratios, according to a Hansberger Global Investors study, the S&P has only experienced six years in which the year-end p/e ratio ranged between 5.2 and 7.4: Two of those years were 1916 and 1917. Of the 15 years in which the p/e was between 7.4 and 9.7, two years were in World War I, one was in World War II, three were in the Korean War, and two—1973–1974—covered the period that included the Yom Kippur War.

In contrast, every year in which the p/e closed above 21 was a peace-time year in which the threat of war seemed minimal: 1894, 1921, 1933, 1961, 1991, 1992, 1993, 1997, 1998, 1999, and the first 20 months of this millennium.

Note that 1961 was the only year of the Cold War in which the S&P closed at a high p/e. That was the first year of the Kennedy presidency, a time of optimism about the magical Camelot personalities who would blow away the stale frost of the Cold War. After Kennedy's troubles in the summit meeting with Khrushchev and the Cuban missile crisis, the S&P multiple went back to its normal Cold War range: 16 to 19.

Why are stocks worth less in wartime?

Because war is one of the two completely inflationary things modern governments undertake on a grand scale. The other is the debauching of the nation's currency through reckless printing of money, a problem among many unstable new nations. The advanced industrial nations, in a temporary spasm of panic, collectively seemed to try to adopt "banana republic" monetarism in 1974 after the oil boycott, and the outcome was double-digit inflation and stagflation.

Thankfully, hyperinflation like that of the Weimar Republic (see "Paper Promises," in Chapter 6) is rare. Apart from foolish monetary policies, governments only contribute to inflation by misconceived spending (such as the 2002 U.S. farm bill), protectionism, and forcing wages higher than the market would dictate. Nevertheless, even grand-scale absurdities such as the European Union's Common Agricultural Policy (which spends nearly half the total E.U. budget on farm subsidies) do not spawn painful inflation because they also contribute to the creation of goods and services. (Both the U.S. and E.U. farm programs drive down global food prices, hurting Third World producers but benefiting consumers elsewhere.)

War is different . . . uniquely different.

War is about taking men and women from civilian production and sending them to kill other men and women and destroy the enemy's means of production. It is the antithesis of the production, distribution, and selling that are the roots of capitalist wealth building.

Governments manage wars on the three C system: command, control, and cost-plus. Railroad cars, transport ships, and planes are requisitioned, sometimes without warning, causing disruptions and supply shocks across the economy. The intense demand encourages strategically positioned unions to make potentially inflationary wage or staffing demands (such as the U.S. West Coast longshoremen's job actions in 2002). Prices for "essential" goods and services are sometimes frozen, creating black markets. The multitudinous variety of goods needed to fight the war are ordered, and if suppliers cannot meet the military's demands, they can be put on a cost-plus basis as long as the emergency continues. (The rebuilding of the outer ring of the Pentagon within 12 months after 9/11, for example, an astonishing accomplishment, doubtless imposed inflationary pressures on the construction industry in the Washington area.)

When governments get big, they become arrogant and inefficient. When governments become gigantic, they become even more arrogant and inefficient. When governments are at war, and move into a command position across the economy, there are no constraints on their arrogance and inefficiency except the individual patriotic and moral impulses of public servants. Those impulses are not distributed equally or universally, either through nature or nurture.

Of the many stories that could be told about the inefficiencies of governments in wartime, a good one is the account of how a patriot took great personal risk in confident reliance on those tendencies.

Bill Rickenbacker, my officemate at the *National Review,* chuckled when he told me his tale of cheekiness and audacity in counting on the Pentagon to behave bureaucratically.

He enlisted as a pilot at the outbreak of the Korean War. He won his wings at a base in Arizona and was ready to be shipped to war. Then his father, the legendary Captain Eddie, America's leading air ace in World War I, came through the base on his barnstorming tour to build enthusiasm for the war effort.

The next day, Bill was assigned a desk job.

He knew his father would never have asked the base commander to exempt his son from war, but concluded that the commander had made a unilateral decision that the Rickenbacker family had already done enough for the nation's war effort.

Bill pondered his alternatives, then reached a decision. The Pentagon, after all, was just a branch of government, so it was unlikely to be much more efficient.

Relying on the slowness of bureaucratic response, he walked out the front door of the base, hitchhiked to the Northeast, doffed his uniform, and won his wings all over again. By the time they caught up to him, he had already participated in air action over Korea. The Air Force blustered about his defiance, but on reconsideration, decided to close its already large file prepared for submission at his court-martial.

THE COSTS OF WAR

Apart from the control given to government in wartime, what are the market distortions that make equities less valuable?

- War puts particular pressure on the prices and availability of key commodities, such as oil, chemicals, and base metals.

- War distorts global trade patterns in at least two ways: It imperils the sea lanes, and it promotes protectionism by narrowing trade options to allies and neutrals.

- War is damaging to civilian productivity because of anticipatory hoarding, National Guard call-ups that break up production groups, and by diverting technology research (and leading scientific brains) away from the development of civilian goods and manufacturing systems and into war-related products and systems.

- War distorts capital investment, as high-priority, cost-plus, military-related projects that have to be completed immediately get top priority. Meanwhile, civilian capital spending is cut back as companies fill defense contracts, awaiting the war's outcome to see where opportunities lie.

- War discourages consumers from making longer-term commitments, such as buying a car or a home, or moving to a new community to take a better job. (The one important exception to that rule is the sudden increase in marriages contracted just before the troopships and planes depart.)

Although most investors can easily understand how World Wars I and II affected equity valuations, few seem to understand how the Cold War hurt the economy and the stock market.

The Cold War was only occasionally a shooting war, but in economic terms it was the most expensive war ever fought. Over a half century, American and British taxpayers—and, to a much lesser degree, other NATO taxpayers and their Japanese counterparts—paid trillions of dollars to prevent Soviet communism from invading Western Europe, and to prevent Chinese communism from taking over East Asia. For much of that period, millions of young men were drafted, thereby removing them from civilian production in farms, factories, and offices, or delaying—and in many cases ruling out—their higher education.

Because the Cold War was a fixed feature of the global landscape, most people came to assume it would last forever, and they planned their lives on the assumption that the Cold Peace would continue.

That is the reason so many investors failed in the early 1990s to understand the huge economic and stock market implications of winning the Cold War. Trade would be freer, defense spending would plummet across most of the world, technology companies that had relied heavily on the Pentagon would fall all over themselves to design consumer products, and capital would move across the globe with relative ease. The fall of the Berlin Wall was one of the great moments in the history of capitalism, not just of Germany. In fact, the war's end was the springboard to greater prosperity in other parts of the world than in East Germany, despite hundreds of billions of deutschemarks in aid from West Germany and massive directed capital investment (such as moving the capital from Bonn to Berlin).

Communism collapsed everywhere except in North Korea, Vietnam, Laos, Cuba, and China (though enthusiastic students thronged Tiananmen Square in 1989, believing that the tide was on their side; it never penetrated into China enough to transform the government).

In one of history's droller ironies, the biggest political winner of the war won primarily by Ronald Reagan and Margaret Thatcher was Bill Clinton, whose contribution to the victory was, at best, nonexistent. He came to office with the conditions that liberals had dreamed about for decades: gigantic, growing Peace Dividends that would let him cut the Pentagon's budget share of GDP to less than half the level it had reached under Reagan. Those dividends let Clinton deliver something Americans had long believed no administration would ever achieve: budget surpluses on a scale that convinced independent voters (and grumpy Republicans) that he was no mere tax-and-spend Democrat.

The end of the Cold War delivered something else, something far more important, but because it came in gradually, on little cat feet, few commentators noticed its appearance until long after the Cold War was over. By removing war's inflationary pull on the economy, it grew consumers' real incomes without big—inflationary—wage increases; it reduced the cost of social security pensions and pensions for retired government employees; it dramatically lowered interest rates on the burdensome national debt and interest rates on consumer and corporate borrowing, including, most significantly, home mortgages.

For me, the end of the Cold War raised a new kind of price risk: deflation. The only previous American experience with sustained negative CPI numbers was during the Great Depression. But history told us that deflation had come after almost every major war since the American Revolution, including the Napoleonic wars, the Civil War, and World War I. It hadn't come after World War II because the Cold War came so quickly on its heels that a peacetime deflationary economy never became entrenched.

An economy that moves from inflation to deflation experiences the good parts of the switch first: plunging interest rates, an end to shortages, bargain prices in stores, and an improvement in the income security position of the aged and disabled.

Deflation's effect on stock prices can be beneficial—if it's controlled and corporate profits are strong—or disastrous—if deflation gets out of control and corporate profits collapse, as in the 1930s or in modern Japan.

As an historian by training, I knew that the sustained inflation of the Cold War was an aberration. Four decades in which the only question about inflation was, "How high?" had long since convinced most people that inflation was ubiquitous and inevitable. Volcker, Reagan, Thatcher, and their allies might drive inflation down to tolerable levels, but it would come back. It always had. ("Always," of course, meant history since 1945. Anything before that didn't have meaning to most people.)

The leading recent work on the question of price stability through the ages is David Hackett Fischer's *The Great Wave* (New York: Oxford University Press, 1996). Fischer analyzes price data from Europe and America for nearly all of the Second Millennium, demonstrating conclusively that, apart from crop failures and other natural disasters, inflation on a multiyear basis is associated with wars and preparation for wars.

The experience of the age of Pax Britannica (1815–1914) is proof of that assertion. Prices were essentially unchanged for a century. The only significant inflationary period occurred during the U.S. Civil War, which had a near-catastrophic impact on the English cloth millers. (Cotton prices in the 1860s, for example, were at times higher than they would be at any time for more than 125 years.)

For readers who doubt the claim of nearly a century of price stability, and who can't face the thought of plowing through a textbook of economic history, here are three palatable research works:

Pride and Prejudice, Jane Austen, 1813

The Adventures of Sherlock Holmes, A. Conan Doyle, 1892

Gladstone: A Biography, Roy Jenkins, 1995

- In *Pride and Prejudice,* Mrs. Bennet and her five daughters would share on Mr. Bennet's death a legacy of £5000 (pounds); invested in the 4 percent War Bonds, they would earn £200 a year, or £33 each, enough to provide genteel subsistence for a gentlewoman.
- In "The Adventure of the Copper Beeches" of *The Adventures of Sherlock Holmes,* Violet Hunter consults the great detective about a mysterious employment offer for a governess. One reason for her suspicion was the salary, which was £120 a year—three times the market rate for the services of an educated gentlewoman. Seventy-nine years after *Pride and Prejudice,* and the cost of living was virtually unchanged.
- In his magisterial biography of Gladstone, Lord Jenkins, himself a former Chancellor of the Exchequer, provides scrupulous detail on Gladstone's budgets when he was at the Treasury, and thereafter as Prime Minister. He suggests in a footnote that the reader multiply the sums by 50 to get modern equivalents, adding that there was essentially no inflation during the 19th century.

Yes, there was—and is—one big difference between the world of Pax Britannica and the world of Pax Americana: Britain was on the gold standard. Paper money was exchangeable for gold, and pounds were circulated in gold sovereign form. The Bank of England couldn't print unlimited quantities of money to buy the government's debt, because as soon as inflation appeared, people would come down to Threadneedle Street to cash their bank notes in for gold.

In the modern era, the restraint on inflationary printing of money comes from modern monetary techniques and from the holders of trillions of dollars of global bonds. Ed Yardeni calls these holders the "bond vigilantes" because they have shown they will dump their bonds and run for cash or gold if governments resort to inflationary tactics. When they sell bonds heavily, interest rates soar, and there are widespread demands for restraint. (In replying to a question about how he'd like to be reincarnated,

James Carville, Clinton's 1992 campaign manager, said he'd like to come back as the bond market, because it's so powerful.)

The other important difference between the world of Pax Britannica and the present is that modern governments have assumed major roles in the economy as income stabilizers. In Elizabeth Bennet's time, the poor had recourse to what might be in their parish's poor box, but not to much else. In our time, governments operate large schemes to protect incomes, including unemployment benefits, social security, legal exemptions for unions, farm programs, winter works programs, and so on. The result is that wages don't collapse when deflation hits, as they did during tough times in the 19th century.

POSTWAR DEFLATION

My view in 1992, and since, was that despite big governments every-where, the risk to the price system was moving rapidly from inflation to deflation. I began telling clients back then that interest rates would con-tinue to fall along with inflation rates, and I told them to buy long-term zero coupon bonds to capitalize on the onset of deflation. (A zero coupon bond pays no interest—ever. What the investor gets is the principal on the bond at maturity. Very long zeros sell for small percentages of face value. When long-term interest rates fall, zero coupon bonds can easily double in value, because they are so heavily levered. Despite the roaring bull market of the late 1990s, the holder of a 30-year zero Treasury bond acquired in 1994 would have far outperformed the stock market had he or she held on to it until today.)

Most clients insisted deflation was dead. I argued that no stake had been driven through its heart. Proof that it still stalked the world could be seen in Japan. A great deflationary drama was unfolding there—a deceler-ating, stately, kabuki dance of death.

Asset deflation—in the form of falling prices for stocks and real estate—was moving into the general economy. Consumer prices had stopped rising and were starting to fall. Huge overcapacity in Japanese fac-tories meant that they kept on producing to maintain global market share and to cover their machinery costs even when prices fell below break-even levels. Because Japan was the world's second largest trading nation, those made-in-Japan deflationary forces were being exported.

Why was Japan hit so hard, and why did deflation begin to engulf that country in 1990?

These questions have been debated by economists for a decade, and there is still disagreement. The Triple Waterfall Crash of prices of stocks and real estate was the driving force of the 1990s deflation, but asset deflation cannot in itself explain the long recession that enervated what had once been a vibrant economy.

From 1987 to about 1991, the Western world had been transfixed by the blinding rays of the new Rising Sun. After the U.S. Triple Waterfall Crash of technology and growth stocks in 1973–1974, Japanese companies became the global standard in any market they seemed to choose. They began with heavy industries—steel, shipbuilding, machinery, and automobiles. By the early 1980s they were moving so rapidly into electronic technology that President Reagan had to negotiate a slowdown on Japanese chip exports to save the U.S. industry.

What Japan was doing on a grand scale was what Sweden did during World War II: winning big from war by neutrality, a stance that permitted trade with both sides. Yes, Japan was not truly neutral; and yes, unlike Sweden, it didn't sell to Nazis. But the Japanese postwar constitution forbade Japanese military aggression (as contrasted with self-defense) outside the islands, while permitting the nation to build up its defenses and its defense industry.

The result was that by 1988, Japan had the world's third-highest defense budget and Japanese manufacturers were huge suppliers to the Pentagon—and, to a lesser extent, to the armies of Western Europe.

In 1989 the fall of the Berlin Wall signaled the coming end of the Cold War. It also put much of Japan Inc. into a quandary.

Where could they replace those lucrative foreign defense markets?

A former National Security adviser told me a story just after the end of the Cold War. He had returned from a visit to Japan. While there, he naturally talked to many Japanese leaders.

He asked them, "With the Cold War over, you now have the world's third largest defense budget. What are you doing with it?"

"Oh, we are conducting extensive research on our new priorities."

"Could you give me some examples of important new research?" the American asked.

"Well, we recently completed a full analysis of what we would need if Korea attacked us, and what we would need if we attacked Korea."

"Can you imagine that?" the adviser said to me. "Suppose it were revealed that the German government had just completed a survey on what would be needed to invade France? That's the Western equivalent of the history between Korea and Japan." Perhaps those plans are being reviewed in the light of North Korea's recent intransigence.

Most observers considered the deflationary pressures emerging from Japan as good news for the global economy since it helped pull down global inflation rates, giving consumers greater buying power and central banks more breathing room (see Charts 4-1 and 4-2).

The sudden, peaceful victory in the Cold War established the United States as sole superpower. Then came the Gulf War, which was pursued by the last of the Cold War leaders, George H.W. Bush, with advanced technology and a display of massive firepower. In light of the current debate on war with Iraq, it's worth recalling the strong Democratic opposition then to fighting Iraq. Even though the United Nations had authorized a military response to Saddam Hussein's invasion of Kuwait, President Bush needed congressional authorization. Senator Kennedy led the impassioned opposition, which evoked predictions of thousands of body bags. The resolution to repel Iraq's invasion of Kuwait carried by just five votes in the Senate. Less than 300 American soldiers died from all causes in that war. Cold War antiwar emotions die hard.

The Gulf War had delayed the onset of the Peace Dividend until after President Bush's electoral defeat. With that rejection, he joined Margaret Thatcher in the roster of Cold War victors who became political losers;

CHART 4-1   U.S. Dollar Index (April 1, 1986 to December 31, 1995)

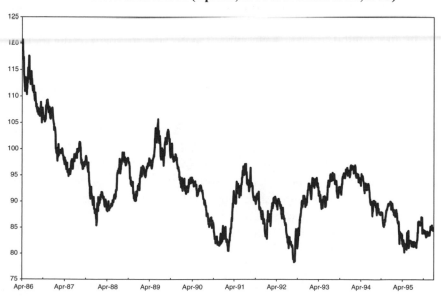

Data courtesy of Bloomberg Associates.

CHART 4-2   Yen/Dollar (January 1, 1986 to December 31, 1995)

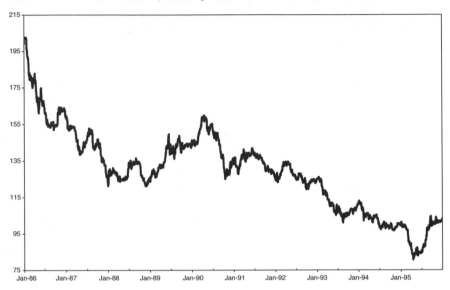

Data courtesy of Bloomberg Associates.

Germany's Helmut Kohl, who had been their staunch ally, would join them later. They were in good company: British voters booted out Churchill in the election whose results were announced while he was attending the Potsdam Conference to arrange the settlement of the victory in World War II.

War-weary voters want different leadership in peacetime. They're tired of being told to sacrifice; they want someone whose attitude is: "Let the good times roll!"

Although few saw it at the time, the war's end meant that there would be a rapid—and likely spectacular—buildup in the domestic technology industry. In particular, a system developed over two decades by and for the Pentagon—now called the Internet—would surely be developed for large-scale civilian and consumer use. Nobody talked of beating swords into plowshares, but that's just what happened—on a scale greater than even dreamy tech futurist George Gilder predicted.

When the Cold War ended, the four largest private sector employers in California were Department of Defense contractors. By 1995, 400,000 defense-related jobs had disappeared in that state alone, with nearly a million more lost in the rest of the nation.

At the peak of the Reagan buildup, defense spending accounted for 6.2 percent of GDP. At the nadir of the Clinton climb-down, it accounted for 3.0 percent.

When that budget number was announced in the fall of the year 2000, a conservative commentator noted that the nation was now back to the same level of defense spending as at the time of Pearl Harbor. Given the risks out there in an increasingly hostile world, he sourly predicted "another Pearl Harbor soon."

That Cassandraesque observation was made less than one year before 9/11.

A NEW KIND OF WAR

The sudden outbreak of the terrorist war blasted the stock market hard, with the Dow Jones Industrials plunging from 9605 to 8920 when the market reopened for trading after 9/11. Many serious market students assumed the reaction of investors had been overdone.

That was not my view, and I had the chance to expound those views to a large gathering of hedge funds and pension funds held at a closed-door meeting of the Greenwich Round Table on September 20. Four of us addressed the group.

Douglas Cliggott, then of J.P. Morgan, spoke first. He had the best forecasting record on Wall Street. He had been deeply bearish on stocks before 9/11, and he was still bearish. His analysis focused on the economy and corporate profits. The two other speakers, both associated with hedge funds, thought falling interest rates would trigger a good stock market rally (and they were proved right—for a while).

I took a different tack, discussing the effect of war on equity valuations. From the comments of other speakers and attendees, this analysis was novel to them. I argued that the correct p/e for stocks should be reduced by about 20 percent to compensate for the effects of war on the efficiency, flexibility, and profitability of the economy.

In that speech and in my writings at the time, I expressed particular concern about protectionism. As I noted, Bill Clinton would probably be taken very seriously as an important president by future historians because he'd had the wisdom, vision, and tenacity to stand up to the protectionist and parochial elements in his party. He was the president who gained legislative approval for George H. W. Bush's program of the North American Free Trade Agreement (NAFTA).

I expressed fear that, like all past wars, the new War on Terror would lead to protectionism. (That's the way it's worked out. The demands of gaining political support to prosecute the War on Terror have driven George W. Bush into the arms of the protectionists. Free trade may not be the first casualty in war, but it is surely the second. Industry after industry and vested interest after vested interest troop forward to claim that the national interest in wartime demands protection for them. 'Twas ever thus. This time the focus was steel, lumber, textiles, and agriculture—so far. As the dour Dr. Johnson noted, "Patriotism is the last refuge of a scoundrel.")

Since that Greenwich meeting, market strategists have been constantly debating the "right" price-earnings ratio for the market. To date, none of the prominent strategists has said that the War on Terror warrants a lower p/e ratio, even those who blame falling consumer optimism numbers on fear of war in Iraq.

My fears about a return to protectionism may have been realized. Because protectionism restricts choice for both consumers and businesses, it is a major negative for the stock market. It was no coincidence that President Bush's surprising (to the markets, at least) decision to embrace the steel industry's claims for protection from foreigners started the stock market down in the spring of 2002. The market's slide became vertiginous as Bush added lumber, textiles, and agriculture to the industries coddled from their economic xenophobic insecurities (see Chart 4-3). While staging the greatest sustained assault on Adam Smith's principles of any recent president, Bush made a brief visit to Latin America and Russia, where he told the locals their way to prosperity lay through free trade. It was as if a prominent atheist were to piously announce that although he hadn't changed his personal views, the nation's problems could only be solved by deep religious revival.

When conservatives rebelled against Bush's protectionism, they were told to "keep the faith." The president was so preoccupied with winning the War on Terror that he was apparently letting his political adviser, Karl Rove, call the shots on which small-scale domestic economic trade-offs with the Democrats were needed to keep control of the House and gain control of the Senate in November.

Some market historians darkly noted that it was the passage of the Smoot-Hawley Tariff that turned the correction at the end of the 1920s into the Crash of 1929 and the Great Depression. Bush had become the second Republican president to go protectionist when the real protectionist goal was protecting his own party's position in Congress. He continued his emulation of Herbert Hoover by making remarks in July (the worst month for the S&P since the Depression) that the stock market collapse was unreasonable, because "the economy is sound." (Yes, it's just a coincidence, but the three worst bear markets in the S&P 500 came with Republicans in the White House—Hoover, Nixon, and Bush.)

The War on Terror, in combination with the recession of 2001, turned the nation's fiscal situation from surplus to deficit. As we are told repeatedly, this is a new kind of war.

Will the war introduce sufficient inflationary pressures into the economy to offset the deflation still being pumped from Japan, and, more importantly, from China? (See "China's Impact on the Global Economy and Corporate Profitability," in Chapter 8.) Readers who take a trip to Wal-Mart or Target store these days will see the large-scale penetration of products made in China, East Asia, and Japan. Not since the colonial era have such large segments of the U.S. economy been captured by distant suppliers whose main competitive advantage is price. The United States is fast becoming a postindustrial society. That means bargains for consumers, but it also means the loss of millions of well-paid manufacturing jobs. No wonder North American unions are so bitterly opposed to free trade.

CHART 4-3   S&P 500 (January 1, 2002 to August 31, 2002)

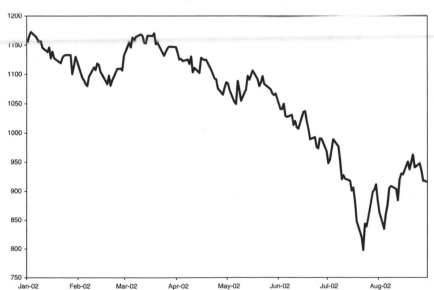

Data courtesy of Bloomberg Associates.

Will the war have sufficient impact on the economy and on corporate profitability to justify a stock market p/e retreat to Cold War levels? During the late 1990s the "New Economy" Shills & Mountebanks justified record p/e levels on the S&P (and astronomic p/e levels on Nasdaq) by talking of endless economic growth and rising profits generated by the economy's growing use of new technologies. Those forecasts have been 100 percent wrong.

One thing that will hold back business enthusiasm is the huge increase in insurance costs arising from the War on Terror. That building owners can face punitive damages (in which lawyers will collect 33 to 40 percent of the payouts) because terrorists fly gasoline-laden planes into their properties means insurers must charge huge premiums even for insurance on office buildings, let alone on planes. That leap in insurance costs comes at a time of crisis in the corporate insurance coverage for companies, their directors and officers, and for the costs arising from lawsuits based on malfeasance (see "Asbestos and the Growing Burden of Insurance Costs" in Chapter 8). No, "Enronitis" and its associated diseases have nothing to do with war, but the combination of premium increases—or outright denial of coverage—arising from the war with premium increases—or, again, outright denial of coverage—arising from malfeasance is a big burden on business, and a big burden on the stock market as well.

By the way, this is a global problem. European stock markets fell as hard as U.S. stocks in 2002; a big factor in those plunges was the forced liquidation of billions of dollars' worth of stocks held by European insurers and reinsurers who were on the hook for 9/11 and corporate malfeasance damages. On the Continent, this became a mutually reinforcing fall in equity values—insurers sold because of balance sheet problems, which drove stock prices lower, which forced more insurer selling, and so on—as European indices fell to multiyear lows. As of August 2002, the nine-year total return on the leading Morgan Stanley international stock index, EAFE (Europe, Australia, Far East), was zero. The fat returns from one of history's greatest bull markets had been completely erased.

There is never a good time for a war, but this one came at a time when America was reeling from the immense economic, financial, and human disasters inflicted from another new kind of war—a war on the ethical (and, in a few cases, the legal) principles of capitalism by a new group of financial brigands—armies of sleazebags, book cookers, unaccountable accountants, and uncountable Shills & Mountebanks who enriched themselves to the tune of hundreds of billions of dollars. Their biggest bases of assault on American wealth and on Americans' belief in their system were Silicon Valley, Houston, and Wall Street.

That latter war, which has claimed so many victims and is being waged on so many fronts, is six years old.

The War on Terror, which has claimed so many victims and is being waged on so many fronts, is not yet two years old.

C H A P T E R

Surviving Wall Street's Predators

[In a trap you are setting] the use of a lure is undoubtedly the most effective way to kill man scent. Urine of the species of animal you want to trap, and urine of the species taken when she is "in heat" or "in season" is an infallible lure for males of that species.
—R. GRAVES

W ALL STREET HAS A LONG, sometimes raffish, record of success at setting out lures to trap unwary investors. Investor survival depends on the ability to see those lures for what they are. Since its commercial beginnings as a slave market (at the Water Street waterfront), Wall Street has come a long way; still, it never seems to quite manage to cleanse itself of the habit of finding profitable ways to exploit defenseless men and women. On occasion it reverts to its worst traditions, but it always burnishes them with a patina of slick modernity.

This book is dedicated to the proposition that investor survival depends, in large measure, on how wisely one deals with Wall Street.

Outdoor enthusiasts know that in nature they can encounter pests, diseases, fires, and powerful carnivores, and they prepare themselves accordingly. They assume those risks because they want to reap the unique rewards of life away from the comforts of urban homes.

And so it is with investors. They could just leave their savings in bank accounts and savings bonds, but they know that the opportunities to grow their wealth in stocks, bonds, and mutual funds make those risks worthwhile. What experts call "capital markets pricing theory" is a simple concept: Rewards on investment are proportional to the risks in that asset class. Or: "No pain, no gain."

Common stocks have delivered superior returns to bonds and bank deposits for most periods in the past century. On a long-term basis (30 years), it is no contest.

Indeed, if stocks did not outperform bonds and bank deposits, the capitalist system could not long exist. Stocks represent the "capital" in that term popularized by Marx, "capitalism." They are the ownership component of the markets, and, as such, have a direct tie to the dynamism that drives capitalism—for better, for worse, for richer, for poorer.

Real estate also represents equity in ownership, and it is at all times an alternative investment to stocks. As American homeowners who didn't have lucrative stock options know, since 1998 real estate has been a much better and safer investment than stocks.

But these comparative returns wax and wane. Unless you are a real estate and property management expert, or unless you can share in partnerships that offer such expertise at reasonable cost, stocks should still be the core of your long-term investment policy. All the horrors and excesses of the late 1990s have not destroyed the validity of that statement.

That means you must become a customer—directly or indirectly—of Wall Street. Even if you have all your money managed by a private bank located a thousand miles from Wall Street, you are one of Wall Street's indirect customers and, simultaneously, one of its indirect prospects.

WHAT "WALL STREET" IS

The term "Wall Street" or the "Street" has long since ceased to mean just that tiny road that ends in a graveyard on Lower Manhattan. By the figure of speech known as metonymy, the term means all the investment banks and brokerage firms and their associated operations and lines of business that collectively underwrite and trade stocks and bonds, and trade commodities and financial derivatives (instruments such as futures, options, and swaps).

The names of the great Wall Street firms are important parts of American history. Nor need that importance be expressed in the past tense.

Unlike so many other American industries that once dominated their field globally—such as automobiles, steel, machinery, machine tools, consumer electronics, photography, office equipment, and computers—the great U.S. investment banks and brokers have maintained their leadership at home, while gaining market share abroad in recent decades. Big banks such as Citigroup, Merrill Lynch, Morgan Stanley, J.P. Morgan, Lehman Brothers, and Goldman Sachs are formidable, well-diversified organizations with global reach. Those firms are headquartered in Manhattan, but their branches spread across the cities and towns of America and the financial centers of the world.

The big investment banks on the Street make most of their money from three kinds of transactions:

- Underwriting and offering bonds and stocks to the public

- Trading existing bonds and stocks, either for their own account or on behalf of clients

- Advising corporations on mergers and acquisitions

They also earn fees for managing investment portfolios and mutual funds, from trading commodities and currencies, and from other kinds of businesses related to the markets.

At various times in the past two centuries, "Wall Street" has become a term of contempt, hate, and fear within the United States and in many other parts of the world. At various other times, "Wall Street" has become a term of admiration, envy, glamour, and sex appeal.

In general, investment opportunities have been best when Wall Street was most remote from the public at large.

In general, investment opportunities have been worst when Wall Street was most accessible to the public at large.

It's like fishing.

Serious fishermen fly in small, dubious airplanes to remote, bug-infested lakes, where they cheerfully fish from dawn to dusk under frequently miserable weather conditions. (I am told that fishing is "the practice of casting, trolling, and spinning while freezing, sweating, and swatting.")

Unserious fishermen fish off crowded piers, where food and beer are abundantly available, and only when the weather is salubrious.

If one is to believe the serious fishermen, as a class, they catch far more fish—and have far more fun—than their unserious brethren.

THE ETHICAL CHALLENGES TO WALL STREET

This book is published at a time when Wall Street is once again in the dock—of public opinion, and in some cases, of criminal and civil trials. Like other cycles, such as El Niños, locusts, and Great Lakes, water levels, this too shall pass. After a series of spasms of moralizing, vengeance, and demagogy, Wall Street will be allowed to get back to its indispensable task of making markets and financing economic progress. Like Voltaire's God, if Wall Street did not exist, it would be necessary to invent it.

By now the public is aware of the internal conflicts of interest that major investment banks such as Goldman Sachs and Merrill Lynch face on a day-to-day basis:

- Their highest-margin line of business, and the one that pays the biggest rewards to senior management, is investment banking, which includes advising companies on mergers and acquisitions, and distributing new offerings of corporate stocks and bonds.

- They have huge research departments where staffs of highly paid analysts study publicly traded companies and advise clients on what those companies are worth. In theory at least, the costs of those departments are covered by the brokerage commissions paid by institutional and retail clients.

When I was on Wall Street in the 1980s, many analysts didn't confine their recommendations to Buy and Hold. They prized their reputations as independent advisers to the institutional investors who paid for their advice with brokerage commissions, and voted for or against them in the annual *Institutional Investor* magazine's survey of analytical excellence.

That professionalism deteriorated during the booming 1990s. By the end of the decade, "Buy" recommendations exceeded "Sell" recommendations by approximately 200 to 1.

On the face of it, that is a preposterous ratio. For every buyer, there must be a seller. All value is relative: A stock is a "Buy" because it offers much greater value than a similarly situated stock, which it should replace in investors' portfolios. Without such comparative exhortations, the Buy recommendations become mere vaporous exhalations.

Three excuses were offered by the Street for this patently absurd ratio:

- Since nearly all stocks worth a high-priced analyst's time were going up, it made little sense to say "Sell." (This justification is the irreducible distillation of the essential idiocy of "never-ending boom" marketing.)

■ Since cash inflows to mutual funds kept setting records each year, portfolio managers rarely required "Sell" stories, but they had an endlessly regenerating requirement for "Buy" stories. (This justification used the seeming priorities of one class of client as justification for the shabby treatment of other clients—notably retail clients.)

■ Big institutional clients with big holdings in a stock that got washed away in a downpour of selling because some analyst broke the cloudless sky over the Street with that seldom-heard discouraging word got mad, and they punished the brokerage firm accordingly. (This is the "No good deed goes unpunished" excuse.)

Admittedly, the Street did find ways to tiptoe through the tulip maniacal atmosphere of the late 1990s, creating euphemisms for the *verboten* word—*Sell*. My personal favorite was "Weak Hold," although such other Nice Nellyisms as "Near Term Underperform," "Short Term Hold; Long Term Buy," and "Medium Term Unattractive" entered the argot of the Street.

The three justifications the Street adduced for its collective ban of the S word were, of course, not the real reasons.

The real reason was the porous permeability of the "Chinese Wall." This imaginary structure that supposedly extended across investment dealers' offices was there to keep investment bankers and research analysts apart.

Because of SEC rules, the Street's research reports have long included a fine-print note that the firm had recently performed investment banking services for the company covered in the report. That alerted clients to possible bias.

What we have learned is that not only did the investment bankers lean on analysts to say nice things about *existing* investment banking clients, they demanded good recommendations for *potential* investment banking clients. Bankers griped that a lukewarm research report on a potential client would prevent that prospect from switching existing investment banking arrangements with enthusiastic research recommendations.

Investment banking clients and investment banking prospects are like men and women: Everybody is one thing or the other. So all publicly traded corporations were either existing or potential investment banking clients for every Wall Street organization.

What are investors' chances of survival in this world in which predators multiply like rabbits and dangerous practices proliferate? And will the new "independent" research imposed on the Street by New York Attorney General Eliot Spitzer really change things?

The seasoned survivor takes note when the balance of nature becomes regionally upset in favor of a potentially dangerous fast-propagating menaces, whether it is gypsy moth caterpillars or Lyme disease or "Mad Deer Disease."

What happened during the technology Triple Waterfall was that the self-corrective processes of the Street broke down. Shared Mistake became Law and Order. Everyone—top management, investment bankers, research directors, analysts, and sales managers—promoted the same story of endless growth in sales and profits for technology and telecom companies. The Street, like any other marketplace, only works well when there's disagreement—and the more vigorous, the better.

When everybody who matters on the Street is getting rich from being on the same side of the story, the natural balance that makes capitalism a good financial ecosystem is imperiled.

Get out while your (financial) health is still sound.

STOCK OPTIONS AND NASDAQ'S TRIPLE WATERFALL

> *Have you ever seen a forest fire? It is terrible. Thousands of acres are destroyed, and many a time men and women and children have been cut off by a tornado of flame and burned alive. The person whose carelessness starts such a holocaust is worse than a fool— he is a criminal and a disgrace to the good earth he treads.*
>
> —H. KEPHART

In one sense, it *is* different this time: No past Triple Waterfall transferred so much wealth from retail investors to corporate insiders and Wall Street elites. The scale of the elites' depredations during the Nasdaq mania is truly majestic. A few CEOs and CFOs accumulated spoils on a scale reminiscent of the Spanish Conquistadors.

That makes this crash unique.

- Few enduring fortunes were made from the Nikkei crash.

- Few enduring fortunes were made from the silver, gold, and oil crashes.

- Few enduring fortunes were made from the Nifty Fifty crash.

- Few enduring fortunes were made from the Great Crash.

- Many, many enduring fortunes have been made from the Nasdaq crash.

Why the difference?

Because in each previous crash, the only great fortunes accumulated that outlasted the catastrophe were those who sold out and those few (like Joe Kennedy in 1929) who sold short. Those who sold out simply protected the wealth they had—they didn't grow it exponentially through the mechanisms of the bubble.

This is the first mania in which the really big winners had seemingly unlimited access to an off-market enrichment device: stock options. In a way that few observers understood, these seemingly obscure and unremarkable instruments allowed insiders to leverage up their position without having to find or borrow more capital. Because of this multiplier effect, they could grow their wealth exponentially in time periods so brief that they would have seemed science fiction to the great barons of the past. It took time—lots of it—to make the billionaires of the past—the Rockefellers, the Morgans, and even Warren Buffett.

But through the leverage effect of stock options and the public's avidity for Initial Public Offerings in which entrepreneurs could sell a fraction of their company and mark up their holdings gigantically, billionaires—and near billionaires—were created in time periods of four years and less.

Moreover, most of these fabulously rich newcomers didn't get that way by building something of enduring value, as had such "robber barons" as John D. Rockefeller, Cornelius Vanderbilt, or J. P. Morgan. Gary Winnick made $735 million from Global Crossing in the three years before the company went bankrupt. Joseph Nacchio, the former CEO of Qwest, and Philip Anschutz, a co-founder, made a combined $1.8 billion in sales of stock before the price collapsed.

Even political history was made during the mania. Maria Cantwell made so much money on a bubble dot com that she largely financed her own winning bid to become a U.S. senator in Washington State (what could be called Silicon Valley North), heavily outspending established Republican incumbent Slade Gorton. She sold her insider shares to pay for her campaign, thereby displaying superb market timing. The dot com was history before she attended her first Senate meeting, but then so was Gorton, and she was now Senator Cantwell. Had she lost, the Republicans would have kept control of the Senate even after Jim Jeffords's defection. That defunct dot com made a few people like Ms. Cantwell rich, changed American history, and made a lot of people a lot poorer.

In past eras, entrepreneurs could—and did—sell off shares of their companies when bubble mania inflated their values. But this time investors had no idea of the scale of fortunes quietly being accumulated by their heroes in Silicon Valley and Wall Street.

How Big Is Big?

- The State of California disclosed that its residents reported *$85 billion* in taxable income from exercise of stock options in the year 2000 alone. To put that sum into perspective, it's more than the total reported earnings of all technology companies; nor does it include the profits earned by the elites in the other 49 states.

- *Fortune* published a list of insiders who had made *$66 billion* from stock options, on big companies whose share prices collapsed by at least 75 percent. They explained that the reason they had limited it to those whose shares had fallen so far—or had gone bankrupt—was that these were clearly cases in which top management had failed stockholders dismally, yet cashed billions in personal gains.

- Larry Ellison, CEO of Oracle, cashed $706 million in option profits in 2001 alone, a grim year for investors in his company.

- John Roth, Nortel's CEO for a brief period, cashed $86 million before the stock fell 99 percent.

- In 2001, when Cisco Systems was announcing terrible sales and earnings, CEO John Chambers, who already cashed in more than $150 million in option profits, blamed the company's troubles on a "100 Year Storm." He was cleverly tying his results into a successful book and movie about a unique storm off New England that engulfed a boatload of brave fishermen.

To this writer's knowledge, not one prominent person in Wall Street or the media ridiculed Chambers for his explanation. None pointed out that he had cashed a fortune in stock options. None pointed out that his reduced reported profits came despite what some financial experts consider unethical cleansing of the earnings to disguise the cost of his option program. (Cisco's unreported option costs were 13,921 percent of the earnings reported to stockholders, according to a Lehman study.) None pointed out that the "100 Year Storm" was the most modest economic downturn since World War II.

As *Fortune* noted, *these gigantic payouts were to men who failed on a gigantic scale.* The stockholders lost heavily—in many cases their life savings—but the men in control made fortunes that had in previous capitalist eras gone only to those who built great companies that were the foundations of America's rise to international leadership. *In this cycle, most of the biggest bonanzas went to those in charge of most of the biggest collapses.*

The system was perverse and anticapitalist in the extreme. It was as if the manager of a baseball team that was in first place by 10 games in July, and then had a record 37-game losing streak to finish in last place, had been rewarded with a $50 million bonus, plus a contract for a further five years at a guaranteed salary equal to all the money that his players would earn in that time. In essence, it was the equivalent of Las Vegas giving insiders the word on slot machines that were about to pay mega-jackpots.

According to the National Center for Employee Ownership, 75 percent of all options outstanding in the year 2000 were to the top five corporate officers, 15 percent to the next 50, and just 10 percent for all the rest of the employees. Yet in 1993 when the Financial Accounting Standards Board—the policy-setting board for the accounting profession—announced that it would be issuing a rule requiring publicly traded companies to report the costs of stock options issued as a deduction from reported net income, Silicon Valley reacted with the horror of a vampire faced with a cross. The chip culture called in its political chips and got the Senate to issue a resolution barring the FASB from promulgating its rule. Leading the charge was Connecticut senator Joseph Lieberman, who would later run for vice president. As the senators agreed in their very brief discussion of the Lieberman bill, stock options were the way start-up companies became great companies, and millions of Americans had stock options.

True, but what might be needed by start-ups should hardly be the basic mode by which men running some of the highest-capitalized firms in America get to make vast fortunes for a few good years from vehicles whose costs are not reported in the companies' earnings statements. Congress draws distinctions elsewhere between small business and bigger businesses with special tax provisions and with an entire government department devoted to the care and feeding of smaller companies. Why did Congress assume that what made sense for privately held start-up companies or even for publicly traded small companies should apply to Cisco, Sun, Microsoft, Dell, and Intel?

Perhaps the senators should stop their fund raising from Wall Street and Silicon Valley and do some financial analysis. Here is a way to understand the impact of stock options on the stock market and the economy.

Let's start with those $85 billion in stock option profits cashed by California taxpayers alone in the year 2000, the year the bear market got rolling. Given that it was Californians, it's safe to assume that the over-whelming proportion of those profits came from tech and telecom stocks.

1.   Their employers claimed the $85 billion as tax-deductible expenses, so the government recognized them as reductions in cor-porate profitability, *even though the companies never showed that $85 billion in reduced profits in their earnings reports.*

2.   Technology and telecom stocks were trading at triple-digit multiples in 2000, but for this exercise, we'll assume that the companies that issued those stock options to Californians were trading at just twice the S&P, or roughly 60 times earnings. That back-of-the-envelope calculation—which, though rough, is doubtless closer to reality than almost any of the tech companies' earnings reports for the year—shows that the implied stock market value of those phantom earn-ings was $5.1 trillion. But total losses by investors in all stocks since the market peak is on the order of $7 trillion. Therefore . . .

3.   The insiders' share of the profits of the tech and telecom compa-nies expressed as market values of stock was on the order of all losses experienced by all stockholders in all stocks (because investors didn't lose $7 trillion in 2000 or even in 2000 and 2001—that $7 trillion figure is as of July 2002. Furthermore, that doesn't include the stock option gains of the top people at compa-nies such as Microsoft and Dell, because Bill Gates, Steve Ballmer, Michael Dell, and their close cronies aren't California residents, so the total stock option profits are far higher).

4.   In other words, the *crème de la crème* of the tech industry cashed profits which, if they had either been properly accounted for or stayed with their companies would have been sufficient to prevent Nasdaq from reaching such perilous heights that its subsequent descent damaged the entire global economy, let alone plunging to levels that devastated the wealth of ordinary stockholders.

Most of those same people are accruing more stock options as you read this, set at the price of those companies' shares today. If Nasdaq does recover, then they'll get another multibillion payday.

But *you* won't.

Stock Option Accounting
It took a crash to get corporate America to focus on the problem of stock option accounting. Not that the battle was easy: Despite the prestigious

intervention of Warren Buffett, Paul Volcker, and Alan Greenspan, the New Economy stars hung tough. They argued (through their political supporters) that the backers of option accounting wanted to ban the use of options.

In fact, Volcker and some others have recommended abolition, but the actual proposals debated in Congress simply called for full and clear disclosure. When the elites find their backs against the wall, they can be formidable: Senator John McCain bitterly denounced his fellow senators for arranging that no vote would be held on his stock option accounting proposal. "The fix is in," he said, comparing the Senate to a boxing ring when a bribe has been paid. Despite alleging serious misconduct, he was not reproved by the president of the Senate pro tem or censured.

Arthur Levitt, the wise leader of the SEC in the Clinton era, recently published a noteworthy book detailing the problems of securities regulation in the 1990s. He makes it clear that his big regret was not standing by the Financial Accounting Standards Board when the Senate attacked it on the options issue.

Professor Niall Ferguson, the eminent British historian, argues that this crash vindicates one component of Karl Marx's analysis: This was class conflict; but it was not the clash of greedy owners against workers, it was an intraclass war within Marx's despised bourgeoisie, between what Ferguson calls "the CEOcracy" and "the suckers."

The rapacity of the CEOs, which he ascribes primarily to the leverage effects of stock options, is beyond any level of greed seen previously in capitalism, and the losses of the suckers—retail investors, particularly those who invested in equities in their 401(k)s—in what has been a relatively modest recession, are on a scale previously seen only from the worst economic cataclysms.

In previous compensation arrangements, the fortunes of the CEO and other top insiders were aligned, over reasonable time frames, with those of the stockholders. But this time, Ferguson believes, there was the creation, across much of the business community, of a cabal of consultants, directors, and senior officers who created overgenerous stock option plans by arguing that "everybody does it."

What happened here was that the CEOcracy could cash fabulous rewards in a huge, brief, stock market run-up, while the suckers who bid up the share prices, creating those option profits, were wiped out—all within a matter of a relatively few months. Nothing like this perverse wealth allotment process had been seen in earlier cycles except in cases of fraud and insider trading. This time, apart from a few crooks, the process of reverse enrichment applied to much of corporate America—and was justified as being of the essence of capitalism.

Ferguson, an avowed Thatcherite, observes that those who should be most eager to change the rules on stock options are capitalists, because history shows that when revulsion against big business becomes widespread, investors and workers naturally seek to shift power away from the private sector to government.

Wall Street was both actor and abettor in the large-scale fleecing of the American investing public by the abuse of stock options. It handled the trades when the insiders sold their millions of optioned shares. It handled the investment banking for the companies the insiders were milking. It created the dot-com mania with its eagerness to issue Initial Public Offerings of companies with no histories of profitability—and in some cases no histories of sales revenues.

According to investigations conducted by New York Attorney General Eliot Spitzer, some Wall Street firms used the dot-com IPOs as "free money" to give to investment banking clients. (During the idiocy era, newly offered shares of dot coms routinely leaped 50 to 100 percent in their first week after going public; investors who got stock in such hot offerings at the underwriting price were virtually guaranteed huge instant profits.)

Wall Street is not a seething den of corruption. But it isn't a safe place for the unwary either. Investor survival means taking Wall Street seriously and not letting Wall Street take *you* seriously.

C H A P T E R

The Dollar and Its Alternatives

In a camp that is liable to be raided by 'coons, porcupines, or other predatory animals, the meat [and] fish should be cached under piles of stones twice as heavy as you think such beasts could move. . . . Bears will demolish any such pile that one man could build.
—H. KEPHART

THE SYMBOL OF FINANCIAL MARKETS that fatten personal wealth is a well-fed bull; the symbol of financial markets that savage personal wealth is a hungry bear.

The carnivorous imagery of market terminology is deep-rooted. Man, as flesh-eater, has survived in the wilderness primarily by two carnivore-driven skills: the ability to hunt and fish for food (vegetarianism being the luxury of residents of agricultural societies with functioning food markets), and the ability to protect himself against becoming food for some other predator.

How does one measure the investor's diet?

In terms of money.

When one has enough money beyond basic nutritional needs, one can acquire stocks, bonds, bank deposits, real estate, and other forms of savings. Poverty is the absence of wealth, as measured in money. Financial survival is the accumulation of enough income-producing financial assets to generate enough money income to live comfortably. Personal financial crisis comes when falling asset values, accompanied by high liabilities measured in money, force investors to the equivalent of killing their cats and dogs to survive. (That some of the failed investments sold to cover margin debts are known as "cats and dogs" is the Street's sardonic summary of the process.)

What is money?

Money is, by far, the most heavily traded financial asset in global markets. Investors, travelers, and businesspeople switch from one currency to another, or to a group of other currencies, on a scale that dwarfs the resources of all but the most powerful central banks.

Yet most Americans tend to think of the importance of currencies only when some far-off country's financial system is collapsing because holders of that country's currency are panicking to get out of it. Television images of Argentinians and Brazilians lining up at banks to try to cash out their plunging pesos and reals show the human drama of wealth destruction when a paper currency suddenly loses its value.

PAPER PROMISES

Paper money not backed by gold or full exchangeability into other currencies is, in reality, little more than the printed paper promises of politicians. It is therefore subject to inflation risk at all times. In general, if the inflation in the country issuing the currency is at or below the average level of inflation in the leading industrial nations, that currency should be able to hold its own in the global markets. It will trade up or down moderately based on economic, political, and financial developments in its host country or in the countries of other leading currencies that are not tied directly to inflation, but it should qualify to be called "a store of value."

If the inflation is significantly higher in the issuing country, the currency's value will fall. In essence, that's what happened to the dollar over the period from 1950 to 1980: U.S. inflation was higher than inflation in Germany and Japan—the next most important economies.

If inflation in the issuing country is completely out of control, then the condition is catastrophic. This is called *hyperinflation*. The most famous example occurred in the fragile Weimar Republic in the 1920s.

When the Weimar Republic began printing unlimited amounts of deutschemarks in a vain attempt to cover Germany's punitive war debts imposed by the victorious allies after World War I, the money soon became worthless, and inflation skyrocketed to hundreds of thousands percent.

The money was literally not worth the paper it was printed on. Proof of that condition came when Neilson's, Canada's leading chocolate company, took advantage of the disaster: It bought hundreds of billions of face value marks for a few hundred dollars and used them to wrap its candy bars. The paper was good quality, and it was cheaper for the manufacturer than buying such paper from local suppliers.

Someone in Germany who was worth the equivalent of $10 million in 1921 in bank deposits and cash who did not switch his wealth into "hard" currencies, such as pounds, Swiss francs, or dollars—or into gold, stocks, or real estate—had only enough wealth to buy a few beers after the hyperinflation had run its course.

The biggest losers from the currency collapse were those who held the currency, or who held mortgages, bonds, or bank deposits in a currency that swiftly became worthless. Who were they? The middle class. The truly rich owned companies, farms, factories, and urban real estate; if those assets were subject to bonds or mortgages, then the rich just got richer. The poor got poorer: Food prices rose faster than prices generally, because farmers sought to export their production to hard-currency countries.

Lenin and Stalin inflicted similar devastation on the Russian ruble. In Russia and Germany, the private cash and bank savings of the middle class was virtually wiped out. "Money under the mattress" became worthless. The bourgeoisie lost heavily and became dependent on the Communist Party for survival, whereas members of the upper class were simply shot.

Hyperinflations lead to political revolutions.

Currency devaluations, in which a currency loses 10 or even 50 percent of its value, may also lead to the collapse of governments. Nations such as Britain have had to accept such humiliating repudiations of their national money, but without resorting to dictatorships. When the pound broke through its support levels in 1992, George Soros became known as "the man who broke the Bank of England" because he bet heavily in the currency market against the pound, and ultimately the pound fell to a lower—but not disastrously lower—level.

Since currency markets began to flourish in the decades after World War II, all currencies' values have been primarily expressed in terms of the U.S. dollar. Therefore, the most important story for investors in terms of long-term wealth planning is to focus on the outlook for the dollar. This may seem obvious to American readers, but it's also applicable to readers abroad.

The dollar is one end of a series of teeter-totters in the playgrounds of currency players. The other end of each teeter-totter is the alternative currency—the euro, the yen, the Canadian dollar, the Swiss franc, the Thai baht, and so on. Because the dollar is the world's reserve currency, the story of global inflation since World War II is largely the story of the rate of decline in the purchasing power of the dollar: When the dollar rose in value against the other leading currencies of the world, global inflation rates moderated or fell; when the dollar fell in value, global inflation rates and the price of gold tended to rise.

The importance of that statement for investor survival is that the dollar experienced a powerful bull market from 1995 to 2002. Since then, it has entered a bear market.

To make that statement is to invite a host of questions from investors. What is the meaning of a bull or bear market for the dollar? Should we be buying gold? Should we be switching into euros? What does a dollar bear market mean for U.S. stock prices?

Answering those questions requires a review of the history of the dollar over the past 75 years.

But, you may be saying, this book is supposed to be an Investor's Survival Guide, not a textbook on global currency trends. Do I really need to go through a lot of history in order to design my own wealth accumulation program?

Yes.

It is quite likely that the biggest investment challenge you'll face in the next decade will come as a result of a crisis—or a series of crises—in the exchange rate value of the dollar.

This is not a book about playing the stock market. It's about survival, and, as billions of people learned in the last century, when your country's currency gets into trouble, you've got trouble—unless you've protected yourself.

THE ALMIGHTY AND NOT SO MIGHTY DOLLAR

The dollar became the unofficial global wealth standard during the Great Depression. Most of the nations in the rest of the industrial world were indebted to the United States in dollars, and America was by far the richest nation in the world. When President Roosevelt revalued gold from $20.67 to $35 an ounce, the United States sucked in gold from all over the world, as bullion holders and gold miners eagerly swapped their metal for dollars.

The dollar's de facto role was made official at the Bretton Woods Conference in 1944. By then, the United States owned most of the world's known supplies of gold bullion, and it agreed to make those reserves available to foreign official holders of dollars (governments and central banks) at a fixed price of $35 per troy ounce, an agreement that laid the basis for Europe's postwar economic recovery. To ensure the ready availability of gold to foreign central banks, and to discourage Americans from speculating against their own currency's value—since Americans collectively held most of the world's tradable financial assets—Washington decreed that it would be illegal for American citizens to own gold bullion.

Until the early 1960s the new system of gold exchangeability worked well. But, as French president Charles de Gaulle complained, the requirement that other central banks hold dollars in their official reserves gave the United States the ability to undergo worrisome levels of inflation without its currency's value being punished: The other central banks were forced to keep swallowing dollars.

In short, it meant the United States had no market-imposed discipline on its government's economic policies, even when those policies led to a sustained Current Account deficit.

The *Current Account* is the balance between exports and imports of goods, services, and short-term interest payments, and is primarily driven by the trade balance.

As de Gaulle noted, the effect of these unforeseen consequences of Bretton Woods was to give the United States the license to export its own inflation.

Why?

Because the rising inflow of dollars into foreign central banks forced those governments to issue more of their own currency than was prudent. Furthermore, a nation's foreign exchange reserves are supposedly held in the most secure investments possible, and Bretton Woods forced governments abroad to stuff their treasuries with an asset whose value was declining because U.S. inflation was higher than rates abroad. The result was inflationary stimulus to European economies.

The prodigal son only repented of his spendthrift ways and came home when he'd run out of money and out of creditors willing to support his dissipation. But in effect, the United States was able to draw on seemingly limitless lines of credit abroad because those central banks had to keep issuing their own currency to absorb the endless flow of dollars.

In the 1960s the United States had the license to print money—hardly a stimulus to discipline.

Since the newly recovered nations of Western Europe had vivid memories of the horrific effects of uncontrolled inflation, they had reason to fear the apparent unconcern of the U.S. government about the gradual revival of inflation. In fact, President Kennedy was surrounded by liberal academic stars who thought the threat of inflation was greatly overdone.

Keynesianism

These academics were followers of John Maynard Keynes, the brilliant British economist who had correctly analyzed the terrible effects of the terms imposed on the Germans after World War I and who had written the classic work about dealing with deflationary depressions.

During the Depression, Keynes asserted that governments should abandon their fear of deficits when the economy wasn't functioning properly. If anyone argued that his policies of government stimulus would lead in the long run to inflation, he would reply with his famous assertion: "In the long run, we are all dead."

To him, the threat to the allied economies in the postwar era was not inflation, but deflation. He knew that deflation had hit after past wars had ended, and he feared that the weakened democracies of Europe would be at risk if their societies were engulfed by a new depression. He was a leading intellectual force behind the Bretton Woods Agreement that enthroned the dollar. He wanted to get rid of gold in currency management, terming it "a barbarous relic."

Keynes's followers used his arguments for government stimulus policies even when the economy was quite strong and when inflation levels were rising. They believed that sustained government intervention would achieve continued economic growth, thereby preventing unemployment. They had arguments to "prove" a direct trade-off between inflation and unemployment—what became known as the "Philips Curve."

In the 1960s, the Kennedy circle did not ridicule de Gaulle's inflation concerns: As we've seen, JFK launched all-out attack on the steel industry when it raised steel prices, triggering the 1962 Teddy Bear stock market plunge. (Republicans joked about the new Washington drink—the Kennedy Cocktail: Stocks on the Rocks.) Nor did President Kennedy and his economic advisers ignore the weakening dollar. They just didn't want to support it by eliminating the economic and monetary stimuli that were eroding its value. Instead they chose a dramatic new form of interventionism: a penalty on those who contributed to the dollar's fall—and the outflow of gold—by investing abroad.

This was the Interest Equalization Tax, a punitive tax on Americans who bought foreign assets. The administration also promoted a "Buy American" program on international trade. Pan American World Airways, one of the nation's flagship foreign carriers, eagerly responded to this new nationalism, running full-page ads asking Americans to fly abroad on Pan Am, rather than on foreign airlines, thereby protecting America's reserves of gold.

Those interventionist and protectionist policies were, of course, doomed to failure.

The dollar continued to struggle. In 1971, with U.S. gold reserves dwindling rapidly as foreign central banks, led by France, kept cashing in their dollars for gold, President Nixon "shut the gold window," decreeing that Fort Knox's gold was no longer for sale.

By breaking the dollar's last link to gold—delivery to foreign central banks in exchange for dollars—he in effect decreed that the covenant of Bretton Woods had been unilaterally repudiated. The dollar had become mere "fiat money"—not backed by anything real. That unilateral violation of a 27-year-old promise set the stage for double-digit inflation, which Nixon tried vainly to control through wage and price controls. In justification for his breach of promise, Mr. Nixon exclaimed, "We are all Keynesians now."

Keynesian economic theories were proclaimed as universally accepted just when events would prove that the theories were in fact inapplicable except in deflationary recessions. *Stagflation* arrived, a new problem in which both prices and unemployment rose sharply during a deep recession.

The stagflation of the 1970s put paid to the liberal economists' arguments that inflation was the trade-off for job creation: Unemployment and inflation soared together, even as the recession across the industrial world was the worst since the 1930s. Those problems weren't supposed to go together.

A whole new concept of macro policymaking was needed. Fortunately, no policymaking vacuum survives long.

Gradually, other voices were heard. The first call was to give American citizens the right to protect themselves against inflation: Let them own gold. Then the government could not cynically continue to be the big winner from inflation—because it reduced the value of the outstanding national debt—while not letting citizens protect themselves. Before the Republicans were driven from office in the Watergate fiasco, they repealed the ban on Americans' ownership of gold. The Comex in New York soon became the world's leading trading center for gold futures, and coin and bullion dealers sprang up across the land.

What began as the right to be able to own protection against inflation soon evolved into a new investment concept: You can get rich from inflation by buying gold (and other precious metals). Investors saw lurid advertisements telling them of the riches to be gained with gold because the government would never do anything to stop inflation. A real debate about the effects of currency depreciation was inevitable.

Monetarism, 1975–1989

Keynes died in 1946, but he retained a special hold among economists for three decades, partly because no new giant had emerged to replace him. (Speaking in Chicago last year, Francis Fukuyama delivered a puckish quote: "Economics progresses one funeral at a time.")

With inflation out of control, it was the time for the Chicago School of Economics, led by the brilliant Milton Friedman, to challenge liberal orthodoxy. His argument that "inflation is always and everywhere a monetary phenomenon" had been ridiculed by those who claimed governments could control inflation through interventionism. The double-digit inflation of the 1970s led to a national sense of foreboding and helplessness—what President Carter termed a "malaise." It was time to try Friedmanesque monetarism and Friedmanesque tax-cutting and deregulation.

Monetarism came first, when it was implicitly adopted as the basis of Federal Reserve monetary policy by Chairman Paul Volcker in October 1979. Previously, Fed policy was loosely targeted toward inflation experience and/or to levels of interest rates. By decreeing that growth in monetary aggregates would be the basis of policymaking, Volcker, in effect, said that the Fed would let interest rates do what the market chose. He thereby implicitly stated that the Fed would not be dissuaded by the onset of towering interest rates—which is exactly what happened, producing a recession.

Volcker made the switch to monetarism in response to the anguished pleas of other leading central bankers at the Belgrade IMF Conference. They said they could no longer keep acquiring dollars in their foreign exchange reserves, and warned of a global inflationary blow-off that would ensue from the coming collapse of the dollar.

Next came the tax cutting and deregulation under President Reagan.

The recession ended. Inflation peaked and began to decline. The bond market rallied powerfully, igniting (on Friday the thirteenth of August 1982) a new equity bull market that would last, with brief bearish pullbacks, until March 2002—by far the longest bull market on record.

The dollar naturally entered a major bull market in 1982 as foreign investors rushed to acquire Treasury bonds—the longer term, the better. So successful was Volcker's implementation of Friedman monetarism that the dollar once again became "the almighty dollar"—soaring against foreign currencies despite soaring fiscal and trade deficits. It became greatly overvalued on a trade basis, putting much of U.S. manufacturing in peril.

The dollar had become the "new Swiss franc"—a currency that traded on its *financial,* not its *economic,* value. In the late 1970s the gold-backed Swiss franc took off against all other currencies, as investors rushed to acquire income-producing assets that were totally protected against inflation. Result: Swiss industry was seriously wounded, including the nation's jewels—its renowned watchmakers. These companies were incurring their manufacturing costs in a high-cost zone, making them uncompetitive with watchmakers based in other currency zones. It was beginning to look as if only oil sheikhs could afford to wear Omegas or Rolexes. The Swiss resorted to an astounding policy: They imposed *negative* interest rates on foreign holdings of Swiss franc bank deposits. Instead of the bank paying the depositor some rate of interest, the bank deducted part of the account value regularly and paid those sums to the government. This had the desired effect—the franc once again began to be valued more closely to its economic rather than its financial value.

The novelty of an overvalued dollar was heartily enjoyed by those Europeans who had for so long fretted about American financial indiscipline and the problems created by a continuously depreciating global store of value. They noted that falling rates of inflation—within the United States and internationally—were the natural consequence of a rising dollar.

The problem was, not everyone rejoiced about the rising dollar and falling inflation. Although few in Washington shed tears for the most obvious losers—those Triple Waterfall victims of the inflation-hedge crashes—the plight of U.S. manufacturing certainly caught attention. Established U.S. manufacturers of such globally traded products as steel, automobiles, machinery, ball bearings, TVs, washing machines, computer chips, and electrical products found themselves in more desperate conditions with the nation in economic recovery than they'd experienced during the recession. Foreign producers whose costs were incurred in rapidly cheapening currencies flooded the U.S. market. Export-driven companies, such as Deere and Boeing, found that their high costs were pushing them out of foreign markets.

To deal with the economic fallout from this now-expensive novelty, the Reagan administration decided on a jointly managed devaluation. Treasury Secretary James Baker organized a private meeting of finance ministers from the leading Western nations at New York's Plaza Hotel on September

21, 1985. They agreed to a managed realignment of the dollar, to be achieved through massive currency intervention in the open markets.

It worked. The stock market soared, correctly anticipating a surge in profits. The economy strengthened.

Those who would rule unruly markets always come a-cropper. The Plaza agreement worked all too well. Driving the dollar down at a time of rising U.S. Current Account deficits turned out to be easier than the finance ministers realized, but stopping its descent at some theoretical level of "fair value" was quite another matter. By late 1986, fears of a comeback in global inflation from a falling dollar had revived—along with gold prices—and central bankers began searching for a new strategy that would keep the U.S. economy humming without reviving global inflation.

By now the world was focused on America's "twin deficits"—fiscal and Current Account. After further bargaining, a deal was struck to jointly stabilize the falling dollar. This agreement was reached in the majestic environs of the Louvre in Paris, in February 1987, allowing U.S. media to announce the deal alongside pictures of the Victory of Samothrace.

The Louvre agreement (discussed in "The Nikkei Crash: 1985 to ?" in Chapter 3) was a last-ditch maneuver that ultimately led to the 1987 crash, which devalued the dollar anew.

For eight years following that crash, the dollar traded up and down, mostly down, but in 1995 it entered the most powerful bull market in decades—a run that raised its value by a range of 33 to 45 percent, depending on which currency teeter-totter comparison you choose. Naturally, the dollar's new strength was to a significant degree the result of problems other currency zones experienced that led to serious weaknesses in those currencies. (See Charts 6-1 and 6-4.) Strength is relative: If your economy is booming and most of the rest of the world economies are struggling, then investors from most of the rest of the world will be clamoring to invest in yours—driving up your currency's value.

Some of these new weights on the dollar's end of the teeter-totters came from currency panics and collapses in Asia that began in July 1997. While the world's glitterati were gathering in Hong Kong to toast that tiny capitalist miracle's ingestion into the maw of the "reformed" communism of China, Thailand was quietly removing the peg that had supported its currency, the baht.

At the time, I was disgusted by the near-zero coverage in Western media of Thailand's forced devaluation, and I warned clients that the real financial story was coming from Bangkok, not Beijing or Hong Kong. I cited a famous H. T. Webster cartoon that depicted farmers chatting in

Hodgenville, Kentucky, February 12, 1809. One asked what was new, and the other said there'd been a new baby, named Abraham, born at the Lincoln cabin, but "Nothin' much ever happens around here." If Thailand was unable to defend its currency, what about the other Asian tigers?

As what would be called "Asian flu" (and I called Thai bahtulism and Malaysian ringgitworm) spread to the currencies in the region, Asian financial markets collapsed, unleashing the worst depression in the region since the 1930s.

That fast-spreading panic moved money into the dollar on a big scale, so the dollar's bull market accelerated.

Currency markets tend to trade according to Newtonian physics: When a currency is moving in a given direction, it will continue to move that way until external forces compel it to change direction. As traders put it: "The trend is your friend." So the dollar's two-year bull market continued into 1998, at which time two more crises drove investors into the greenback.

First came Russia's default on its external obligations, a blow that the markets had inexplicably failed to anticipate. Financial markets worldwide slumped, as fears of financial collapses from institutions holding devalued Russian paper proliferated. The thermometer of global financial health, the TED spread (see "The Ted Spread: Global Finance's Thermometer," Chapter 7) leaped, but not into the crisis zone.

The dollar's role in times of trouble once again asserted itself. When a global crisis is unfolding, the greenback is a traditional haven. (Why do so many people call it a "safe haven"? That is an ignorant redundancy. Any unsafe place or market hardly qualifies as a haven.)

Then came a made-in-America financial crisis that just might have broken the dollar bull market had the Fed not responded with such vigor.

Long Term Capital Management (LTCM), a huge hedge fund based in Greenwich, Connecticut, had a galaxy of stars in its partnership, including two Nobel Economics laureates (Myron Scholes and Robert Merton) and elite alumni from Salomon Brothers from the era when its swaggering traders were "Masters of the Universe" (as described by Tom Wolfe in *Bonfire of the Vanities* and Michael Lewis in *Liar's Poker*). It was supposed to have foolproof computer-based hedging strategies that profited from small distortions in the markets.

What they were certainly expert at was in finding complex tax avoidance—or evasion—strategies with complexities beyond Enron's wildest dreams. (The *Wall Street Journal* quoted the esteemed Myron Scholes as saying, "Nobody really pays taxes," a concept currently being tested in a suit brought by the Treasury against the partners. The previous member of the Greenwich glitterati who spoke similar words was Leona Helmsley, and she ultimately went to jail for tax dodging.)

Then, as global markets were still reeling from the Russian default— and from a major bank loan restructuring for Indonesia—LTCM began to crumble. Word spread that those supposedly fail-safe formulas had failed. (It would turn out later that the geniuses who worked out these programs only used trading data dating back to 1990. Thus, they had no precise information about how various kinds of financial assets had behaved during the major TED spread crises of the 1980s.)

The partners at LTCM called on all their powerful friends in Wall Street and Washington to bail them out. They got by, with more than a little help from their friends. The Fed participated in a bailout package that wound LTCM down gradually and had the charming attribute of protecting much of the wealth of the key insiders who had claimed to possess infallible formulas for making investors rich. The Fed also injected massive liquidity into the system. But the most crucial help came from an unlikely source: The beleaguered Japanese revalued the yen upward, a move that ended what was potentially a bigger financial crisis than Russia and LTCM combined.

As Chart 6-1 shows, the yen had been declining steadily, and there was widespread talk in currency desks that Japan was prepared to let the yen collapse as a means of kick-starting its economy out of a deflationary recession. This threat alarmed China, Japan's biggest trade competitor. The Chinese let it be known that if the yen were to fall further, China would competitively devalue its currency, the renminbi or yuan. Given that China had already become the most formidable force in international trade, that was the equivalent, in trading terms, of threatening nuclear war. By its upward revaluation, Japan took pressure off all the Asian currencies and off the share prices of leading global banks that stood to lose heavily from a new wave of global deflation.

Charts 6-1 through 6-4 illustrate the interrelationships among the Fed's crisis management, the stock market, and the currency markets.

The debate still continues about the Fed's response to the LTCM collapse. Most observers believe it did the wise thing in helping to orchestrate a bailout that prevented a massive default. It eventually came out that LTCM was levered far beyond what the marketplace assumed. It may have been indebted to 50 times its equity, depending on which valuations one accepts. Some of Wall Street's biggest names—including Merrill Lynch Chairman David Komansky—were investors in LTCM, and at least one central bank—the Bank of Italy—had a large investment in the partnership.

CHART 6-1   Yen/Dollar (January 1, 1998 to December 1, 1998)

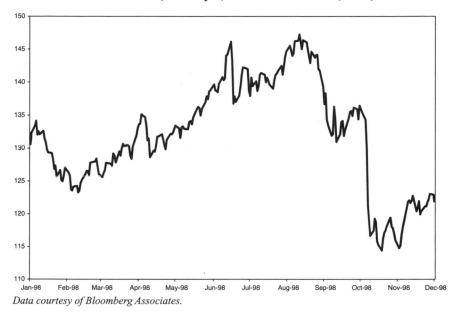

Data courtesy of Bloomberg Associates.

CHART 6-2   U.S. 90-Day Treasury Bill Yield (January 1, 1998 to December 1, 1998)

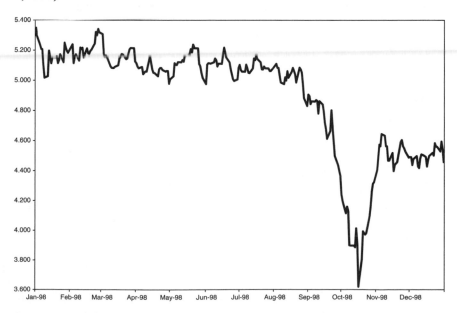

Data courtesy of Bloomberg Associates.

CHART 6-3   S&P 500 (January 1, 1998 to December 1, 1998)

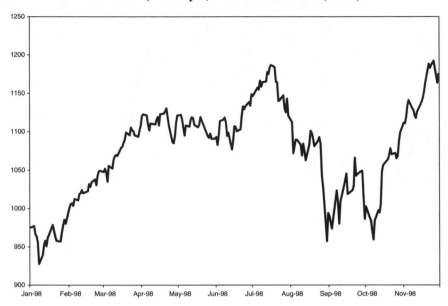

Data courtesy of Bloomberg Associates.

CHART 6-4   Dollar/Deutschemark (January 1, 1998 to December 1, 1998)

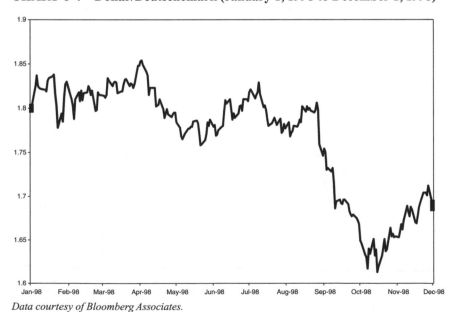

Data courtesy of Bloomberg Associates.

I argued then, and continue to believe, that the Fed should have let LTCM go down, relying on the beneficial effects of its massive monetary ease and the yen revaluation to carry financial markets through the crisis. The United States—including Fed chairman Alan Greenspan—had long lectured Asians of the evils of "crony capitalism." Those lectures had grown louder and longer after the 1997 Asian collapses disclosed webs of partnerships, deals, paybacks, and other sub-rosa arrangements that contributed to the depths of the disasters.

So what was the bailout of LTCM if not crony capitalism?

Moreover, by both bailing it out and embarking on a massive liquidity expansion, the Fed spawned a new monster that would dwarf LTCM, bahtulism, and ringgitworm: Nasdaq had been on a simmer through the summer of crises. It was trading in the 1600–1700 range, and it responded to the Fed's furious monetary injections like Popeye to spinach.

The rest of the world saw that breakout, and global investors rushed into American technology stocks. Nasdaq's nonstop run to 5048 was fueled by massive global inflows that also boosted the dollar.

Those two bull markets moved in tandem: Through 1999, the weekly price changes of the euro against the dollar had a sustained, superb inverse correlation to the performance of Nasdaq in general and Cisco Systems in particular, as can be seen in Chart 6-5. Inverse correlations (see "Analyzing Your Portfolio Risks," in Chapter 9) are assets that trade in opposite directions to each other: When the euro fell, for instance, which was most days during 1999 and early 2000, Nasdaq went up, usually led by Cisco. Positive correlations—such as the share price of Cisco and the changes in Nasdaq's value—are, of course, more common: In a bull market, most stocks go up, and in a bear market, most stocks go down. That the value of a new foreign currency would trade inversely to a U.S. stock index was an important indicator of a major global trend.

By this time, any discussion of the strength of the dollar was focused overwhelmingly on its strength against the euro. Japan was bogged down in another deflationary recession. The Canadian dollar was bedeviled by a global perception that the nation had poor politics and an overdependence on commodity exports at a time of long-term commodity deflation. The British pound was rising strongly, but this was really at the expense of the euro, not the dollar, and reflected Britain's better economic performance under the enlightened, moderately leftist Blair government, at a time when Eurosclerotic policies on labor, regulation, and taxes were seen by investors globally as reasons to avoid investing in the Continent.

CHART 6-5   Nasdaq/Euro (January 1, 1999 to June 30, 2000).

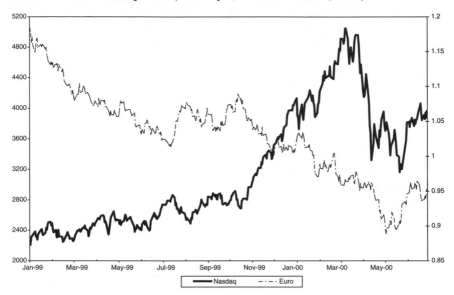

Data courtesy of Bloomberg Associates.

Why was the currency of the region with the greatest reliance on red tape now trading inversely to the market value of a U.S. technology-heavy index, and to the share price of Cisco, one of the glamorous components of that index?

To answer that trillion dollar question, we need to go back to 1991.

THE EURO: A CURRENCY CREATED BY COMMITTEE

At the Maastricht Summit in 1991 a group of Continental politicians eager to build a new colossus—Europe—agreed on the complex terms of a new treaty. This document was to a considerable degree the brainchild of French Socialist Jacques Delors, president of the European Commission.

It had long been the goal of Delors and his associates to create a counterbalance to the economic and military power of the United States. They were particularly opposed to the free market traditions of the "Anglo-Saxon nations"—the United States and Britain. During the years of the warm relationship between Margaret Thatcher and Ronald Reagan, those countries had achieved strong economic growth with falling inflation by—*horreurs!*—cutting taxes and government regulation, weakening the powers of large unions, and imposing monetarism. In other words, they had achieved success that had given them worldwide admiration by following policies that were the exact opposite of those advocated by the European Socialist parties.

But the Anglo-Saxon sins didn't stop there. The willingness of Thatcher and Reagan to expand defense budgets, place Pershing nuclear missiles in Germany, and generally raise the ante against the Soviet Union to new heights, had been crucial factors in triggering the collapse of Soviet communism.

This was a deeply disturbing development to Eurosocialists such as Delors. Their parties routinely formed electoral alliances with local Communist parties against center-right coalitions. Indeed, when the French center-right ruling coalition fell in the parliamentary election of 1997, the Communists were crucial in supplying the margin of victory and got key cabinet ministries in the government. France had quit its role in the NATO military command under de Gaulle, so it was not as if the French Socialists could claim any part in the sudden collapse of a system they had never truly opposed. (Georges Marchais, noted French Communist politician for decades, backed Stalinism to the hilt, including the Soviet Union's crushing of the freedom fighters in Hungary in 1956 and Czechoslovakia in 1968.)

What made matters worse for the Eurosocialists was the obvious delight the inhabitants of Eastern Europe and even Russia had in demolishing the signs, symbols, and systems of "socialism." The fall of the Berlin Wall, which was greeted with such joy by millions of rejoicing young people, was a troubling event for Socialists, who had for decades maintained that East Germany was a respectable political and economic system to West Germany.

Although it seems hard to believe now, until the actual collapse of Communism, leftist parties and intellectuals in the West believed that the Communist system worked to deliver the greatest good to the greatest number of people. As social democrats, they rejected the idea of "the dictatorship of the proletariat" and opposed the brutality of those regimes, but they did believe that socialism was a vast improvement on capitalism, so the economic statistics published by the "Socialist" countries were to be treated with respect.

(Even such a distinguished liberal economist as J. K. Galbraith spoke glowingly in the early 1980s of the superior economic achievements of the Soviet bloc compared with the poor performance of the U.S. and British economies.)

When Delors was sketching the vision of a Europe united in one economy and one currency, he didn't dwell on his party's barely observable contribution to Western victory in the Cold War. He pointed instead to what he called the unfair advantage the Americans had because there was really no currency alternative to the dollar. Japan had already begun its descent into a long deflationary recession, but was continuing to run a Current Account surplus. That meant there could not be enough yen available abroad for central banks and other major currency holders to use as an alternative to the dollar.

Echoing de Gaulle's complaints of three decades earlier, Delors noted that this status of unchallenged eminence meant the arrogance of power. This meant, he claimed (correctly), that U.S. businesses got an indirect but important subsidy from the rest of the world, because foreign central banks were forced to hold dollar-denominated instruments, which meant U.S. interest rates were lower than they would be if the United States had to finance its own economy. Delors calculated this subsidy to U.S. corporations at close to 1 percent on dollar-denominated bonds and Eurodollar loans.

Delors understood something few Americans did: Being the reserve currency issued by the world's largest single economy and free trade zone, with the deepest and most liquid capital market, is a unique advantage. In contrast, the markets where securities are denominated in francs, guilders, deutschemarks, lire, escudos, and pounds are small and illiquid. In terms of financial markets, bigger is most definitely better.

His arguments carried the day. The Continental countries signed on to the Maastricht Treaty of the single market and the new single currency. Denmark and, most important, Britain finally agreed to the rest of the treaty, but deferred agreement on currency union. (John Major, Margaret Thatcher's successor, knew that giving up the pound for a new currency in an economy dominated by the Germans and French would be profoundly unpopular at home; his predecessor and Delors had clashed frequently: Thatcher claimed that increasing the power of "the Eurocrats" in Brussels would be "socialism by the back Delors.")

Although the rest of the Continental members of the EU signed on to the euro, few of the governments ever submitted the question to a direct vote of the populace. Chancellor Helmut Kohl wanted to be known as (1) the longest-serving chancellor—longer even than Bismarck, (2) the chancellor who had reunited Germany, and (3) the chancellor who had been the key player in the formation of a united Europe, which would never again face the threat of war. Since the euro was the linchpin of this unity, he couldn't let his people vote on it in a referendum. He knew that the nation was deeply proud of its deutschemark, the one German national institution in which his guilt-ridden nation believed. His agreement to sacrifice this precious national symbol and unifier to achieve the New Europe was the highlight of Maastricht—and a major factor in his ultimate electoral defeat.

Although the euro was agreed to in 1991, it took nearly a decade to make it a full reality. It began trading as a financial—but not paper—currency in 1999, and replaced all the predecessor paper currencies in 2002.

This lengthy discussion of the origins of the euro is necessary, because the story of the Fall of the Dollar needs a challenger: No king is dethroned without a pretender, and no champion loses his title without a defeat. The dollar had been king for 60 years when the men met at Maastricht. It was looking strong at that point because for a few months the massive payments to the United States for the Gulf War from Germany, Japan, and some of the Arab oil states gave the United States a Current Account surplus, an event that had occurred about as frequently as the reappearance of Halley's Comet (which also arrived and, as swiftly, departed).

However, once the United States was no longer being paid for global peacemaking, the dollar's problems resurfaced. It gained a new lease on life in 1995, however, and seemed to have imbibed from the Fountain of Youth when the euro was born and thrust into the global currency markets in 1999. (See Charts 6-6 and 6-7. Note that Chart 6-6 uses the deutschemark's exchange rate for the period prior to the beginning of trade in the euro.)

Before the euro was launched, there were widespread predictions that it would swiftly become the new global store of value, replacing the dollar. It was the currency of the world's second-largest free trade zone, a region with a Current Account surplus and one that boasted fiscal deficit control imposed by treaty. A bond market for euro-denominated securities developed rapidly. It looked like the euro would shortly be a worthy substitute for dollars in global exchange reserve accounts. The noted American economist, Fred Bergsten, testified to Congress that the advent of the euro threatened the dollar and, thereby, the continued strength of American capital markets and the American economy.

In part because the hype had been so hot, the newborn baby became an instant embarrassment. The euro came, was seen, and was conquered—by the newly mighty dollar. Among its other misfortunes, it had the bad luck to be born at a time when the U.S. economy had never looked better.

The whole world was agog at the talk of the "New Economy," and the connubial bliss flowing from the union between Silicon Valley and Wall Street was where it was at. With the promise of everyone becoming wired on the Web, a new era of peace and prosperity loomed—just in time for the New Millennium.

CHART 6-6   Deutschemark (January 1, 1994 to December 31, 1998)

Data courtesy of Bloomberg Associates.

CHART 6-7   Euro/Dollar (December 31, 1998 to December 31, 2002)

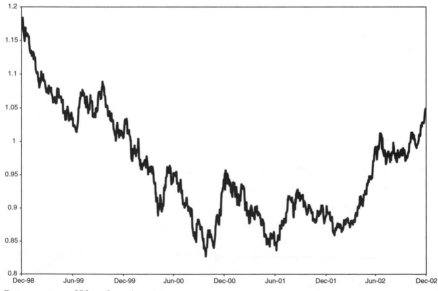

Data courtesy of Bloomberg Associates.

This American triumphalism was easier for the rest of the world to take because it didn't involve military actions or trade embargoes. Companies such as Microsoft, Intel, Cisco, and Dell were bringing the wonders of the most advanced technology to the whole world—they weren't imposing it on anybody. Young people in repressive societies such as Iran, China, and the Arab states could plug into these liberating forces in their own homes, through the incredible power of the Web. As the TV commercial put it: "Is this a good time to be alive or what?"

A basic component of this great time to be alive was that it was a great time to invest. Stocks were chic, stocks were cool. Europeans discovered the joys of equity mutual funds during the 1990s. Until then, most Continentals saved through bank deposits and real estate. Until as recently as the early 1980s, for instance, the Frankfurt Stock Exchange had been open only a few hours a day, during which time the trading was largely conducted between representatives of the big German banks.

In part because of the Web, the Equity Love Affair that had been enrapturing American Boomers and Gen-Xers spread across the ocean. But another reason for this un-Continental upsurge in enthusiasm for stocks was the force of demography: European economies were aging even more rapidly than the United States, and the outlook for viability of the extremely generous European social security programs was grim.

Besides, Europeans had lots of something of which Americans had little: savings. This lack had long been part of the dollar's problems, but for a few years it would become a factor in a remarkable dollar bull market.

The Expatriate Dollar:
The Eurodollar

[G]roup sensitivity . . . This sense is seen when you watch a flight of birds, pigeons are particularly good examples. The flight, moving in one direction, turns, all together, and changes direction. The movement is not made by one bird who acts as a leader but simultaneously by all the birds in the flight.

—R. GRAVES

THE UNITED STATES HAS HAD, for decades, the lowest personal savings rate of any of the industrial nations. It is but a slight overstatement to assert that in the post–Cold War era, saving is the only remaining un-American activity.

On the surface, this is remarkable, because Americans do not have government pension schemes as generous as those enjoyed by citizens of most leading industrial nations, and health care is primarily provided by private plans rather than by government programs.

It is not that Americans don't put money aside for rainy days, although they do it less than people in any other advanced economy.

They don't save, because they find it so easy to borrow.

The U.S. economy is built on readily available—and astonishingly flexible—consumer credit. America is justly proud of having the highest percentage homeowner rate among the leading nations. That didn't just happen. It was driven by (1) giving homeowners full income tax deductibility for mortgage interest, and (2) the development of unique mortgages. In the United States, homeowners can borrow up to 80 percent (and sometimes more) of the value of their homes with fixed-rate mortgages for 15 and 30 years. And those mortgages can be repaid in whole or in part at any time, without notice, and at no cost (except, in the event of full prepayment, modest service charges).

If that were not enough, American banks developed another tax-deductible product—the home equity loan—a second mortgage, at a rate usually below prime, which, depending on the aggressiveness of the lender, can inflate the indebtedness beyond the full market value of the home.

But there's more. Americans were the pioneers in the development of painless automobile financing—through loans and leases. Americans pioneered the credit card loan, whereby offerings of (initially) cheap funds come through the mail, with seemingly little or no credit checking on the part of the card issuer.

To take an example, one of my clients, a sophisticated institutional investor, has a credit card in the name of his dog. He uses that card, whose credit line he capped at $500 (but only after mail arguments with the bank, who wanted the dog to have a far higher line), to make Internet purchases, having heard horror stories about what happened to people's credit when they made Web purchases on their credit cards.

A further example: A New Orleans bank that had suffered heavily from credit card losses retained consultants to analyze their experience so they could fine-tune their future card offerings. They learned that their default rate was almost zero when the cardholder had lived at the same address for more than five years. So they assembled the data on southern Louisiana and then mailed out credit card offerings—with generous credit lines—to people who fit that description.

Thus it was that the mail brought an offer from the good ol' folks at their friendly bank to all long-term inmates at the local prisons (some of whom were doubtless there for having robbed that bank). The unanimous acceptance rate dazzled the bankers.

Where does all the money come from to finance the federal deficit, the Current Account deficit, U.S. home mortgages and home equity loans, U.S. corporate debts, car loans and leases, credit card borrowings, brokers' margin accounts, and all the other ways Americans manage to go deeper into debt each passing day if American savers don't provide it?

The nation of grasshoppers has been sustained by the nations of thrifty, industrious ants abroad. Foreign savings have made up the U.S. savings deficit as well as the Current Account deficit (which is mostly the trade deficit), an outflow that moved steadily up during the 1990s, exceeding $1.2 billion per working day as the old millennium went.

Foreigners—particularly foreign central banks—have long been heavy buyers of Treasury bonds and bills. In recent decades, they also became big buyers of corporate bonds.

During the 1990s, foreigners eager to invest in dollar-denominated securities got hooked on the allurements of mortgage-backed securities issued by Fannie Mae and Freddie Mac. Why did Europeans—led by the thrifty Germans—suddenly take to these instruments?

Because they were marketed by investment banks and dealers as having a government guarantee.

In fact, that is not legally true, and Alan Greenspan got very upset when his European central banker colleagues inquired about the big surge in U.S. mortgage sales.

Thrifty foreigners supported the dollar—and thereby the American borrowing binge—by:

1. Buying American equities
2. Buying American bonds—Treasurys, mortgage backs, and corporates, with a particularly great appetite for telecom bonds
3. By continuing to load up on eurodollars

EURODOLLARS FORCE FED BY PETRODOLLARS

It was this seemingly insatiable appetite for eurodollars that was the most important foreign contribution to the American Way of Debt.

What are Eurodollars?
They are American dollars deposited in banks outside the United States. They can be—and most certainly are—loaned back into the U.S. financial system, but they are resident abroad. They can be demand deposits or, more commonly, are loaned for weeks, or months, or, in some cases, years. That means the money loaned into the U.S. banking system can be recalled at any time the deposits mature.

Where Did They Come from Originally?
All eurodollars started off as ordinary American dollars. They went abroad and stayed abroad because they were spent abroad to buy foreign-made goods,

or by American tourists, or by drug dealers and other underworld characters who wanted to keep their money outside the purview of American authorities. The interest paid on those deposits also accumulated abroad, so that what used to be a few billion dollars became trillions of dollars.

Because they have been for many years the primary source of global financial liquidity, eurodollars are naturally subject to trade in the financial futures markets. The primary place they're traded is a few blocks from my office at the Chicago Mercantile Exchange, where the basic futures contract—for 1 million eurodollars—is the most active and important term financial futures contract in the world.

By the late 1990s those elusive, ubiquitous, largely tax-exempt dollars were being repatriated heavily into the U.S. banking system to make up for the modest growth in bank deposits. By the end of the century, the U.S. banking system was growing its loan portfolio nearly twice as fast as it was growing its deposits—a feat of financial prestidigitation possible only by daily increases in repatriation of eurodollars from abroad.

Long before the year 2000, eurodollars—which are deposits not created, directly or even indirectly, by the Federal Reserve—had become the world's most important source of financing for banks and for dollar-denominated bonds and financial derivatives traded globally.

The good news for the American appetite for borrowing—and for the growth of world trade, which the eurodollars financed—was that the eurodollars were so readily available.

The potential bad news was the ever-present possibility that the foreign holders might decide not to roll over their deposits.

If or when that happened, the U.S. financial system would have big, big problems. If it happened now, the crisis could be more acute than the financial system faced in 1987 when many foreign holders simultaneously decided to switch their investment from eurodollars into other eurocurrencies or other assets denominated in other currencies.

Who owns eurodollars?

Eurodollar holders are persons, partnerships, and corporations who seek good interest rate returns in highly liquid investments in a strong currency, and appreciate the anonymity and, in many cases, the freedom from income taxes, available through dollar deposits in banks outside the United States. These can be U.S. banks' foreign offices and agencies, or—as in the greatest volume of deposits—they can be any other nationality of bank.

What is the interest rate on eurodollars?

Eurodollar interest rates, being rates on bank deposits, are naturally higher than U.S. Treasury bill rates. How much higher they are on any given day depends on how global investors see the two risks that together set eurodollar rates: (1) the risk for the value of the dollar itself as against key foreign currencies, and (2) the risk that a major global bank will be unable to meet demands for withdrawal of its eurodollar deposits.

The Federal Reserve has great influence and control over U.S. Treasury bill rates, but the Fed has no direct influence or control over eurodollar rates. The global rate for eurodollar deposits is virtually set out of London each day when the London InterBank Offered Rate (LIBOR) is quoted—the rate set for large banks' eurodollar deposits with one another. However, it trades widely around that rate when the market becomes unstable. In the past five years, the spread has ranged from a low of 20 basis points 0.2 percent) to a high of 120 basis points (1.2 percent). That yield spread is called the TED spread (T for Treasury bill, and ED for eurodollars). It was for decades one of the most important financial data in the world, as will be discussed shortly.

Eurodollars started multiplying in their billions when the U.S. Current Account regularly went into deficit in the late 1960s. (The deficit became perpetual after 1981 and has risen steadily, except for the brief period during the Gulf War when the United States received huge subsidies from its allies.) Because the Current Account includes the balance of trade, including tourism, and the balance of short-term interest payments, it is the best measure of short-term capital flows.

Why Did the Current Account Go into Deficit and Stay There?
Initially, economists tended to blame it on the Vietnam War, which put extra inflationary pressures on the U.S. economy, making U.S. manufacturers less competitive. But the United States has run trade and Current Account deficits nearly full-time since the 1950s, though the outflow has been far more severe since the Vietnam War.

Ironically, it was another war that gave the United States its only big Current Account surplus. During the Gulf War, Germany, Japan, and the Gulf states paid most of the costs. In effect, the U.S. military became modern Hessians—an army paid by foreigners.

The real reason for the imbalance was the revival of Europe and Japan as formidable trade competitors, and a long decay in American industrial productivity. Americans acquired a liking for such foreign-produced products as Japanese cars and electronics, German cars and machinery, French wines and fashions, and Italian wines and clothing.

When a German automobile manufacturer sold a car to an American, dollars flowed abroad. The German could cash them in at the bank for deutschemarks (and they would probably end up on the books of the Bundesbank), or use them to buy a factory in the United States, or hold them as U.S. cash in a eurodollar account.

It was convenient for many of those exporters who acquired dollars to keep some of them, rather than trading them in at their bank for deutschemarks, francs, pounds, or yen. Eurodollar accounts were exempt from almost every kind of control—and the biggest growth came in places with low or nonexistent income taxes, such as Switzerland, Hong Kong, the Cayman Islands, and the Channel Islands. For many decades after World War II, businesspeople in most countries faced exchange controls on using their own currencies abroad. Eurodollar accounts were useful caches to pay for international purchases, or corporate acquisitions, or just to have available to cover foreign travel for corporate executives.

Eurodollars are the Rodney Dangerfield of financial economics. They get almost no respect from financial economists. Statistics on them have always been hard to obtain, and they remain elusive even when the global financial system depends on them for survival. Doing research for this book, one of the most comprehensive books on eurodollars we found was published by a very smart analyst, Jane Sneddon Little, a remarkable 28 years ago: *Euro-dollars: The Money Market Gypsies* (New York: Harper & Row, 1975).

Her book begins well:

> A latter-day specter is haunting Europe—haunting the entire world, in fact. That specter is the vision of $100 billion on the loose in the Euro-dollar market, free to rush with next to no restraint from one nation to another, scattering well-ordered government policies and exchange-rate systems in its path. Not even the wealthiest nations in the world have been able to protect their economies from the meddling of this phantom. . . .
>
> One reason that the Eurodollar market appears formidable to central bankers is its extraordinary freedom from regulation. As a market for dollar balance deposited outside of the United States, it is a truly international creature beyond the control of any single national authority. . . . It now reaches $100 billion and produces huge monetary waves, which can flood into national economies or drain them with a powerful undertow . . .

Ms. Little deserves some sort of award for having analyzed the way eurodollars were changing the world's financial markets while economists were still (and still mostly are) focusing only on monetary aggregates compiled by the Federal Reserve. Her prescience is impressive. Just add zeros to her data and you'll have a useful analysis of the system in every year since she published her book. Today, eurodollars are measured in trillions. They are still, to use her term, "gypsies."

What made the eurodollar supply multiply exponentially from that $100 billion level was the sudden wealth of the oil-exporting nations after the two 1970s oil shocks. Countries such as Saudi Arabia, Iraq, Iran, and Abu Dhabi found themselves awash in dollars, because oil was dollar-denominated. Their own Third World economies were unable to absorb and use most of this cornucopia, so, after buying planes, guns, palaces, baubles and bangles, the rulers invested it abroad. Few of them were financially sophisticated, so they bought obvious investments, such as government bonds and Treasury bills. But they also deposited tens of billions of dollars into global banks. Leading banks, such as Deutsche Bank, Chase Manhattan, and First National City Bank, found themselves with an embarrassment of riches, as they were deluged with a flood of what became known as "petrodollars."

Money supply growth in the industrial world was rapid in the 1970s—far too rapid to slow the rise of inflation. That meant, however, that the banking system had enough domestically generated liquidity to meet loan demand—most of which was coming from the New Economy borrowers—oil, gas, mining, forestry, and agriculture.

By the late 1970s, eurodollars had become the most liquid and flexible liquidity source in the world. London became the center of the eurodollar market (and the new euromarket in other offshore currency deposits, including markets in all major currencies).

By 1978 there already was insufficient demand from credit-worthy borrowers in the industrial world to absorb the inflow of petrodollars. Then came the fall of the shah of Iran, and a redoubling of oil prices. What had been a somewhat unmanageable flow of dollars into the banks became an unimaginable flow.

Yes, the banks *could* have declined to take all the petrodollars offered, based on an inability to find clients to borrow such mind-boggling sums. Had they done that, the history of the world would have been very different. For one thing, there would have been no crash in 1987.

Instead, bankers found a new class of borrowers with nearly unlimited demands for loans to balance their supplies from a new class of major depositors who were lavishing them with a nearly unlimited supply of funds.

It seemed a stroke of genius: Since previously unimportant Third World countries were now the world's biggest bank depositors, why not lend the funds to previously unimportant Third World borrowers?

Some of these new borrowers were struggling democracies, but many (or most) were dictatorships and kleptocracies. Politics were irrelevant. Bankers fell over one another trying to get the nod to be lead bank in syndicates arranging massive deals for such sterling borrowers as the Congo, Sudan, and North Korea.

Why were capitalist banks willing to bet their very existence by making hundreds of billions of dollars in loans to countries with primitive economic structures?

A new theory had emerged to meet the new needs of new times. Citibank's Walter Wriston, the most publicized of the new breed of swashbuckling eurolenders, in explaining why country loans were a better deal for banks than corporate loans, announced a banker's epiphany: "No country has ever gone bankrupt."

On that rationale, banking syndicates made gigantic loans to countries previously notable in international trade mainly for sales of postage stamps and purchases of armaments. Lending to them was the kind of "aggressive lending" you had to do if you wanted to be in the big leagues. By the late 1970s, billions of petrodollars were being "recycled" (another splendidly convenient new term) to almost any nation or nationette that qualified for membership in the UN General Assembly, and many who didn't meet even that minimal test.

Another colorful (but unpublicized) term emerged to cover the explosion of global banking syndications: the "Secretary Loan."

The Secretary Loan was the participation limit in a new banking syndicate loan offered over the Teleprinter that a secretary in a bank in places such as London, Zurich, Frankfurt, Geneva, Luxembourg, or Hong Kong could agree to while her boss was out having a three-martini lunch. (Yes, back then they actually did have three-martini lunches. Nowadays, we are given to understand, global financiers' lunch breaks involve workouts in the gym, followed by drinks of designer water.)

When dealing with dictators, it wasn't considered smart to press them on what they would do with the petrodollars you were advancing. As an example of salutary neglect in asking tough questions, consider what happened after North Korea got a huge loan from a syndicate headed by a major Canadian bank. Canadian newspapers began carrying a series of full-page advertisements (usually in the business section, where ads cost most), in which North Korea's Stalinist leader published very long answers to long questions about Marxist theory raised by Communists abroad. This kind of dense intraparty dialogue had been filling pages in *Pravda* and its kind for decades. It was a first to have such long-winded Marxist musings published in expensive ads in capitalist newspapers financed by loans from capitalist banks.

By 1980, Wriston and his colleagues were shocked—shocked!—to discover soaring default rates on their eurodollar loans to Third World borrowers. To make matters worse, critics were showing the insensitivity to question the way the borrowers had actually spent those hundreds of billions of dollars. In too many cases, the critics alleged, little or none of the money was used productively to help their struggling economies and impoverished citizens.

This unpleasant turn of events came at an extremely inconvenient time for Walter Wriston, David Rockefeller, and other globetrotting petrodollar pushers.

The Iranian revolution had once again sent oil prices skyrocketing, triggering a worldwide recession in the oil-consuming economies.

And the determined Paul Volcker was sticking to his pledge to impose Friedmanesque monetarism on the U.S. financial system. This restraint was proving to be an ever-tightening tourniquet on the big banks with big portfolios of bad loans.

Enter the TED spread.

THE TED SPREAD: GLOBAL FINANCE'S THERMOMETER

With domestically generated dollars becoming scarce, at a time when banks' balance sheets were seriously impaired by bad Third World loans, eurodollars moved from a backup source of liquidity to the primary source of global financial liquidity. Volcker's defense of the dollar had the unforeseen effect of raising the value of the trillions of eurodollars and dollar-denominated eurobonds sloshing around the world.

The 1980s were the decade of the Reagan Recovery, a robust but disinflationary boom that put a sickly banking and Savings & Loan system under sometimes intolerable strains. Hundreds of financial institutions would fail, the stock market would crash in 1987, and the whole process of debt-unwinding would end with the real estate bust of 1990.

From the time investors and regulators began worrying about the banks' exposure to Third World loans, a new stress indicator—the TED spread—became indispensable for market watchers.

The TED spread measures the daily—and on occasion, minute by minute—change in the interest rate spread between U.S. Treasury bills and eurodollar deposits. As the world's premier short-term investment medium, Treasury bills are the basic financial rate, responsive to Fed policy. As the rate on uninsured dollar deposits in banks around the world, eurodollars always traded at higher yields than T-bills. When problems developed anywhere in the global banking system, eurodollar rates would rise as bankers and investors moved out of euros into T-bills. That change in rates would also occur if investors became worried about the value of the dollar and moved their deposits into other currencies.

The TED spread has been the thermometer for the international financial system now for a quarter century. Investors have been able to chart it by checking spot rates through their banks or by watching the yield spread between the two key short-term financial futures contracts traded in Chicago—Treasury bills and eurodollars. That yield spread was (and still is) low double digits in confident times (of which there were few in the 1970s and 1980s), and leaped above 100 basis points (1 percent) each time the system was at bay.

In every financial crisis from 1978 through 1998, the TED spread climbed sharply. In every case that the TED shot up, stocks fell sharply. The TED had a 100 percent accurate forecasting record.

The worst TED spread crisis came in May 1984 when the Continental Illinois National Bank and Trust Co. collapsed. As the Fed official who helped manage what they considered "the worst global financial crisis since 1930" told me, when the TED leaped from the 100 range to 415, alarm bells went off. What Paul Volcker did that day was brilliant, audacious, and gutsy.

The Continental was a mismanaged Illinois bank with pretensions to being a major global bank despite being hobbled by an archaic Illinois law that prevented local banks from operating branches. So, from one location on LaSalle Street (across the road from where this is written), the Continental tried to become one of the global biggies by bidding aggressively for extra-large (wholesale) eurodollar deposits. Japanese and German banks were among the major participants in these funding operations. Through them, Continental managed to become the seventh largest commercial bank in the United States.

When word leaked out that the bank faced collapse because of bad (even by the loose standards of the time) lending practices, major foreign holders of Continental's eurodollar deposits declined to roll them over. Continental desperately bid up to try to replace the matured loans, but the euroflow worldwide seized up. As rumors of the collapse of a major U.S. bank spread through the system, other banks declined to roll over their eurodollar deposits, switching to Treasury bills or other eurocurrency assets. In a matter of hours this became a worldwide "flight to quality" within the banking system.

At one point during the morning, it looked as if the world faced the worst financial crisis since the Depression.

Then Chairman Volcker averted catastrophe by announcing that the Fed would cover Continental's eurodollar liabilities and that the Continental would be restructured and recapitalized. (The only deposit insurance existing at that time was Federal Deposit Insurance, which insured domestic deposits—not eurodollars—up to a limit of $100,000; what Volcker did was doubtless illegal under U.S. regulations, but it was unquestionably the right response to a crisis. The TED spread plunged to normalcy. The ultimate cost to the taxpayers was trivial, and the financial world resumed functioning until October 1987.)

EURODOLLARS AND THE CRASH OF 1987

The Crash of 1987 came barely six months after I moved to Wall Street as portfolio strategist for Wertheim Inc., a respected research firm. One reason they recruited me was because my eurodollar-based stock market forecasting record had been good. The reason I kept my job after that debacle was because I had alerted so many major institutional clients to the risk in the financial system, as demonstrated in the rising TED spread. (Some clients would for years afterward call me "Mr. Ted Spread.")

The 1987 crash was born in a eurodollar squeeze at a time of rapidly dwindling foreign faith in the dollar. The stock market was vulnerable to correction because of relatively high valuation, but what occurred was a crash caused by the financial equivalent of severe heart attack. The leap in the TED was a signal that the blood flow in the system was experiencing blockage.

I was in Dallas to see institutional investment clients of Wertheim on Monday, October 19. I was deeply worried because the TED had leaped from the 120 range to 145 on Friday.

The problem was a falling U.S. dollar, which was being defended by newly minted Fed chairman Alan Greenspan. He had succeeded Volcker on August 11 and quickly arranged two tightenings of monetary policy. They were designed to stop inflation in its tracks and also to put a safety net under the falling dollar.

On Monday, I phoned my assistant in New York from my hotel room at 7:20, when the eurodollar futures started trading at the Chicago Mercantile Exchange.

When she heard my voice on the line, she giggled nervously. "Don," she said, "the TED is at 215."

I told her I'd see the clients booked for that day, but would fly back to New York that night. I told her to expect the most exciting day of her career.

I then awakened my son Stuart, who was with me because we'd planned to attend the Dallas Cowboys Monday night game. "Stuart," I said, "You're going to have to go to the game by yourself. I've got to fly back to New York, because there's going to be a stock market crash today."

"Oh, Dad, you always exaggerate," he grunted, and went back to sleep.

I went to the client meetings in their offices. I explained what a TED spread crisis was, but the meetings were difficult. People would exit to check the market, return and announce the latest number, and we would gasp.

The big lesson from that terrifying bear raid was that one ignores a leap in the TED at one's cost. That lesson served me and my clients well in the years to follow.

There has not been a TED spread crisis since October 1998. The TED signaled "All Clear" during the major sell-off of 2001–2002, which meant that this was the first full-blown bear market since the eurodollar market began in which the viability of the financial system was never in question.

THE DOLLAR AND THE EURO

When eurodollar holders switch out of dollar deposits, they have a wide choice of eurocurrency deposit vehicles for their money. A Swiss holder of eurodollars might decide to switch into Swiss francs or euros or into other currencies such as British, Canadian, or Japanese deposits, based on two considerations: the relative interest rates available and the outlook for the currencies. (Just as eurodollars are dollars on deposit in banks outside the United States, eurocurrencies are any other currencies on deposit with banks outside of the currency's issuing country.)

Eurodollars were fine investments for Continental Europeans from 1995 until 2002 because those investors earned competitive rates of interest and, more important, they profited from the rise in the value of the dollar. Yet the dollar had entered a bear market against the euro on January 31, 2002 (see Chart 7-1).

A German holder of eurodollars from January 31, 2002, to June 30, 2002, would have had little reason to be happy with his investment. The interest rate paid on his deposits was significantly lower than was available in euro or British deposits, and he lost 14 percent on the sudden fall in the dollar. At then-prevailing eurodollar rates, it would have taken him more than six years of interest income to offset his currency loss—assuming he was paying no income tax. That also assumed that the dollar fell no further.

Why did the dollar and the euro suddenly switch roles from winner to loser? Why did a dollar bull market suddenly become a dollar bear market at the end of January?

CHART 7-1   U.S. Dollar/Euro (January 1, 2002 to June 30, 2002)

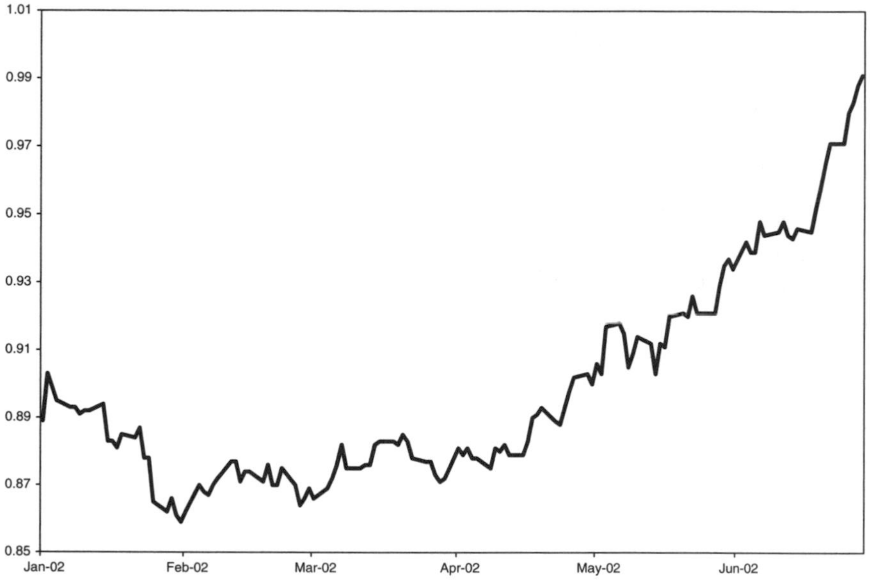

Data courtesy of Bloomberg Associates.

To answer that question, we have to go back to the dreams and delusions of Jacques Delors and his fellow eurocrats.

They planned ahead for the day when all holders of deutschemarks, lire, francs, guilders, pesetas, drachmas, and escudos would be trading in their paper money for the new euro paper money.

When they announced agreement on creating this new supercurrency, they exulted in the thought that the faces on the bank notes would be the great Europeans—those whose achievements transcended the narrow nationalism of most of the visages on the existing money.

Naturally, a committee was struck. Its job originally was to select the great people of the past who would make holders of those notes proud to be Europeans. This was to be a big part of the process in which Europeanness subsumed the parochialism and nationalism that had been such curses for Europe over the centuries.

What did the committee choose? Structures.

Yes, structures. They were apparently unable to agree on any great European people for the back of the bank notes, but they were able to agree on great European architecture. They couldn't agree on a bridge—because everybody had a bridge in his or her country that was truly special. They compromised with generic bridges; they look a lot like bridges you've seen, but you can't quite identify them. One engineering expert wrote that one design wasn't the design of any bridge in Europe he knew, but it did look like a famous span in India.

So much for the new European consensus! I took this eurocommittee paralysis to be confirmation of my view that most of the hype about the new Europe and about the inevitable attractiveness of the new currency would be proved wrong. The bureaucracies, committees, red tape, euroscle- rosis, and excessive taxation that had bedeviled the European Union would continue. I told clients to sell the new currency short, or to borrow in it— because they would be repaying the loan in depreciated currency.

Europe's heavy taxes and the insatiable demands of Europe's farmers for costly handouts were at the root of a eurocratic decision that would help sink the euro in the months leading up to the issuance of the new paper money. (That issuance, let it be noted, was a splendid organizational accomplishment, and was a sign of a turning point from ugly duckling to swan for the euro.)

As the date for issuance of the currency neared, Brussels announced that, as of the date of distribution, all previously issued banknotes would become nonnegotiable.

This was a shock to millions of people who assumed they could hang on to their cherished deutschemarks and guilders and francs, which would be accepted at any time at the official exchange rate.

Even more shocking was the ukase that said that when people exchanged their existing currency for euros at their banks, the banks would be required to report all sizable transactions to the government. Jacques Delors and his friends had all along assumed that this unpublicized aspect of the conversion would expose massive tax dodging. All that paper money under floorboards and mattresses would have to come out, and then the gleeful tax men would have grounds for some very interesting inquiries. "And just how did you manage to accumulate 275,000 deutschemarks when your tax returns showed no income and you have been collecting welfare for six years?"

The Italian authorities were awaiting the appearance in Sicilian bank branches of mafiosi who would have huge fortunes to explain.

Well, of course it didn't work out that way. There was one big remain- ing loophole. All a holder of these currencies needed to do was to swap them for foreign currencies at the ubiquitous exchange wickets and the tax man wouldn't be any the wiser.

Result: a frenzy of sales of European currencies, mostly into dollars, in the waning months before the financial portcullis clanged shut. In January

2002, the dollar's exchange rate against the euro peaked as the last tax-sensitive holders of big supplies of paper money completed their cleanouts of mattresses, floorboards, and safety deposit boxes.

Then the dollar's bear market—particularly against the euro—began.

THE FED AND THE DOLLAR

How big was the demand for dollars by holders of the expiring European currencies? The best way to measure it is to take the year-over-year growth of the currency component of American M-1* and subtract it from the year-over-year growth of the American Monetary Base. For the year beginning the end of July 2001, the currency component of M-1 grew by $132 billion, and the Monetary Base grew by $135 billion.

That background leads to a discussion of what the Fed does and how it does it.

The Fed raises and lowers monetary growth and interest rates by adjusting its own balance sheet. It holds U.S. government debt—plus some minor miscellaneous items, like the gold in Fort Knox. Its main liabilities are currency in circulation and U.S. bank reserves. (It creates bank reserves by buying U.S. government debt, primarily Treasury bills, and it reduces reserves in the system by selling U.S. government debt.)

Everyone in the world knows the Fed slashed interest rates and grew the money supply after September 11.

Except that it did not do it by growing bank reserves, which is the monetary method for moving a torpid economy. Reserves grew with the glacial speed associated with prerecessionary periods of Fed tightening.

The Fed's supposed "activism" was confined to printing all that paper money, which has no "multiplier" effect on the economy. What happened to that money and why was it suddenly in demand?

Did Americans stop using credit cards and bank charge cards? Did drug lords quadruple their sales, thereby increasing their cash holdings? Of course not.

The most reasonable explanation is that the huge demand for greenbacks from foreign exchange traders who were absorbing expiring European currencies created extraordinary demand for dollars. Anecdotal reports from foreign exchange traders confirm this sustained rush into dollars by those who wished to retain some confidentiality about their affairs.

*Bank and other short-term deposits plus currency in circulation.

Another aspect of that puzzling piece of data is that it helps to explain why U.S. economic growth in 2002 was so disappointing. The Fed was actually not stimulating the economy, a point noted frequently by Dennis Gartman, a shrewd market commentator. The Fed was more spectator than actor in the dramatic events of 2001–2002.

By most accounts, the Fed has kept the accelerator to the floor. It cut the Fed Funds rate 12 times. Isn't that monetary stimulus?

Suppose you are managing a store in an outlet mall and your owner gives you a huge batch of merchandise to sell, telling you it must be sold within a few days. He comes by a week later and your store is still jam-packed with the stuff. When he blasts you for not getting rid of it, you answer, "I lowered the price 12 times in five days. I'm doing my damnedest." To which he says, "But you haven't got the price down to the level where it clears. I don't care how many times you cut prices. Slash prices to the level where you unload the merchandise."

The Fed Funds rates kept getting lower, but economic activity was sluggish, as indicated by weak credit demand and massive loan loss write-downs across the system. The Fed, relying on the statistics showing robust growth in the savings-oriented monetary aggregates, such as M-3 and MZM, didn't really move to counteract those deflationary forces.

The problem with using those monetary aggregates to show Fed activism in stimulating the economy is that they are largely composed of large Certificates of Deposit (CDs) and Money Market Funds, not what Milton Friedman calls "transactional balances"—which are the banking components of M-2—checking and savings accounts and small ($10,000 and under) CDs. These millions of little accounts are the monetary muscle of the day-to-day economy—money that is likely to be used in transactions, including the day-to-day expenditures for mortgage payments and trips to the supermarket, but also for discretionary expenditures—such as on trips, automobiles, furniture, and appliances.

The multi-million-dollar CDs and Money Market Funds are mainly parking places for investment capital temporarily withdrawn from the stock and bond markets. They are savings accounts, not economic activity accounts. (The exception is corporate Money Market Funds arising from issuance of securities; these funds get drawn down within months after a bond or stock issue, but until actually spent, they stay in Money Market Funds.)

The flaccid U.S. economy since 2000 is the seriously wounded victim of the drunken drivers of the tech binge. That interest rates have fallen so far, so fast, since then is more a measure of the collapse in demand of an imploding economy than the exploding expansionism of an aroused Federal Reserve. Had it not been for the euro conversion, the Monetary Base might not have grown at all, and every economist and strategist in the United States would have been screaming for the Fed to get moving to stimulate the moribund economy.

THE DOLLAR BEAR MARKET BEGINS TO BUILD

When the global reserve currency enters a major bear market, it tends to fall against nearly everything except the collapsing currencies of distressed emerging nations, such as Argentina and Brazil in 2002, or African kleptocracies.

That the greenback fell against the yen in 2002 was a sign that the dollar's problems were suddenly truly serious (see Chart 7-2). Japanese interest rates are submicroscopic, making the 1.75 percent return on U.S. Fed Funds look like a shogun's ransom. (Those tiny Japanese yields may help explain why the TED spread stayed very low in 2002, despite all the problems in U.S. financial markets and the decline in the dollar; eurodollar

CHART 7-2   U.S. Dollar/Yen (January 1, 2002 to December 31, 2002)

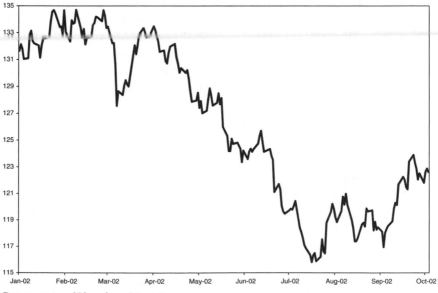

Data courtesy of Bloomberg Associates.

holders may have decided that a 1.75 percent yield with currency risk was better than .15 percent in Japanese deposits.)

The Japanese government was alarmed, and sought to get the Bank of Japan to drive the yen back down by massive reliquification. The Bank of Japan resisted being drawn into another dollar-propping exercise such as it had engaged in after the 1987 crash (see "The Nikkei Crash: 1985 to ?" in Chapter 3), a reflation that drove the values of Japanese stocks and real estate to ridiculous heights, setting the stage for 12 years of deeply deflationary recessions interrupted by brief periods of modestly deflationary recoveries.

But the Bank of Japan finally caved and began buying Japanese Government Bonds (JGBs). That got the money supply moving and increased the supply of yen, thereby holding back its rally against the dollar.

That Japan sought to hold down its currency was natural: Just about the only segment of the Japanese economy showing good growth was the export operations of Japan Inc.—the Sonys, Hitachis, Toyotas, Hondas, and Toshibas that make "Made in Japan" the standard of quality worldwide. Those five companies collectively stood to lose nearly all their corporate profits in 2002 if the yen were to rise to par (100) against the dollar.

Lest the reader assume this is because Japan Inc. exists almost solely on sales to Americans, let me explain that the new powerhouse of mainland Asia—China—pegs its currency, the renminbi (or yuan) to the dollar. Because it holds more than 300 billion dollars in its exchange reserves, and it refuses to let the renminbi float in global currency markets, China, already the fastest-growing export-oriented economy in the world, grows faster and gains market share from its major competitor, Japan, when the yen rises in value against the dollar (see "China's Impact on the Global Economy and Corporate Profitability," in Chapter 8).

The yen's rise was part of a new trend. *Behind this trend was the changed attitude and growing numbers of a special group of investors.*

THE GROWTH IN GLOBAL INVESTING AND ITS INFLUENCE ON THE DOLLAR

When you hear somebody speaking of "a strong dollar" or "a weak dollar," what do they mean? What are they comparing it with?

Those expressions generally refer to the dollar's strength or weakness against a "basket of foreign currencies." The U.S. Dollar Index is a collection of foreign currencies of leading industrial nations weighted in relationship to U.S. trade with those countries or regions. It is the index used by most forecasters when they say "the dollar will be strong" or "the dollar will be weak." They aren't speaking of its performance against Russian rubles or Brazilian reals.

The dollar's bull market was bound to turn into a bear market at some point, even if there hadn't been that fascinating last fling as the dollar danced with the artful millions who didn't want eurogovernments to learn their secrets (see Charts 7-3 through 7-5). Once the dollar entered a major bear market, a major bull market for gold would be born.

What had been a major underpinning for the dollar during the 1990s would inevitably become a major threat to the dollar in this decade: global investors' strategies.

During the late 1980s and the 1990s, global investing for pension fund, endowment fund, and high net worth clients became a profitable, glittering business.

During those decades, some of the best jobs in portfolio management for a Baby Boomer chartered financial analyst were with the fast-growing global investment firms and private banks based in London, Paris, Edinburgh, Zurich, Geneva, Luxembourg, Munich, Milan, New York, Fort

CHART 7-3   Euro/U.S. Dollar (January 1, 2002 to December 31, 2002)

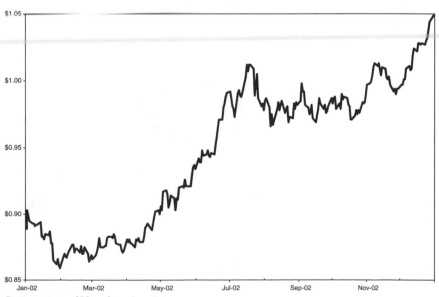

Data courtesy of Bloomberg Associates.

CHART 7-4   U.S. Dollar/Canadian Dollar (January 1, 2002 to December 31, 2002)

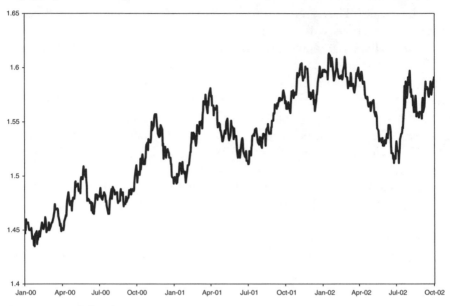

Data courtesy of Bloomberg Associates.

CHART 7-5   U.S. Dollar Index (January 1, 2000 to December 31, 2002)

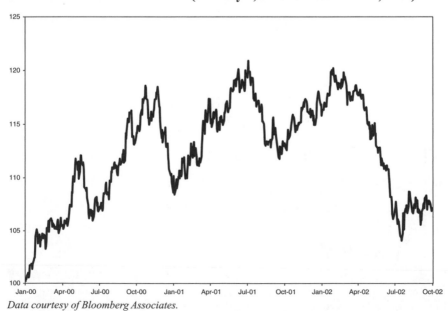

Data courtesy of Bloomberg Associates.

Lauderdale, Abu Dhabi, Hong Kong, and Singapore. Everything was First Class.

Like all institutional investors, a London-based firm offering its services to pension funds and high-net-worth individuals worldwide needed to compare its investment returns to major indices. The S&P 500 wasn't appropriate, nor were such relatively small national markets as the German DAX or the French CAC 40.

Morgan Stanley met this new need by creating three kinds of indices for globe-trotting investment firms:

1. Morgan Stanley Capital International: a global index that included stocks traded in most of the significant markets of the world, including the United States.
2. Europe, Australia and Far East (EAFE): an index that included the significant established markets outside the United States (except for Canada). Latin America wasn't included because its markets were all included in the third, Emerging Market, index.
3. Emerging Markets: an index that included dozens of countries from around the world. All they had to do was have a local stock market with enough transparency and liquidity to be measurable and they were counted in this subgroup of the world.

In practice, foreign-based suppliers of services to U.S. clients concentrated on the latter two indices.

U.S. pension funds and high-net-worth clients already had managers expert in U.S. markets, and they weren't interested in paying offshore-based managers to figure out which U.S. stocks to buy.

This industry's impressive growth in the 1990s was in part due to a new trend among Continental European pension plans to invest heavily in equities. Britain had pioneered the concept of prefunding private pension plans with heavy equity exposure, but it took a long time for the Continentals to make that move. A major reason for Europe's rejection of equities for pensions was that private pension funds were insignificant on the Continent. Governments assumed the pension responsibility, and they used pension contributions from companies and self-employed persons to fund their deficits.

That hangover from the dominance of Socialist thinking among euroelites in the 1950s and 1960s was at last addressed during the 1990s, as Europe came to the belated recognition that its fast-deteriorating demography had created a fast-developing crisis for its social security and government employee pension programs.

A study conducted in 2001 showed that, thanks to the redoubtable Margaret Thatcher's imposition of prefunded pension plans on employers, the share of Britain's GDP represented by pension fund assets is hugely higher than the minuscule accumulation of pension investments in the eurozone. Although its authors did not draw any conclusions, I was struck by the realization that if Britain does not join the eurozone quickly, it will not be able to afford to join it later, because the taxation implications for the euro countries of the Baby Boomers' retirements will be drastically higher than those facing Britain, and members of the eurozone are under annual pressure to "harmonize" their taxation levels.

When, all of a sudden, a whole gaggle of new pension fund investors appears, loaded with money, what would those high-living investment advisers do?

They would explain to all these eager new committees how they make money for their clients by investing globally, more or less in the following terms: "It's all quite simple, really. Two-thirds of global equities are in the United States and Japan. Our firm did brilliantly in the 1980s by overweighting Japan and underweighting the United States (according to the MSCI Global benchmark). That way we caught the strongest currency and the strongest stock market: no surprise that those factors go together. We have done brilliantly in the 1990s by underweighting Japan and overweighting the United States. Furthermore, within the United States, we've overweighted technology stocks, because the hottest tech companies are located there. So we've once again overweighted the best currency and the best stock market. That's why you should let us invest for you. As for the rest of the world, we try to match or exceed EAFE returns by venturing into interesting emerging markets, such as South Korea, Brazil, and Taiwan."

From 1995 to 2002, such firms delivered roughly one-third of their investment returns to European and Asian clients from the huge rally in the dollar; the rest came from stock market performance.

What happened in late 2001 was that global investors, who had been worrying about an overvalued dollar for some years, finally began to conclude the game was up:

- U.S. stocks were now 58 percent of the value of all stocks in the world, up from 24 percent at the dawn of the 1990s. Roughly one-third of that increase had come from currency.

- The price-earnings ratio in the United States was the highest in the industrial world, and the U.S. economy looked to be among the most vulnerable to a global slowdown because of its excessive reliance on technology.

- It had become apparent that Nasdaq was the greatest mania of all time, and this meant that those European inflows that had boosted Nasdaq in 1999–2000 would ultimately reverse.

- Although 9/11 was a horrendous shock, and though it soon became apparent that some al Qaeda supporters lived in the Moslem communities of Europe, it was also soon apparent that the War on Terror was a war between the United States and Britain on one side and Islamic radicals and such threats as Saddam Hussein on the other. This meant that the United States was likely to be the primary focus of any major new terrorist attacks.

To sum up: The great global players who had been such big boosters of the dollar through the 1990s became frightened of their dollar and U.S. equity exposure in late 2001 and 2002, creating a new long-term threat for the dollar.

WHAT DOES A DOLLAR BEAR MARKET DO TO AMERICAN ASSETS?

Obvious answer: It makes them much less attractive to foreign investors. A more complete answer: It makes them much less attractive to the group of investors who have the most savings available to invest. Even less obvious answer: It makes them much less attractive to the group of investors who increased their exposure to U.S. assets most heavily at and near the top of the twin bull markets—Nasdaq and the dollar. These investors have been, therefore, huge losers to a degree even bruised Americans haven't suffered. They lost on the stock market, and also lost on the currency.

History tells us that major currency moves take years to play out. The dollar experienced a bear market in each decade since the 1950s, but it escaped through the 1990s. In reality, it simply deferred the inevitable until 2002 and beyond.

This time, the consequences could be worse than the sudden dollar bear in 1987 that crashed the stock market 22.6 percent in one day.

Then the dollar started to break free from its Louvre support, and eurodollar holders started switching into other currencies. The reason: It was revealed that the U.S. Current Account deficit had climbed to roughly $79 billion a year.

To accumulate a $79 billion trade deficit now takes less than two months.

In 2003, the eurodollar overhang has reached proportions that seem almost apocalyptic compared to the problems of the 1980s. So if eurodollar holders were to decide, en masse, that they can't take the currency losses any longer, the squeeze on the U.S. financial system could be on a scale unlike anything ever seen before.

The reader may well grumble, "Stop muttering about vague threats! Give us the data on these blasted eurodollars!"

The problem is, I cannot.

Nor can anyone else I know. I've asked all the leading economists, Federal Reserve governors, and major global investors I meet whether they have any data. Everyone says current data don't exist: *The principal source of global financial liquidity is a largely unknown quantity*. I understand, however, that major banks in the U.S. banking system now routinely rely on eurodollar funding for 30 to 50 percent of their corporate loans, which is worrisome when one realizes the other side of those transactions is a collectivity of foreigners who have no legal requirement to hold dollar deposits, and who face serious currency risk.

For those reasons, I have long believed that the next serious Baby Bear attack—one that could easily become a Papa or a Mama—will come from a runaway breakdown in the eurodollar market.

Fred Bergsten, the distinguished Washington economist, recently told Congress that the dollar is "the third bubble." (The other two bubbles he mentioned were tech stocks and the stock market generally.) He sees no way that the Current Account problems can be resolved without a contraction in the dollar's value and a rise in American savings, and warns that the adjustment process could be painful.

What will happen to the value of U.S. financial assets if foreign investors refrain from outright panic but just refuse to inject new funds into dollar-denominated assets?

No Wall Street strategists consider that a risk. They point to the depth and liquidity of U.S. capital markets, and say there are no serious alternatives abroad. Japan is sinking slowly into a bog; the eurozone is mired in red tape; China is booming, but its capital markets are rigidly controlled; Canada, Australia, and New Zealand are only about 4.5 percent of the global index.

So like it or loathe it, you've got to be in the dollar and in U.S. markets.

I guess I would be more convinced of this argument if I had not heard it before.

In the late 1980s, Japan was on its way to global economic dominance. It had become the price and quality setter in a wide range of industries. It could buy any foreign asset it wanted—whether a Van Gogh or a Rockefeller Center—if it were for sale.

And then it was all over.

CAN THERE BE GOOD NEWS FROM A DOLLAR BEAR?

In one sense, a dollar bear is like global warming, which could produce widespread deleterious effects on the environment.

But on the plus side, global warming also means longer growing seasons in the temperate zones, helping to explain why world food output has tended to be above forecasts during the 1990s.

Similarly, a dollar bear could be just what a global economic doctor might order as a bracing tonic. Because the dollar is the global reserve currency, when it falls in value, global inflationary forces get a boost. That could be just what the world needs at a time of powerful deflationary drag emanating from Asia and Japan.

A third bonus from a dollar bear: Oil is denominated in dollars. Most industrial nations—with the exception of Canada, Australia, Britain, and Norway—and most Third World nations import some or all of their petroleum needs. It was bad news for the global economy in 2001 when oil prices and the dollar rose in tandem. But the dollar's break has been very good news for many countries that lack indigenous hydrocarbons.

A fourth benefit: A major dollar bear move would be great news for most U.S. manufacturers. They are suffering ruinous competition from Asia and Japan, and the sky-high dollar has been another ineradicable problem. They incur their costs in the world's most overvalued currency, hardly a recipe for global competitiveness. If the dollar can slide gently down to its trading value—and stop behaving as a financial currency—the U.S. Midwest in particular would greatly benefit.

Fifth and last, a fall in the dollar can be good news for U.S. multinationals. Some great U.S. corporations, such as Johnson & Johnson, IBM, and Intel, earn a large proportion of their profits abroad. When those earnings are restated into rising dollars, then companies' overall earnings shrink. Again, a gently sliding dollar would be good news for most multinationals.

How can you profit from a dollar bear?

Most obviously, by investing in gold and in gold mining stocks. You then own a pre–Bretton Woods store of value. As long as the dollar remains in a bear market, gold remains an extremely attractive asset.

What the investor should watch is the dollar's trend and the TED spread, to see if foreigners are giving up on the greenback. If they are merely cutting back on their new commitments, this could be a good outcome for the U.S. economy and most U.S. equities.

To sum up, the U.S. economy and financial system are the financial equivalent of a patient on a dialysis machine hooked up to foreign suppliers. The relationship is symbiotic: They finance us, and we buy goods from them and travel to their countries, and, historically, we have been the guarantors of their liberty (although they don't talk about that so much anymore).

There is no historical precedent for a relationship on such a scale. Therefore, there is no sure way to predict how it will end—or even whether it will end at all.

No long-term investor survival plan would be complete if it did not make allowance for two possibilities: a gradual downward adjustment in the dollar's value, and a violent, short-term, TED spread-activating plunge.

The expression "sound as a dollar" went out of date long ago. It is now in the same category as "What this country needs is a good five-cent cigar."

The Challenging Financial Landscape Ahead

The chief difficulty in forest travel, especially in flat lands that are heavily timbered, is the lack of natural outlooks from which one could get a view of distant landmarks. Although there are plenty of marks in the woods themselves by which a trained woodsman can follow a route that he traversed not long before, yet these signs are forever changing, vanishing, being superseded by others.

—H. KEPHART

TRIPLE WATERFALLS ARE ECONOMIC and financial cycles writ large. They magnify growth in the economy and in personal wealth on the way up and the shrinkage on the way down. They are the product of bad planning on a grand scale, based on Shared Mistake about the inevitability of sustained growth.

The story of Joseph (Gen. 41) is history's first account of a boom/bust cycle. It is also history's last account of a brilliantly planned and managed boom/bust cycle.

Pharaoh has a dream that Joseph interprets. He predicts seven fat years followed by seven lean years. Having made his economic call, Joseph then switches to strategic advice: Hire an economic boss to call in the annual grain production excess. Then there will be enough food for the lean years. Pharaoh believes the climatoeconomic forecast, hires the consultant, and profits immensely over the next 14 years.

This was, essentially, a government-imposed savings system. By buying the surplus grain for all that time, the government kept prices high enough to keep the farmers producing, thereby maximizing output under especially favorable growing conditions. By conserving it from decay and rats, they kept it available. Egypt became the mightiest economy of the eastern Mediterranean when the drought ravaged crops as far east as Canaan.

The essence of the long-range plan was an assumption that a long-term drought somewhere far up the Nile (wherever that might be) would slash the river's flow, reducing much of Egypt's arable land to desert. If you accepted that such a climate shift was coming after seven years of high floods that permitted the farming of vaster tracts of land, then the strategy of price maintenance and saving made sense.

Today in capitalist democracies, that kind of long-term planning is impossible. It was tried in the Soviet Union in the form of Five-Year Plans and Gosplan, but it failed. On 4500 years of evidence, Joseph's strategy is probably the only recorded sustained success of central economic planning.

Yet governments, private forecasting agencies, corporations, economists, and Wall Street persist in planning far into the future on the basis of economic forecasts that assume good GDP growth will be the sustained norm. The Congressional Budget Office has for years been issuing long-range deficit and surplus forecasts that have never been right, yet they are continually trumpeted by politicians and pundits in support of their own particular programs.

This Gosplanism is doubtless inevitable with governments, whose bureaucracies love to wallow in the meetings, graphs, and bafflegab of long-range plans that attain a false air of reality by predicting GDP and tax revenue and—most important—spending growth in precise percentages. Most of these ventures in futility do little harm, because they occupy bureaucrats in discussions with each other, leaving the economy to fend for itself. Smart investors don't rely on them. The harm comes when private sector CEOs and CFOs find it fashionable to mimic the Commissariat of Gosplan.

In the 1990s the leaders of New Economy companies learned to drive up their stock prices and enrich themselves through stock options by convincing investors that they had extremely specific growth plans for five and ten years into the future. These spreadsheet-spawned fantasies were designed to justify price-earnings ratios based on earnings to be achieved off in the mists of the new millennium. Wall Street analysts joyously joined in these computer games. Their spreadsheets confirmed the splendidly precise and gloriously profitable forecasts excreted by the companies' spreadsheets. (If management says it will grow sales and earnings 40 percent a year for the next five years, then the CFO's numbers will be validated when supine Street analysts plug in "40 percent" and click. Hey Presto! Shills & Mountebanks Technology is the next Cisco!)

All such so-called corporate plans were based on assumptions of endless growth in product demand backed by sustained pricing power. No technology company—and no Wall Street analyst who remained employed—allowed for the possibility of an economic downturn coming from oversupply and overinvestment. No technology company—and no Wall Street analyst who remained employed—ever allowed that the record of railway and canal booms and busts in the last century had any relevance in modern forecasting. No technology company—and no Wall Street analyst who remained employed—believed the tech boom was a cycle that would end, like all the others, in the inevitable pattern of slowdown, disappointment, price-cutting, disbelief, financial stress, anguish, terror, finger-pointing, and collapse.

Cycles, natural disasters, wars, and other catastrophes are *always* perils for investors. They always have been, and they always will be.

Without the shocks capitalism is heir to, the risk premium on equity investing would soon begin to shrink to the vanishing point, and over the long run stocks would probably return little more than bonds.

Joseph had divine guidance in formulating his long-term forecast and suggesting the optimal strategic response. Beware of prophets who predict profits far into the future without Joseph's backing.

THE BLESSED 1990s

The 1990s were truly special.

What gave them the chance to be so uniquely rewarding for investors was that they were the grown-ups of the 1980s, the era of the Reagan and Thatcher revolutions and the collapse of Bolshevism.

The so-called Clinton Bull Market was really the continuation, compounding, and climax of the "Reagan Bull Market." It was born on August

13, 1982, when Paul Volcker looked at the world of disinflation he had wrought and saw that it was good. He announced he was resting from his labors and proclaimed the interest rate cut that became a pattern. The inflationary devil had been driven from the land, and the United States was on its way to two decades of falling inflation and falling interest rates that would come to seem to most homeowners, corporate borrowers, and investors like a New Eden in contrast to the years of punishment from double-digit borrowing costs.

It is only a slight overstatement to say that the U.S. economy of the late 1990s was characterized by the sustained operation of an inverse Murphy's Law. Nearly everything right that could happen did happen, and nearly everything that could go wrong did not. That felicitous combination even extended to the national statistics—the data published by Washington overstated what was a good story and made it a magnificent story.

The nation experienced peace, falling inflation, falling interest rates, falling costs of basic commodities, rapid technological gains, rising productivity, and the aura of global success that attended its newfound status as *the* global superpower.

Vince Lombardi is credited (perhaps falsely) with asserting as his credo, "Winning isn't everything, it's the only thing." That slogan was both a call to excellence and the recognition that winning tomorrow is much easier if you win today. Losing is habit-forming. The great sports dynasties, such as the New York Yankees (of most decades), the Chicago Bulls (of the Michael Jordan era), the Montreal Canadiens (of the 1950s through the 1970s), and the Nebraska Cornhuskers (of recent decades) showed that nothing succeeds like success. Conversely, teams with losing records can stay that way for what may seem eternity. The Chicago Cubs are justly famed for futility, having failed to win a World Series since baseball became a national obsession. At one point during the 1990s, the manager of another team with a dismal record told reporters, "Any team is entitled to have a losing decade." When the Cubs manager was asked to comment on that statement, he replied, "Any team is entitled to have a losing century."

During the late 1990s, American triumphalism was an irritant at G-8 gatherings of heads of state, but American culture, technology, and economic policies had growing allure globally. For example: Iranian mullahs grew more and more angry at the United States, but young Iranians grew more and more envious and impressed with America and with its model of freedom.

Francis Fukuyama's seminal book, *The End of History and the Last Man,* made a persuasive case for the proposition that winning the Cold War could prove to be the most enduring victory in history. The West's victory in the Cold War (the consequence of the policies of Reagan and Thatcher) and the prosperity of the West on free trade and private property models (of which the Reagan and Thatcher models were the purest form) had answered the two major nonmetaphysical questions sages had debated since Plato's time: What is the best system of government, and what is the best economic system for maximizing the creation and distribution of wealth?

Democracy was the best system of government and capitalism was the best economic system. No intellectually credible alternatives remained. Anyone who advocated dictatorships or theocracies had to base his case on essentially irrational arguments. Anyone who advocated government control and management of the economy had to base his case on utopian claims, not logic.

If democratic capitalism was now the only logical way to create good economic growth and distribute its fruits fairly, then more and more people across the world were naturally bound to look at the U.S. economy to see how and why it worked so well. What helped to stimulate that global fascination with America was the disappointing performance of other economies.

The 1990s began with Japan as ruling economic superpower and ended with Japan mired deep in a deflationary bog. Asia went through two major financial crises that produced the region's deepest recession since World War II. Germany began the decade with the ecstasy of reunification, then slid slowly into despond, and with the engine of Europe gradually running out of gas, growth in the rest of Europe came in fits and starts. Russia was imploding. Whatever strength Canada and Mexico showed was overwhelmingly dependent on those economies' benefits from exports to the United States under NAFTA.

One wellspring of this strong U.S. economic performance was the size of the so-called Peace Dividend compared with the effects of peace on economies abroad. America had shouldered most of the burden for waging the Cold War, so it naturally benefited the most from winning it. Bill Clinton and Robert Rubin were dealt the strong hand of an economy blessed with that dividend, which would grow throughout their terms in power, and they played that strong hand well.

Too well, as we were to learn too late.

By near-continuous cuts in defense spending, they freed up funds for social programs, yet produced a string of fiscal surpluses. They kept contracting the Pentagon's share of GDP and cleansing the intelligence services of wiggle room for what could be deemed dubious counterintelligence activities. This sustained sapping of the nation's defenses continued through their term in office, despite an attack on the World Trade Center, on U.S. embassies abroad, and on the USS *Cole* that showed that a new, sophisticated, and remorseless global terror organization had emerged.

On August 13, 2002, in the midst of the bear market, historians observed the 20th anniversary of the beginning of the Great Bull Market that had endured, with some brief bearish intervals, until March 10, 2000.

Credit Suisse First Boston published some fascinating historical data for that anniversary, noting that only six companies included in the list of the 20 biggest market capitalization companies on that date had been on the 20 biggest list the day the Reagan-Bush-Clinton bull was born: IBM, Exxon Mobil, General Electric, Johnson & Johnson, Procter & Gamble, and Philip Morris. The industry that lost relative stock market capitalization most heavily over the two decades was, of course, oil, which was entering its own Triple Waterfall as the bull was born: Nine oil companies made the mega list then, but only Exxon Mobil remains.

The report included a listing of the biggest winners in 20 years. Among the names that would have rewarded the buy-and-hold investor most were these success stories:

Name of Company	Percent Market Cap Increase
Countrywide Credit	49,699
Home Depot	45,471
Applied Materials	24,008
Tyco International	17,715
Wal-Mart	9,547
Intel	6,400
Walgreen	5,985

What most investors probably found most remarkable in that list was the high ranking for Tyco International, one of the poster bad boy stocks of 2002. Tyco's investment performance ranking near the top of all American companies over two decades came after the stock had already fallen 75 percent from its all-time high amid revelations of accounting sleaze and indictments for tax evasion against its CEO, Dennis Kozlowski. Had the company's financial affairs been clean, it might have been the top-performing stock of all.

There will be other long-lived bull markets.

But not soon.

To justify that prophecy, I cite some sound reasons for believing that, for the foreseeable future at least, the felicitous combination of events, forces, and trends that made that bull so great will not be repeated.

THE PROBLEMS AHEAD

As the Papa Bear of 2000–200? has matured, his reasons for grouchiness have changed. He was born as twin to the technology and telecom Mini-Mama Bear, sent to deliver Triple Waterfall punishment for the idiocy of the technology mania. His arrival, drowned out by the cacophony of collapsing technology stocks, signified the onset of a recession that economists denied. He seemed to have been driven into hibernation by the post 9/11 rally, but because none of the major indices got back to their March 2000 highs, he was still out there. He became vicious amid burgeoning evidence of accounting problems, ranging from the overenthusiastic to the overaggressive to the over-the-top to the over-the-line-of-the-law.

Since then, he has been performing his classic function of forecasting the outlook for the economy and for corporate profits—something the stock market does better than any economist, strategist, or Federal Reserve committee. At its low on October 9, 2002, the S&P was 776, down 49 percent from the high, exceeding the index's 48 percent crash in the Nifty Fifty Triple Waterfall of 1972–1974.

Floyd Norris of *The New York Times* noted a neat coincidence: 776 was the closing level for the Dow Jones Industrials on August 12, 1982, the day before the greatest of all bulls was born.

The stock market is troubled by what it sees:

- Another Day Older and Deeper in Debt

- Slower Corporate Earnings Growth

- The New Buyers of the 1990s: Once Is Enough?

- Demography's Tourniquet Starts to Tighten

- The Legacy Crunch

- Asbestos and the Growing Burden of Insurance Costs

- Global Turmoil

- Endangered Species? Animal Spirits

- After the New Economy a New Price Risk: Deflation
- China's Impact on the Global Economy and Corporate Profitability

  The list is long! Let's look at these problems one by one.

Another Day Older and Deeper in Debt
The wondrous 1990s saw explosive growth in the technology, telecom, and biotechnology industries. Passage of the Telecommunications Act of 1996 led to what proved to be cancerous growth in development of wireless and fiberoptic facilities as hundreds of new players rushed into the business, backed by seemingly unlimited amounts of venture capital and Initial Public Offering (IPO) funding. Ordinarily, the telephone business is a slow, steady grower; this explosion of growth from an unlikely sector came at a time when the Internet was creating billions of dollars in capital spending, and the two new technologies overlapped and reinforced each other, ultimately creating *the spectacle of a fiberoptic system in which only 4 percent was "lit"—in use*. By another test—what percentage of all cable is linked to a switch—the excesses seem even more preposterous: Only 15 percent was linked to a switch as of mid-2002.

Nothing succeeds, we are told, like success. There are times when nothing succeeds like excess. During the 1990s, Americans managed to build the Internet, homes, factories, schools, universities and stadiums, pay for a huge research budget, get richer, and in general have a great time.

Without the nuisance of having to save to pay for it.

During that period the U.S. personal savings rate—long the lowest in the industrial world—collapsed. But the economy boomed even as American personal savings went negative. Americans learned the pleasures of "living off the fat of the world."

Private sector debt grew faster than GDP during the decade, which meant that to produce one dollar of GDP growth, more than one dollar had to be borrowed—through bonds, eurodollars, mortgages, credit cards, bank loans, and so on.

As noted previously, the status of the United States as hegemony and haven, and the slow or erratic growth in economies abroad, let the United States tap global savings on an unprecedented scale. According to the *Financial Times,* the United States draws down more than 70 percent of the entire world's cross-border savings flows to finance its lifestyle—which means, more than 70 percent of the world savings invested across national borders are going to the United States. Since U.S. GDP is only 24 percent of global GDP, this U.S. portion is disproportionately high, and it's a drag on economic growth in other capital-short regions of the world. (A dollar saved by a Taiwanese that is invested in the United States is a dollar that is not available to Thailand or Indonesia or, for that matter, Canada.)

One of the defining characteristics of Triple Waterfall mentalities is the Shared Mistake that a new perpetual wealth machine has been invented. Eliza Doolittle's ecstasy at the ball where she "Could have danced all night" is the kind of sustained joy that permeates stock exchanges, board-rooms, governments, and media.

Until the music stops.

What is certain is that as Asian economics grow more rapidly, and as Europe begins to face up to the daunting financial problems of paying for its pensions and health care, savings from abroad will not be so readily available to Americans.

So in this decade, Americans will finally have to confront the challenge faced by the trade-off between savings and growth.

When a nation has grown faster than the rest of the world by serially using—and serially abusing—the savings of the rest of the world, the process is inherently unsustainable. That the world's biggest economy could rely permanently on its ability to go deeper into debt to the rest of the world each working day, while (1) setting the price of servicing most of those debts itself (through the Fed's ability to influence short-term rates) and (2) assuming that the world forever owed it a living . . .

Now *that's* chutzpah.

A more realistic outcome is that the nation's savings rate will be forced higher—if only to service private, public, and international debts.

Any increase in the savings rate will be a transfer from consumption, which means the nation's growth rate must slow. (Do not assume that any increase in personal savings would mean big new cashflows into U.S. stocks. That increased savings could come from reducing household indebtedness. If the average family were to (1) add $100 a month to its mortgage payment, thereby prepaying part of their mortgage, and (2) freeze its credit card and automobile lease debt at existing levels, the national savings rate would climb sharply, but it would depress stock prices because retail sales growth would shrink or disappear, forcing cutbacks in business capital spending.)

We should update the old saying that there is nothing certain but death and taxes: There is nothing certain but *debt,* death, and taxes. Most of these debts are owed domestically, but apart from borrowings spent on productive capital spending, the debts represent the seemingly perpetual payment burden for past consumption.

As long as Nasdaq was soaring, the value of U.S. assets was rising more quickly than the value of U.S. debts to foreigners. Nasdaq has since fallen by three-quarters, but most of those debts remain and must be serviced out of current economic activity. (The debts that do not remain have not been discharged from the proceeds of American thriftiness. Billions of dollars of foreign loans to American borrowers such as WorldCom and Global Crossing have been written off, and billions more from the bleeding bad will join them in the global debt graveyard.)

Prodigal sons ultimately become broke beggars. The 1990s were the time Americans lived splendidly but far beyond their means, relying on the seemingly inexhaustible thrift of foreigners. This decade's economy will be struggling under the weight of debts accumulated during those good times that already seem so long ago. The American economic situation in much of this coming decade could be summed up in the words of Captain Ahab: "I feel bowed, as though I were Adam staggering beneath the piled centuries since Paradise." No—it has only been a few years since our earthly Paradise, but a substantial proportion of all those debts will remain to haunt our great-grandchildren. Man is mortal—most debt is not. It gets rolled over, but is immediately resurrected. The only stake that will ever be driven through its heart comes through bankruptcy.

It is dispiriting to note that the nation slides deeper into debt even when the economy slows to a walk, suggesting that we are now borrowing from abroad to cover the payments on the debts accumulated in the good times. As *Barron's* reported (October 7, 2002), the debt buildup has continued even as the U.S. economy struggled under its mountainous debts. In the first seven months of 2002, foreigners pumped $308 billion into the United States—10 percent more than the Current Account deficit (according to Joseph Quinlan, senior global economist of Morgan Stanley). In July alone, foreigners bought $25.4 billion in Treasurys (according to the credit research firm CreditSights).

By late 2002, the huge rally in gold and gold stocks showed that time was running out for U.S. borrowers and, perhaps, for U.S. assets as global winners.

Slower Corporate Earnings Growth

If things seem too good to be true, the proper response from a prudent investor is to assume they are. In the late 1990s, bad accounting practices took over in Washington and in large sectors of corporate America. The economy was not quite as strong, total corporate profits were not as high, and the profits earned by large public companies were nowhere near as high as we were told.

In July 2002 the Department of Commerce announced a revision of its National Income and Product Accounts, slashing corporate profits for the years after 1997. The effect was to *drive the direction of earnings from up to down* for those years, meaning that corporate profits actually peaked in 1997 (when the S&P was trading in the 900 range), not in early 2000 (when it was trading at 1500). Corporate profits as a percentage of GDP peaked at 10 percent in 1997—far above the 6 percent range of 1983 but well below the 11 to 12 percent range of the mid-1960s.

What these restated numbers meant was that during all the years of tech mania, and most of the years of the Cult of Equities, corporate profits were actually *declining*. As Josh Billings long ago observed, "The trouble with people is not that they don't know, but that they know so much that ain't so."

What the Pied Pipers and Shills & Mountebanks were doing to millions of novice investors in early 2000 was the equivalent of taking thousands of schoolchildren for an extended skating trip far out on a lake that was already in advanced stages of spring breakup—and then surreptitiously fleeing to shore to watch, in safety, as the children drowned.

The Internal Revenue Service reported that in 1998—the most recent year for which its studies are complete—the widening gap between earnings reported to shareholders and profits reported to the IRS had reached $155 billion. Double-talk from double-entry bookkeeping had reached unprecedented levels. *The biggest returns on business creativity in the New Economy came not from innovation, research, production and marketing, but from "creative accounting."* With stock options profits for corporate insiders running into the hundreds of billions of dollars in the late 1990s, the gap between stated and actual earnings reached new peaks of mendacity. Arthur Andersen would later be hanged for having assisted Enron in the creation of false financial statements, but to assume that Andersen was the sole practitioner of accounting sleaze is the equivalent of buying into the single cockroach theory. ("If you see a cockroach in the kitchen, don't worry: It's the only one.")

[Amid the endless revelations of New Economy sleaze, it was natural that the only tech company whose corporate name was the Latin word for Truth would eventually have to own up to a fib. Veritas, a software company, announced in October 2002 that its CFO had resigned after admitting he had lied about his academic accomplishments. With Veritas down to $12 from $160, it was touching to see the company affirm the fine old motto *Veritas omnia vincit* ("Truth conquers everything") in purging an insider for not being the Stanford MBA he claimed to be. In retrospect, it's too bad he had to go because he was so clearly the right man for airbrushing and gold-plating a New Economy company's accounts. He will, we are sure, be missed, although his trailblazing approach to covering tracks will doubtless live on.]

Why are we finding out about all this malfeasance now? As Warren Buffett observed: "The recession uncovers what the auditors missed."

The New Buyers of the 1990s: Once Is Enough?

The stock market of the late 1990s was one gigantic love-in, as the Sixties Generation took charge. They took to equity investing with the infectious enthusiasm they had poured into political causes during their youth. For most of the Baby Boomers, this was their first real experience with stocks, and they found it almost as exciting as their first experience with sex. Nearly everything they bought went up in price. No postcoital depression in the form of Buyer's Remorse. This fabulous process meant they would not have to save much to be able to look forward to a great lifestyle in retirement. They could continue to spend heavily while getting richer. Was this a great time to be alive or what?

Not only did the Boomers invest in stocks heavily for themselves, producing a boom in brokerage accounts and equity mutual funds, but they moved into management of large pension funds and boosted those funds' equity exposure substantially. If stocks were cool, they were not just cool for one's personal brokerage account, they were right for the pension plan.

According to *Pensions & Investments,* the leading pension trade journal, corporate–defined benefit pension plans' average equity exposure during the mid-1980s was 48.5 percent (excluding private equity). By 2000 that was 63.3 percent. Corporate 401(k) plans, which in 1985 were small potatoes and generally invested in guaranteed investment contracts, had by the year 2000 grown spectacularly, with 69 percent exposure to equities.

State and local pension funds joined the parade. In 1985, equity exposure averaged just 30.1 percent, but by 2000 it had reached 61.2 percent. States such as Indiana, which had never permitted their public funds to own stocks, changed their laws during the 1990s to mandate equity exposure.

When individuals and pension funds are investing far more heavily in equities than they have in the past, the stock market is likely to rise substantially. Why should we not expect a continuation of this kind of growth in cashflow to equity investing in this decade?

First, because betrayed lovers are more likely to be cynical the next time. The Cult of Equities of the 1960s, which flowered just before the Triple Waterfall Crash of 1973–1974, did not survive. Although the stock market eventually regained its previous heights, the generation that lost heavily during that first mutual fund boom never regained its previous enthusiasm. It took the maturing of a new generation into middle age for the next Cult of Equities to appear.

Second, the major upward adjustment in defined benefit plans' equity exposure was a single event, even though it occurred over more than a decade. A similar percentage growth from these levels is impossible. In retrospect, as some of us noted at the time, this national swing away from investment traditions that had existed for decades was a reliable sign that the stock market was nearing a top. Those consultants and "experts" associated with getting public funds to sell billions of dollars in bonds (which rose significantly in value thereafter) in order to invest those billions of dollars in stocks (which plummeted thereafter) will be hymning the virtues of prudence, caution, and diversification until well into the next bull market. Indeed, these committees and consultants have historically moved together in a mutually reinforcing process that tends to immunize them against being fired for being different. Since they went down together, the more likely conclusion is that they will collectively reduce equity exposure, thereby missing much of the returns from the next bull market.

Third, defined benefit pension plans as a group have gone from rejoicing in huge surpluses (which generated extra gains in reported per-share earnings for corporate sponsors) to gasping under the weight of huge deficits (which are now beginning to drag down corporate sponsors' reported per-share earnings). If anything, pension plan sponsors will be more risk averse after the huge losses of recent years.

Do we recognize the signs of Shared Mistake? Consultants eager to grow their businesses came up with meretricious PowerPoint presentations about the inevitability of high equity returns. The demographic makeup of pension committees shifted toward Boomers, who were personally enthusiastic about stocks. Changes in compensation arrangements for CFOs and other officers involved in corporate pension funds frequently tied their bonuses and stock options to gross (not risk-adjusted) pension fund returns. Academics chimed in with Efficient Frontier analyses based on Modern Portfolio Theory that made bonds look truly bad. The process reinforced the appeal of joining what would be the Shared Mistake majority.

Seemingly everybody who mattered became convinced that pension funds should increase their equity exposures to levels that would have been characterized as "very aggressive" in any previous stock market cycle.

That is how Shared Mistake has always operated. It leads to the wrong conclusions, generating huge losses, but lets nearly everyone involved plead "Not guilty" because they did what everyone else did.

Capitalism is supposedly all about risk taking. But many corporate committees can be all about personal risk avoidance. They take on the protective colorations of their environments and pay heavily to external consultants to prepare slick reports that are virtually identical to the reports sent to hundreds of other committees. When everybody is wrong, then, paradoxically, no one is wrong—and the story has a happy ending in which the insiders get to cash their stock options, retire on generous pensions, and live happily ever after.

Demography's Tourniquet Starts to Tighten
Across the industrial world, this will be the decade in which population growth stalls, then begins to turn negative.

That kind of demographic event has historically been associated with such catastrophes as major wars, plagues, and famines. This time it will come from human progress—in the form of wider educational, lifestyle, and career opportunities for women—and medical science—in the form of birth control and improved longevity.

One of the generally overlooked aspects of the 1990s was the low Dependency Ratio level across the Western world. (DR is the ratio of those under 16 and over 65 to the rest of the population.) There was much discussion about the aging population mix, and much political rhetoric about the coming crises in social security and Medicare, but little talk about the fact that the millennium was ending with a DR that was the lowest it would be for many decades. The 1990s could, and should, have been the Golden Age of Pension Prefunding. Instead they were the Golden Age of Excess. We needed a Joseph. We got a group of Belshazzars.

As Pogo would say, "From here on up, it's downhill all the way."

The aging of the population will increase health care and pension costs each year for at least the next half century. Abolishing mandatory retirement, postponing the onset of social security benefits, and other Band-Aids will be used to deal with the explosion in pension and Medicare costs after 2011, but health care costs will be climbing even faster before then, as the number of people over the age of 55 escalates.

The United States has serious financing problems in coming decades, but it is in the strongest position of any of the leading industrial nations, primarily because youthful Latino immigrants swelled the ranks of productive workers (see "The Latino Advantage," in Chapter 10). However, apart from immigrant populations, the collapsing fertility rate in the industrial world outside the United States ensures that the costs for pensions, social security, and Medicare after 2020 will be far higher than planners had assumed. Coming events cast their shadows; long before then, societal changes and convulsions will be occurring.

Europe is aging rapidly. Britain's Office of National Statistics reported last year that for the first time since the nation began taking a census, there are more Britons 60 and over than under 16. More than 1 million people are 85 and over, five times as many as a half century ago. By 2050, according to the United Nations, Britain's pensioner population will rise from today's 21 percent to 34 percent.

Continental Europe is facing more serious problems: That UN report says Italy's pensioners will be 42 percent of the population in 2050. The Continent's already low fertility rates for European whites continues to drop, while fertility rates for African and Asian immigrant groups remains high. Germany's longstanding approach of importing "guest workers" (*Gastarbeiter*) is causing social and political strains. The murder of populist politician Pim Fortuyn in easygoing Holland is a sign that tensions are already eroding parts of the sociopolitical fabric.

At some as-yet-undefined point, the aging of the population will begin to erode dynamism, optimism, and risk taking—the pituitary hormones of capitalist growth. Without continued production of those hormones, the system will be gradually weakened by sclerosis, complacency, and timidity. It is not that the young are smarter than the old. (Nasdaq performance confirms as much.) It is that an aging economy dominated by the instincts and theories of mature, cautious, prudent people is as much at risk as a species in nature that collectively ages (like the Ents in *Lord of the Rings*). This subtle, but lethal, process has been contributing to the growing torpor in Japan's economy since 1989. One study simply compounded the negative numbers forward to zero, showing that the last living Japanese would die during the 24th century. Apart from the obvious impact on the building of homes and schools, the "we're all growing old together" syndrome suppurates through the system in insidious fashion.

History shows that when wealthy nations with stable populations are in proximity to needy nations with rising populations, tidal forces develop that usually prove irresistible.

Yet no country has shown itself willing to do serious planning for demographic collapse. Why?

1. Because, until recent years, Club of Rome neo-Malthusianism dominated the thinking of the elites. They were so concerned about an endless population explosion that would pollute the planet and (by the way) kill hundreds of millions with starvation,

that they chose to ignore the evidence of collapsing birth rates in the industrial world and falling birth rates in the Third World. After the fall of the Berlin Wall, the stunned elites of Europe strove to find a new unifying anticapitalist cause. They swung en masse to aggressive environmentalism, which was part Romantic nostalgia, part bad science, part good science, and partly hatred of capital-ism—a hatred that became a force in the fast-developing antiglob-alism of the 1990s.

2. Crucial to this new cause was the conviction that human popula-tion expansion was putting "Earth's future in the balance." At no time did the elites revisit their erroneous population forecasts in light of evidence from across the world that educating women past elementary school produced plunging birth rates. The ready avail-ability of birth control and abortion gave women options they had not had since the dawn of time, and a majority of them are choos-ing not to be birth machines.

3. That the elites chose to downplay evidence that population growth was not just slowing in the G-8 but in most of the world was not because of stupidity. They just found it useful to maintain the apocalyptic vision of billions of people whose bodily wastes and use of chemicals would make the planet uninhabitable—a vision useful for the rest of their program. Although environmentalists have never managed to elect a Green government anywhere (though they have participated in coalitions in some European countries, like the current government in Germany), that failure at the ballot box only reinforces their desire to achieve their goals through other means. Through their dominance in non-Govern-mental Organizations (NGOs), United Nations committees, and foundations, they exert real power.

4. Voluntary demographic collapse, or what some call "racial sui-cide," seems to run counter to human nature.

Since the advent of the Industrial Revolution, and particularly since the spread of public health practices—including water purification and immu-nization in the 19th century—industrial societies have known only rapid population growth (except for the two world wars and the great influenza epidemic). The collective failure to prepare advanced industrial societies for negative population growth means that people and families will gradually reach their own conclusions about such matters as the wisdom of investing in real estate. Judging by the boom in house prices across the G-7 since

1999, that realization has not yet sunk in. Big question: To whom will today's buyers of high-priced European homes sell after, say, 2020? Oil-rich Saudi immigrants fleeing the overcrowding of the teeming cities of Jeddah and Riyadh?

The Legacy Crunch

Two of the reasons Americans have to be proud about their economic system are the nation's private health care and private pension arrangements. Two of the reasons Americans have to be frightened about their economic system are the nation's private health care and private pension arrangements.

When President Bush, a lifelong free trader, imposed tariffs on foreign steel, he was not just capitulating to pressure from a local vested interest. He was responding—simplistically, and probably cynically—to arguments about the essentially hopeless position of the established steel companies: Even if they invest in the most modern equipment, and even if their unions are quiescent, there is no hope for Big Steel over the long run in a global free trade environment. Moreover, the same arguments are beginning to apply to other big industries, such as automobiles and machinery.

Pension and health care plans are the towering "legacy" costs for long-established American industries. (Two statistics out of many: General Motors paid $55 million for just one drug—Prilosec—for its U.S. employees and pensioners in 2001. General Electric said its health care costs are $6500 per U.S. employee far more than the total wages and benefits paid to workers in most Asian countries. Seeking to control the cost increases, General Electric triggered a strike in January 2003.)

There was a time when the factor costs of production were land, labor, and capital. Companies who used those resources effectively could sell competitively. Changes in currency values would affect a company's international competitive position favorably or adversely, but currency advantages and disadvantages would even out over the long term.

There was a time when an industry that could not compete using its existing structure would downsize until it could match production and demand profitably.

But what happens when the employer assumes the burden of health care for its workers, during and after their working lives, and . . .

What happens when the employer assumes the burden of income support for its workers, during and after their working lives, and . . .

What happens when downsizing mandates extremely expensive costs for early retirement, and . . .

What happens when the number of retirees begins to equal or (as in the case of General Motors and some steel companies) even exceed the number of production workers?

How can that employer—and that industry—compete with

- European manufacturers, whose health care costs for active workers and retirees are paid by governments out of general tax revenues, and whose pension costs are largely paid by governments.

- Third World manufacturers, whose modest health care and pension costs are either paid by governments or whose work force is still youthful—and will remain that way for decades to come.

- Canadian manufacturers, whose health care costs for active workers and retirees are largely paid by governments. (Joseph Califano, a former HHS secretary, said some years ago that it was $700 per car cheaper to build new cars in Windsor, Ontario, than in Detroit because of Canada's universal medical care system; that differential is probably higher today.)

What is at stake here is a basic deterioration of the American competitive position in terms of trade. It's hard enough to compete with a Third World producer who is using Western technology and who pays his workers a fraction of U.S. wage rates. But the disparity in health care costs is even greater, given the sophistication of American medicine and the costs of operating a system in a nation that has far more trial lawyers than in the rest of the world combined. America is the only industrial nation that pays for most of its health care through private arrangements. This unique system has been enormously successful in delivering superior medical benefits to much of the population, but it creates insuperable competitive problems in the nation's foreign trade. Europeans pay for their generous health care, vacations, and most of their pensions through stiff value-added taxes (which run from 15 to 25 percent on final sales of most goods and services). But the costs of those programs for manufacturers are applied only to products sold within Europe. Exports of manufactured goods from Europe are VAT-exempt.

European manufacturers can therefore export products such as cars, steel, chemicals, machinery, and electronic goods to the United States, undercutting the prices of leading American firms because the government has exempted those sales from the costs of health care and pensions for workers and retirees—costs that are onerous burdens for American companies. Meanwhile, the attempts of American firms to exempt exports from federal taxes through offshore sales corporations produced a multi-billion-dollar penalty on major U.S. exporters after a World Trade Organization investigation.

How onerous are health care costs to American employers? Health care is now 15 percent of GDP, and its share rises annually. Health care is the only major sector of technology in which the newer the product, the more it costs. A survey last year of rate increases for health care in large group programs showed that employers were paying 10 to 18 percent more than in the year previous. CalPERS, the California Public Service program, said it expected to pay as much as 25 percent more. CalPERS is not competing with public service groups abroad, so it can just pass those costs along to taxpayers.

The U.S. trade deficit exceeds $1.6 billion per working day. As noted previously, the overvalued dollar is a big contributor to that daily bleed.

But so is health care.

And so are pensions.

And the situation can only worsen as the nation ages and the ratio of American retirees to active workers deteriorates. It could be ameliorated somewhat if the costs associated with litigation could be brought even remotely closer to health care operating costs abroad, but that assumes President Bush will succeed in controlling the power of the trial lawyer lobby. (See discussion below, in "Asbestos and the Growing Burden of Insurance Costs.")

Demographers and futurists like to say that "Demography is destiny." Although demography is of merely marginal value in short-term economic and financial forecasting, it is of great value in longer-range forecasting.

As worrisome as these demographic statistics are today, they will quite probably become far worse. The billions of dollars spent annually in research on such major killers as cancer, heart disease, diabetes, Alzheimer's, and cirrhosis will surely produce breakthroughs in coming decades. That means people will live longer in retirement, even if the retirement age is postponed substantially. The longer you live, the more it will cost you—or your employer—particularly for health care.

All the people who will be retiring between now and 2050 are already alive. As they cease to be providers of goods and services and become consumers of accumulated savings and tax dollars, much of the story of the economy of the next half century will be told.

Asbestos and the Growing Burden of Insurance Costs

If you thought the 9/11 attacks were the worst news for the insurance industry in decades, you were wrong. The cost of those assaults to insurers is estimated at more than $75 billion. The costs of asbestos litigation are currently estimated at $280 billion, and that estimate rises sharply every year.

If you thought that the only people who could collect in an asbestos lawsuit were the sick, you were wrong. The greatest volume of lawsuits filed is on behalf of people who have had no contact with asbestos for decades, and who show no symptoms for whatever casual contact (such as sitting in a schoolroom) they might have had.

If you thought that the greatest challenge for corporations and insurers was paying the actual costs of illnesses, disability, and death for those who had asbestos exposure, you were wrong. Lawyers are demanding punitive damages (even for companies who acquired other companies decades after those companies ceased using asbestos). Plaintiff lawyers treat asbestos as a "health risk" of tobacco proportions, worthy of their 40 percent fees.

Asbestos, like tobacco, is a health risk in which trial lawyers stand to earn more money than all the profits of all the pharmaceutical companies. Most of the claims come in suits filed on behalf of healthy people. As for sick people claiming large awards, they are under no great burden to show direct asbestos causality.

There is disagreement about the cost to the U.S. economy and American competitiveness of unbridled tort litigation. What blocks a solution to this growing problem for the U.S. economy and U.S. capital markets, according to the *Wall Street Journal,* the insurance industry, and major business groups, is the influence through fund raising that these lawyers have in the Democratic Party. They were even able to delay passage of legislation in 2002 that would have made the federal government a major insurer in terrorist attacks.

After the Trade Center assault, the government agreed to insure for actual damages from terrorist attacks—including personal injuries, loss of income, and death—but declined to pay punitive damages above $250,000 if buildings were destroyed by terrorists. The government would limit coverage to actual damages, including personal injuries and death. That would stand in the way of lawyers who might otherwise have collected billions of dollars from taxpayers following a terrorist attack. Democrats in Congress blocked the bill, citing consumer protection, and after the 2000 election, President Bush pressured congressional Republicans to accept a bill that would prevent the collapse of the insurance market for major commercial buildings.

Insurance rates are climbing rapidly. Many European reinsurers are on the edge of insolvency because of reinsuring companies with major asbestos exposure in the United States.

Insurance is a basic cost of doing business, and because of this nation's addiction to expensive litigation, it has always been more expensive, from an insurance standpoint, to operate a business in the United States than in any other industrial nation. In most jurisdictions, there are constraints on vexatious litigation because when a plaintiff loses, he or she is responsible for the defendant's court costs and lawyer fees. Only in America does the winner have to pay his own lawyers' fees. Because court costs are so high, and because juries are so inclined to side with plaintiffs against big-pocketed companies headquartered out of state, insurers routinely pay to settle cases they are confident they could win. So the plaintiffs' lawyers win even with what might be losing cases.

A jury awarded a 64-year-old lung-cancer sufferer *$28 billion* against Philip Morris for failing to warn her of the health hazards of smoking. Her lawyer stands to collect up to 40 percent of the ultimate payout. (On appeal it has been reduced to $28 million but her lawyer is appealing that.)

Global Turmoil

It is already becoming fashionable to deride the allegedly naïve optimism expressed in Francis Fukuyama's *The End of History and the Last Man*.

New democracies in Africa are falling in military coups. Fragile Mideast and Asian countries are being destabilized by violent groups whose *raison d'être* is rejection of democracy, free enterprise capitalism, and the rule of any law other than a strict form of *shariah*. Latin American governments committed to freer markets have been collapsing.

A war with terror had been in existence for years before 9/11. Groups such as the Irish Republican Army, the Basque ETA, Colombia's FARC, Hamas, and Hezbollah had been sniping and bombing in their own regions for decades; Kashmir was an ever-present *casus belli* between Pakistan and India. Few observers noted the links between the radicals, and even fewer commented on the support some of them received from wealthy and powerful persons and organizations outside their own regions. (Wealthy Irish Americans funded the IRA, and Syria and Iran and various wealthy Saudis funded such radical Islamists as al Qaeda, Hamas, and Hezbollah.)

What 9/11 laid bare was the new challenge to what is known as the West—the civilization that is the collective inheritor of two traditions: the Judaeo-Christian religion of monotheism and equality before God and the Greco-Roman humanist traditions in art, literature, philosophy, music, commerce, and science.

The West has been the cradle and nurturer of the concept of individual liberty and of the idea that there must be limitations on the powers of the state. The U.S. Declaration of Independence and Constitution are two of the high watermarks of Western civilization, particularly of the bifurcated ideal of a nation under God that separates Church from state. As such, these radical-sounding documents were—and are—summations of traditions that have been evolving since Mosaic times.

Al Qaeda and the various other Islamic terror organizations are also the inheritors of two traditions. One is a great religion rooted in an inspiring text that dates back 13 centuries. The second is a political philosophy rooted in the Jacobinism of the French Revolution. That political viewpoint of the unlimited power of a state over an individual has come to the terrorists by way of Marxism and its various emanations—Communism, fascism, and Nazism.

To the radical Islamists, "Islam is the answer" to everything. Since the Koran does not address the concept of statecraft as such, theocratic "Islamic Republics" such as Khomenei's Iran and the Taliban's Afghanistan have apparently become the models for what these various groups aim to achieve. They have made the Palestinian cause their centerpiece of protest against the West because of their continuing resentment at the amazing success of Israel, the lone democracy in the region. However, these new revolutionaries have only a marriage of convenience with the predominantly secularist ambitions of the Palestine Liberation Organization, or of Saddam Hussein and other foes of Israel.

Radical Islamists understand that it is the West that is their real challenge, because it offers so many opportunities (read "temptations") to young Islamic people—particularly women. Although they speak in historical terms of the Crusaders and the imperialists, their wrath is focused on the United States and Israel as coexemplars of Western traditions of freedom, equality, education, and free markets. Their own nations have failed to deliver the economic progress craved by burgeoning populations, forcing the radicals to blame Israel and the United States for their own dysfunctional economic and political structures.

The West confronted remorseless challengers to its traditions in World War II and the Cold War—and won, at great cost. It now faces a different kind of challenge. War with Iraq is merely one front in a much broader confrontation with forces whose goal is the destruction of Western philosophic, religious, economic, and humanist traditions. To the extent that this new war takes place against true believers in a great and enduring religion, it may prove more intractable than those other wars. The descendants of Robespierre, Marx, Stalin, Hitler, and Mao Zedong had secular utopian creeds to inspire them. These warriors have one of the world's most powerful texts—

the Koran—and more than a millennium of cultural and intellectual development. (It also seems to help the recruitment process that "martyrs" get an instant trip to Paradise, where 72 ardent virgins await; an even more attractive incentive system than a Silicon Valley stock option package.)

What has been unfolding over the past two years is a pattern closer to Samuel Huntington's *Clash of Civilizations* than Fukuyama's benign world of market-oriented democratic economies.

Fukuyama has felt it necessary recently to point out that he never actually predicted that we would glide effortlessly and inevitably into a world of irenic democracies prospering with market economies. He merely said there is no intellectually respectable and rationally demonstrable alternative to democratic capitalism.

Failed democracies, failed economies, and failed states can—and doubtless will—continue to inflict misery on their citizens, leading to coups, rebellions, and wars. Given the proliferation of advanced technologies that make killing and destruction easy for leaders of even relatively poor states, the world is probably facing a period of prolonged instability.

If this is in fact the basic geopolitical situation for the next decade, then investors should not assume that the stock market will return to its previous price-earnings ratio range. A world in which the United States and, perhaps, the West will face the threat of terrorist attacks for years to come is not the cheerful world of the early 1990s. North Korea's admission that it has nuclear materials and the rocketry to deliver them is just another sign that the post–Cold War optimism was naïve. Insurers have already changed the ratings on their exposure. Equity investors are unlikely to restore peacetime p/e ratios as long as insurance rates rise and each month brings new stories of actual and attempted terrorist attacks.

What 9/11 also exposed was how a few well-organized terrorists could use the West's own technologies to disable it. They commandeered passenger jetliners, choosing those carrying full loads of fuel for transcontinental flights, thereby making them flying bombs. This audacious act raised anew the fears of thoughtful American analysts, such as Senator Richard Lugar and former Senator Sam Nunn, about the hoards of weapons of mass destruction—particularly nuclear bombs—stored in locations around the republics that formed the USSR. In the chaos following Communism's collapse, there was erosion of the tight security arrangements that had prevented nuclear war by mistake during the Cold War. With U.S. financial aid, that situation has been addressed in recent years, but audits disclose that some nuclear weapons are missing. (Depending on which reports you believe, the number of missing nukes ranges from 44 to 200.) What is also missing are many Soviet nuclear and germ weapon scientists who helped build those fearsome arsenals. When there was no longer a superpower state to provide them with the pay and prestige commensurate with their training and skills, some of them went abroad, where dictators such as Saddam Hussein eagerly embraced them.

The threat that a few terrorists, or an otherwise inconsequential terrorist state, could cause devastation on a scale previously associated only with major wars, is unlikely to disappear. It appears that the West will return to mankind's position in the Age of the Titans, as told in the Greek myth of Pandora, in which a stream of calamities—including diseases, death, disasters, and wars—were released from Pandora's box, and have beset mankind ever since. Just as the last force in the box was about to escape, as the story goes, she slammed the lid forever, leaving Hope locked in the casket.

The week after 9/11 I spoke at a meeting of the Greenwich Round Table, a group of leading hedge funds and pension funds that meet in Greenwich, Connecticut, to exchange investment views. More than a trillion dollars of managed money was in the room.

I argued that the outbreak of war meant that stocks were worth approximately 20 percent less than they were under peacetime conditions (using the arguments set out in "The Costs of War," in Chapter 4). The effect of my analysis was to agree with the grim outlook for the S&P given by the first speaker, Douglas Cliggott, the Wall Street strategist who had been the most accurate forecaster over the preceding two years. We both came up with a number in the low to mid-800 range for the S&P 500 over the ensuing year.

Even if the West is somehow able to prevent terrorists and their terrorist-state sponsors from inflicting horrendous damage on its territory, we would be reckless to believe that nothing but peaceful years lay ahead.

History shows that a particularly dangerous time comes when a long-dominant power faces a challenge from an upstart impatient for its own place in the sun. The rise of Prussia and Austria to power was a direct threat to the Pax Britannica that had been the basis of one of the most peaceful centuries in history, and that challenge finally produced World War I, which in turn led to World War II.

Such a challenger looms to Pax Americana. If economic trends of the past 15 years are projected forward, China will have an economy which, on a purchasing power parity basis, could be of American proportions by 2015, and its military might would be so formidable that, at the least, the world would be back to the bipolarity of the Cold War.

To date, China has only posed a threat to its adjoining neighbors, but in the era of nuclear intercontinental missiles, all nations are its neighbors. As a dictatorship trying to evolve into a more representative society without yielding the perceived benefits of central control, China from time to time shows signs of a paranoid insecurity that could unleash terrifying aggressions.

The United States has no real choice except to rebuild its depleted weaponry, aiming for such an overwhelming technological advantage (including missile defenses) that neither China nor a terrorist state would choose to attack it.

The European Union is wrestling with the challenge of backing up its claims to be recognized as a major global power while having relatively insignificant military strength. Britain and France are the only members of the E.U. that appear to understand that those who would speak loudly must be prepared to carry a big stick. Not only do such members as Ireland, Greece, and Sweden resist participation in serious military operations abroad, but as last year's elections showed, Germany is retreating from such investment in armaments and participation in NATO as it displayed during the Cold War.

Without a long list of real allies who have real military resources and the real will to use them when necessary, the United States is a lonely superpower. At the very least, that unpleasant reality means no peace dividends for the foreseeable future.

Endangered Species? Animal Spirits

Keynes gave us a useful term—"animal spirits"—for one of the basic drivers of capitalism. They are the enthusiasm, greed, and eagerness to assume risk that are the roots of entrepreneurialism. The 1990s were one of the greatest playgrounds for animal spirits ever seen. They got out of control, but along the way they did stimulate the economy, and for a while they also created enormous wealth for investors other than corporate insiders.

An unlikely way of illustrating these animals at play came in a *Wall Street Journal* article about baseball team owners at the time another strike loomed. A remarkable number of the owners had made their money from the New Economy.

- Texas Rangers owner Tom Hicks's investment firm had lost nearly $1 billion in a telecom investment and had roughly an equal amount at stake in an Argentinian media venture.

- Cleveland Indians owner Larry Dolan was known as a billionaire for his position in Cablevision, but its stock price was down 90 percent.

- San Diego Padres owner John Moores, another of those nouveau billionaires, had watched shares in his software company plunge from $80 to merely $1. (Not to worry too much for the Padres arch-bishop, though; he had previously had the inspiration, from some source, to sell $646 million worth of stock.)

These stories are worth retelling, because they illustrate a trend that will surely have major impact on the economy in coming years: The con-centric ripples spreading outward from the technology/telecom plunge into the chill waters of reality. *Nouveaux* billionaires are significant economic players, and a cautious forecaster will studiously resist the temptation to indulge in schadenfreude at their sudden miseries. They may have levered up their business assets in ego-building sports ventures, but they represent the dynamism and wealth creation that had been a big part of what made the 1990s such a strong decade for the economy and for investors.

Although "animal spirits" may be hard to quantify, one statistic will illustrate how robust those spirits were during the 1990s. Venture Capital funds (VCs) raised $186 billion in the year 2000, many times what had been raised in any of the early years of the decade. In 2001, inflows fell 56 percent. They doubtless fell further in 2002.

What we now know is that a substantial percentage of that great national resource—the supply of animal spirits—was diverted and cor-rupted away from building great companies with great futures by the allurements of short-termism, with its attendant rewards in stock option profits. Short-termism involved such mountebankery as issuing "aggres-sive" earnings statements that overstated the companies' true profitability; issuing "aggressive" forecasts for future growth; and radiating optimism at public meetings, on CNBC, at employee gatherings, and in meetings with analysts and reporters. It also involved huge sales of optioned stock while telling the world that the future looked sensational.

Entrepreneurs such as John Chambers, who was a driving force in Cisco's surge from tiny company into colossus, were great stories in the 1990s. But in economic as well as in political terms, it would seem, power can be corrupting. A new kind of power emerged—the power to enrich oneself in a matter of a few years, or even a few months, to the level greater than the Robber Barons—by getting consultants to design over-generous option schemes, which were approved by tame boards with heavy representation from CEOs of other companies with similar com-pensation schemes.

Even as Cisco was beginning to unravel, and even as Chambers spoke glowingly of its future prospects, he was cashing in $150 million dollars' worth of stock. As the company was at pains to explain to financially pained stockholders, they were the rewards for his creation of shareholder value and the golden manacles that would ensure he would not take his talents to some other firm. How much incentive to work in the stockholders' interest did he need? And why did he keep getting more largesse when he presided over a 70 percent drop in the price of Cisco stock? What should one of the nation's greatest apparent shareholder devaluers get? If the stock's collapse was blamed on a bear market, then shouldn't most of its rise be credited to the biggest bull market of all time? And why didn't anyone ask?

We may never know whether Chambers and the other heroes of Silicon Valley would have been more prudent managers, content to issue conservative earnings statements, had they not been seduced by the prospect of sudden billionairedom.

What we do know is that their perverted animal spirits led them—and the entire economy—astray. It will take years—or decades—for the former focus on company building to return in a way that will help public stockholders' wealth building.

Contrary to Gordon Gekko in the movie *Wall Street,* greed is not good for the company, its employees, its stockholders, the financial markets, or the economy when that greed is not sated with $50 to $100 million in personal wealth gains for the CEO over a few years. If those gains merely raise the CEO's greed lust to higher levels, then a new Greek tragedy is unfolding—in which the sins of the heroic leader produce disaster for his stockholders and employees, and for the economy at large.

Human nature has not changed since the Greek tragedians wrote about the horrible consequences of hubris, greed, envy, and lust. Could the Triple Waterfall have been averted if the leading business schools had included Sophocles, Aeschylus, and Euripides in their core programs?

After the New Economy, a New Price Risk: Deflation

For 60 years North Americans have only been concerned with one challenge to price stability: inflation. A new threat has emerged, which raises new challenges for investors: deflation.

Deflation is a sustained fall in prices. It is more insidious than inflation, and, as Japan has demonstrated, potentially more dangerous.

What can make a heavy but tolerable debt burden intolerable is a deflationary recession. The recession weakens the economy's income statement, while the deflation weakens its balance sheet.

The Economist summed up that problem in its issue of September 14, 2002:

Deflation is much more harmful than inflation. Falling prices encourage consumers to postpone spending in the expectation of cheaper goods tomorrow; they also make it impossible to deliver negative real interest rates if these are needed to drag an economy out of recession. Most dangerous of all is a cocktail of deflation and debt. Deflation pushes up the real burden of debt, while the value of assets linked to that debt, such as house prices, may have to fall even more sharply in nominal terms to return to a fair level.

The debate over the future of the U.S. economy took an ominous turn last year when more observers began to question whether the United States was destined to repeat the deflationary Japanese experience of the 1990s. Alan Greenspan commissioned a special Federal Reserve study of the Japanese experience, and assured Congress that appropriate policies would prevent a U.S. reprise of that long slide into deflationary recession.

Princeton's Paul Krugman, an economist who writes for the *New York Times,* joined the debate with an insightful column published August 16, 2002. He noted that as he had pondered the possibility of deflation in recent years, he had always concluded that the United States would escape, for four reasons:

1. The Fed has plenty of room to cut interest rates.
2. The U.S. long-term budget position is very strong.
3. The United States need not worry about an Asian-style collapse of confidence in the business sector because of strong U.S. corporate governance.
4. We may have a stock bubble, but we don't have a real estate bubble.

He then noted that he had abandoned the first three arguments and was now worried about the fourth. He had not been convinced that the Nasdaq leap was a true bubble, although he did allow for that possibility.

Krugman went on to castigate the Fed for not cutting rates from the (then existing) 1.75 percent. Since monetarism is anathema to liberals, he assumed that all that mattered was the *price* of money, not its actual growth rates. He made no comment on the fact that the Fed had lowered rates 11 straight times without growing the "high-powered money" component of the Monetary Base (see "The Fed and the Dollar," in Chapter 7). To a monetarist, that meant Fed policy resembled a retailer who lowers prices on a load of inventory 11 times without making a sale. To characterize him as an aggressive marketer would be missing the point; what he should have done was lower prices to the level that would get the merchandise moving.

Krugman's dilemma illustrates why academics, politicians, and businesspeople have become far more cautious about the future. During the 1990s, it was fashionable among those groups to ridicule the Japanese for their dysfunctional economy and policymaking. Since the technology and telecom Triple Waterfall poured cold water on their assumptions of American invulnerability, they have sharply lowered their expectations of growth for both the economy and corporate profits, and sharply escalated their expectations for the challenges to mainstream long-range forecasts.

Among those who are most worried about deflation is Stephen Roach, Morgan Stanley's economist. He argues that the United States and Germany are on the cusp of outright deflation, and could follow Japan into that grim situation soon. He worries, in particular, that a collapse in housing prices here would have the effect that the real estate bust had in Japan. He notes that goods prices have been in deflation for some time, with the services sector supplying all the inflation the economy experiences. He regards the data on services inflation as suspect, compared to the relatively hard numbers on goods prices.

Japan exported its deflation to the West in the 1990s. It still does. But the new global deflationary champ is China.

China's Impact on the Global Economy and Corporate Profitability
The deflationary forces emanating primarily from Japan produced continued pressure on corporate profit margins globally during the last economic cycle. China will be the major global deflator in this decade.

The next time you shop at Wal-Mart or Target, spend some time trying to find products (other than candy, food, and personal and health care products) made in the United States. Note how many items come from China.

That unscientific research will help you understand the challenge facing business leaders in the United States, Canada, and Europe, but it would only be your first step: Products made in other nonindustrialized nations—whether Mexico, Malaysia, or Mongolia—must be price competitive with China to enter global markets. China has become the global price setter on a dizzying range of products—and it adds new products to that list each month. China's niche used to be T-shirts, flags, socks, sneakers, and batteries, but it has been moving relentlessly upscale. By 2001, for example, it was a bigger exporter of computers and servers than Japan. It is now the world's biggest cell phone market, and its decision to choose a Siemens-developed third generation technology is a potentially crushing blow to struggling technology companies like Ericsson.

Two statistics show why China's drive to global power will not reverse, but must accelerate: Chinese wage rates are 5 percent of Japanese rates (which tend to be close to U.S. rates), and an industrial park site near Yoko-hama costs 60 times as much as an industrial park site near Shanghai. Japan Inc., the industrial powerhouse that nearly brought heartland America's industries to their knees in the 1980s until the dollar was devalued, cannot compete with almost any product line China chooses to manufacture.

China's low costs, rapid growth, and serious unemployment make fur-ther industrial expansion based on deflationary pricing inevitable. To date, China has not been a factor in the global automobile business. That is about to change. *Ward's Automotive Reports* issued a study on September 16, 2002, detailing a long list of joint ventures that will make China a formida-ble auto producer within a few years. Examples: Toyota's new venture there will increase its current production 500 percent; Hyundai claims it could be building as many as 500,000 automobiles in China by 2010; Kia is plan-ning to start its facilities there at 50,000 cars annually, with an eventual objective of 300,000; Toyota has announced plans to build luxury SUVs in China.

Already, China is becoming a formidable force in chip making and PC assembly, as such global companies as Celestica and Taiwan Semiconduc-tor build huge operations there. Some analysts argue that most of the major U.S. players who have been outsourcing production to such countries as Singapore, Malaysia, and Taiwan will switch most of their operations to China in this decade. In all cases, the reason is costs.

A recent article in the *National Post* cites a study by Chen Zhao, chief emerging markets strategist at Canada's respected *Bank Credit Analyst*. "The deflationary impulse coming from China is so strong, and the timing is so bad—it is hitting a North American economy already swimming in excess capacity—that Mr. Zhao thinks it will trigger currency devaluations across Asia, and eventually lead to interest rates of about 1 percent in major western economies," the article explains. "In 1990, goods from China made up just 5 percent of U.S. imports. Today they make up 11 percent. The Chi-nese have an unlimited ability to drop prices."

Tell those stories to groups of investors, and they become uneasy. But at every gathering, someone sticks up a hand to say, "But so many of the big U.S. and European companies are opening plants in China, so they'll be okay."

I then tell them the story of the Honda motorcycle plant in China.

Honda looked at booming demand for motorcycles in China, and decided it could no longer rely on exporting from Japan. It built a state-of-the-art plant there. Once it was in full production, Honda was selling every-thing it could produce.

For six months.

Then a new Chinese brand of bike suddenly appeared, which cost almost exactly half Honda's price, and it swiftly took over the market. Honda bought one of these hot sellers and took it apart. They found it was an exact, superb knockoff of Honda's product, down to the smallest detail, and with components of equal quality.

China's impact on the global economy and on global capital market returns in this decade will be felt in many ways. Here are a few:

- As global price setter to a continuously widening range of goods, it forces manufacturers abroad to cut their prices or withdraw from that line of business. This is a sustained, widening deflationary force. It works somewhat differently depending on the stage of the global trade cycle: If global trade is not expanding, because of slow or contracting growth in the OECD nations, China's price competitiveness drives foreign manufacturers out of production; if global trade is expanding, China's influence is to restrain efforts by manufacturers abroad to bolster profit margins. This weakens them in good times, so they are more likely to throw in the towel in the next slowdown. Deflation is a force that undermines much of what we have come to take for granted about the economic cycle.

- Because by Western standards Chinese cost accounting is primitive, and because capital is so plenteous for Chinese firms because of (1) the nation's 40 percent personal savings rate and (2) the nation's current account surplus, Chinese firms can penetrate foreign markets by quoting prices far below what producers abroad require—or what a well-managed, publicly traded Chinese firm would require. This is the equivalent of the old poker player's maxim, "The most dangerous player in a game of table stakes is a fool with unlimited money."

- China controls the foreign exchange value of its currency, the renminbi (or yuan). It effectively pegs it below the dollar's global trading range, guaranteeing Chinese exporters a strong competitive position globally, but also making commodity imports (which tend to be dollar-priced) reasonably priced. As China keeps building its foreign exchange reserves, it becomes a bigger threat to global financial stability should it choose to diversify its hoard away from the dollar at a time of dollar weakness. Last year, as the dollar was hurting in the foreign exchange markets, Beijing announced that it was the fourth biggest holder of dollars in the world and was diversifying into other currencies, particularly the euro. This announcement was made just after the president of Taiwan had declared that his island should be regarded as a nation, a statement that provoked a furious response from Beijing and worried reactions from capitals in the rest of the world.

- China is by far the fastest-growing economy in the world. Unlike the growth model of most Third World economies, its strategy is built on the import of commodities and the export of finished goods. Already, the Chinese trading operations have become crucially important in the pricing of copper, zinc, nickel, and even soybeans. As China's importance grows, the nation will doubtless adopt the Japanese strategy of building reliable supply lines overseas for the raw materials most crucial to its development, such as oil, liquefied natural gas, and base metals.

- Some Australian analysts used to worry that the Japanese strategy of long-term contracts with Australian mines threatened to make Australia almost a Japanese colony. The Nikkei Triple Waterfall ended that "Southeast Asia Co-Prosperity Sphere" threat (if there ever was one). China is far more likely to be able to achieve—and manage—a form of economic imperialism in commodity markets. To the extent China manages to make such long-term arrangements with commodity producers abroad, it will tend to hold down commodity pricing through future economic cycles, because the most important marginal buyer will not be easily panicked into bidding up prices stratospherically to keep its factories humming. That will be another deflationary pressure over the long term.

- Future American administrations will have no choice but to regard China as a potential military threat to U.S. interests—including the U.S. homeland itself. The important American military confrontations (hot or cold war), since World War I have been with dictatorships—Nazi Germany, the USSR, North Korea, North Vietnam, and Iraq. No one knows how Mao's successors will evolve. Deng Xiaoping, surely the most outstanding true revolutionary of our time and one of the great men of the past century, clearly believed that China's road to national greatness lay in the opposite direction from Mao's Long March. He squared the circle—building a dynamic form of state-sponsored capitalism while maintaining Socialist rhetoric and control of politics, the economy, and the army by the party responsible for maintaining the "Dictatorship of the Proletariat," as if guided wholly by Leninist principles. (John O'Sullivan of National Review says the Chinese are Communists the way the French are Catholics.) Given the risks that China will behave more like a Communist dictatorship than a capitalist society, Washington will have to maintain heavy expenditures for research, development, and production of advanced military technology to maintain America's lead. It will also have to do a far better job in the future of protecting its military secrets from Beijing's ubiquitous intelligence operatives.

LOOKING AHEAD AT A CHALLENGING LANDSCAPE

This summary of the challenges to investors in the next economic cycle may make it sound as if a traveler would ask, "Is this trip really necessary?"

The answer, of course, is that life is a journey, and we must make the best of the opportunities it offers. Any review of American economic history will quickly reveal that the nation has faced worse challenges before—and investors have still somehow managed to pile up those famous 9 percent compounded returns on equities over a century that included two world wars, the Korean War, the Vietnam War, six Triple Waterfalls, and other tribulations too numerous to mention.

Survivors make the best of what is out there. They adapt.

The world of the 1990s—peace, falling inflation, falling interest rates, rising confidence in the future, and rising productivity—was hardly typical. The least likely occurrence in this decade is a replay of that benign era.

Does that mean there will never be another bull market?

Of course not. There have been bull markets under many kinds of external environments.

A Triple Waterfall collapse and an ensuing recession are not in themselves reasons for investors to give up on equities. What investors need to abandon is the hope that the 1990s will return. The next fat years will be better than the current lean years, but will have their own unique characteristics. Nor will they seem fat compared to the late 1990s.

The terrain ahead offers more in the way of challenges than easy money. Yet for shrewd, patient, disciplined investors, there will be rewards. Those rewards may seem scanty compared to the 1990s, but they will not have to be shared with a fast-growing pool of investors, and most companies will have to show their real stock option costs, so there should be enough to sustain the wise and the prudent.

CHAPTER 9

Setting Your Course to a Secure Retirement

Given a free choice it is always advisable in cross-country travel to choose a route up spurs and ranges and down streams, unless in very mountainous country.

—R. GRAVES

IN THE 1990S, MILLIONS OF PEOPLE set out cheerfully and confidently on the course to a secure retirement, only to discover they had received grossly misleading intelligence from scouts about the terrain, the climate, and the predators.

■ *Campers learn their craft from their elders, respecting wisdom accumulated over the generations back to aboriginal times.*

Investors rejected their elders' lore as soon as it became inconvenient. They came to assume that whatever was new was good, and whatever was old was bad.

■ *Campers prepare their campsites each night, guarding against bad weather, critters, and bears.*

Investors went with the flow, believing that only sunny weather lay ahead and that bears were extinct.

■   *Campers practice their powers of observation, looking, listening,*
    and sniffing for signs of opportunity and trouble, ready to move their
    campsites if danger appears.
    Investors attuned their eyes and ears only for good news, believ-
ing they could dwell forever on the "sunny side of the Street."

THE WAY WE WERE

In the late 1990s, Greed was ubiquitous, and socially triumphant.

At social gatherings, people loved to tell me how smart they were about
the stock market. Considering me a conservative investor of the old school,
it gave many novices particular satisfaction to brag about their triple digit
returns from New Economy stocks.

The worst of those who lorded it over me were those who checked the
returns on the value-oriented mutual fund I managed in the *Wall Street
Journal,* which looked painfully low compared to the spectacular results
they were getting from aggressive growth funds and participation in hot
Initial Public Offerings (IPOs). (That the fund had been a consistent four-
or five-star-ranked product in the Morningstar mutual fund survey until
1999 was not of any interest to them, and I never bothered to point out the
fund's excellent long-term returns. What was the use?)

One of the Street's oldest maxims is, "Never confuse genius with a bull
market." It is a wise observation, and it contains two insights. First, just
because somebody made a pile in a roaring bull market does not mean that
person is smart. Second, the people who make the most when the market is
gaining the most are never the most knowledgeable and smartest investors:
They're mortgaging their homes to bet big and are winning big, while
really smart investors are betting less and are taking more off the table as
the market runs ahead, toward the abyss.

An annual summer sight on beaches in the Northeast is the sudden
appearance of a huge, fast-moving dark shape in the ocean. Lifeguards call
swimmers back to shore to get them out of the way of the feeding frenzy of
a gigantic school of bluefish, who chew anything within reach.

When Nasdaq ran up 88 percent in 1999, it seemed like bluefish time
nearly every week. What was on display was a near continuous feeding
frenzy, and it was scary—yet strangely fascinating—to watch. Roving
mobs of greedy snobs are as subhuman as roving mobs of drunken yobs.

Nasdaq's run from 1300 to 5000 left insiders with stock options rich on
the scale of wealth that took a Carnegie or Morgan a lifetime to accumu-

late, riches grabbed from the savings of millions dumped into the market during the feeding frenzies.

In the 1990s the idea of planning for retirement suddenly became a hot topic. It was not because Baby Boomers were looking ahead to 2011 or thereabouts, when they would reach 65. It was certainly not because the Boomers had suddenly discovered that thrift was sexy. Why should they consider saving desirable or necessary when they had made it into their thirties and forties by living the good life financed by borrowing? To make retirement a chic concept, there had to be a hedonistic motivation.

And so it was that the Street discovered the sales appeal and sex appeal of Early Retirement. Instead of trying to entice Boomers with TV ads showing elderly people reclining in hammocks, they showed fit, trim fortyish folks at play in swank locations or in magnificent wilderness settings.

What made those sales pitches so successful were the real-life stories of people who were "doing their own thing" full-time, thanks to the stock market.

There were various versions of these stories:

- The most frequently heard stories were about the people who decided at age 50 or thereabouts to "get out of the rat race." Why wait to 65? Those who'd managed to accumulate a couple of million or so found that by leaving it in the stock market (which was a perpetual money fountain), they could start *really* living.

- Then there were those who were in their thirties and forties who had found the key to getting rich while having fun: They had packed in their dull jobs in favor of day trading.

- Finally, there were the stories of the bonanzas. There were lots of those during the dot-com era, when it seemed there was a new billionaire a week. A young Chicagoan who ran a shoe store quit and joined a few buddies in setting up a Web site for the distribution of mugs, sweatshirts, etc., with college and fraternity insignias. Within two years they were bought out for more than $200 million.

Early retirement 1990s style was an easy sell. It promised you all the time you wanted for what you wanted, whether painting, pottery, golf, tennis, travel, fishing, or camping. With Viagra in vogue, you could even count on great sex in retirement, something you were sure your parents never had. And, best of all, you did not have to sacrifice to accumulate the wealth to make the last half century or so of your life more fun than what came before. You just had to make sure your 401(k) and your brokerage account were in stocks—and the more aggressive, the better. (Your parents saved with bank accounts, S&Ls, life insurance, savings bonds, and maybe a smattering of blue chip stocks; no wonder your dad worked till he dropped: He was earning maybe 5 to 6 percent a year on his investments, which meant almost nothing after tax. So he didn't have the time to take long vacations, even if he could have brought himself to squander his savings on having fun. Too bad about Dad.)

When the Reagan administration created the 401(k) program, it started its life as an annuity and fixed-income program. By 2000 more than two-thirds of all 401(k) assets were invested in equities.

By 2002 the market value of the mutual funds held by the average investor—including 401(k) accounts—was below the investor's cost. Despite the biggest bull market of all time, despite the biggest commit-ment to equities of all time, despite greater levels of advice by planners and professionals than in any earlier era, most investors were losers. They would have been better off in bank accounts, S&Ls, life insurance, and savings bonds. And they had lost 10 years of wealth accumulation time.

THE WAY WE ARE

Today's challenge is to conquer paralytic fear, rebuild the savings lost in the feeding frenzies, and accumulate adequate resources in the time remaining before retirement. The camper who has decided to spend the winter at a remote cabin in the mountains must accumulate the food, fuel, and provisions needed before the salmon runs end, the deer leave the high ground, blueberries rot, and the game birds fly south. The camper may lament the time he wasted during the spring and summer, but calculates how much time he has left before the deep snow arrives, and how that time must be spent.

It was easier two decades ago than today. Back in 1982, you could have bought an S&P Index Fund that would have delivered 15 percent returns for the next two decades, or you could have bought a long-term Treasury bond that would have guaranteed you 12 percent for that same time span. Yes, you could not have known that the stock market would have been so sensa-tional for so long, but you did not need to know that to lock in double-digit returns free of all risks except inflation.

THE WAY TO GO

Which comes first when thinking about nest eggs, the chicken or the egg?

Sometimes it makes sense for an individual to try to think like a group. In the case of personal financial planning, the prudent practice is to emulate pension funds by constructing a balance sheet. Your balance sheet would show you and your family as the liabilities and your retirement fund as the asset.

Pension funds calculate their liabilities first, then figure out how to invest to fund those liabilities.

So should you.

Most people invest as if there were no offsetting liabilities. That makes no sense, because for every pool of assets, there must be some liability.

When one invests without considering the nature of the liability, the temptation is to look only at the potential rewards. That opens the door for Greed to take over the investment function.

When you ignore the nature of your liabilities, you're prey to predators who tell you what percentage of your portfolio should be invested in aggressive growth, what percentage in growth, etc. They brag that they know the winning formulas.

Know Then Thyself

Consider, then, your personal equation. . . . The personal equation, then— your own—regardless of what other folks do, or think you ought to do . . . . Weigh the essentials. . . . Finally, will you go in company or alone?

—H. Kephart

Before you invest another dollar, sit down with your spouse or partner and review:

1. Your health risks, considering such relevant data as mortality statistics in your family
2. Your current financial position
3. Your life insurance arrangements
4. Your retirement goals
5. Your high-confidence forecast of employment income between now and retirement
6. Your risk tolerances

You will then have an idea of what your personal liability structure looks like. If, for example, you have congenital health problems that virtually rule out working past age 60, then you have less time than people in great health whose parents lived into their eighties. If you're a self-employed person with wide swings in income from year to year, you may not be able to use dollar averaging as the basis of your plan. (Dollar averaging assumes regular contributions, every year, and preferably every quarter. That kind of consistency allows you to ignore short-term market swings. Dollar averaging is the most reliable long-term wealth-building program.)

The biggest problem faced by people who ignore their liabilities is that they are prey for those who cite very long-term statistics on asset class returns. That was the allurement peddled by the Shills & Mountebanks during the 1990s: They were able to cite those very long-term average returns on stocks and make people think there was little risk in equity investing—that great returns were virtually automatic. What never was cited at the big Greed gatherings of that era was Keynes's dictum: "In the long run, we are all dead." When you and your spouse are likely to die are not just important considerations to you for obvious reasons: Those dates are crucial components of your liability structure.

Your likely years of work, income, health, retirement, and the likely financial demands on you from nonspousal family members are basic questions.

When you've answered them, you're ready to design—with the help of some external professionals, such as your broker, financial planner, lawyer, life insurance agent, and accountant—your own Survival Pak. (You may even have enough information to get what is called a Monte Carlo simulation from firms who offer this sophisticated program. This process, the brainchild of W. H. Sharpe, is a leading-edge Modern Portfolio Theory program based on long-term asset return data. It can be helpful—in the hands of experts who are not awed by its precision—but it should be used as a tool, not blindly as a totally scientific exposition of Truth. You may not live long enough or work long enough for all those averages to work out with such beautiful predictability. Besides, as you may have gathered by now, the next decade or two is unlikely to match up with the time periods used in the machine's database. Long Term Capital Management—Nobel prize winners and all—went bust using an analysis system that sounded very much like Monte Carlo.)

A good starting point when thinking about long-term asset accumulation is a summary of the process in 25 words or less. Here is one such formulation.

Investment Survival Statement

Investment survival leading to investment contentment comes from consistently compounding an acceptable level of risk-adjusted real rate of return on one's portfolio.

The component parts of this strategy statement are (1) consistency, (2) compounding, (3) maintenance of an acceptable level, (4) risk adjustment, and (5) real rate of return.

1. *Consistency.* You will not get from here to there effectively by subjecting yourself to wide swings from positive to deeply negative annual rates of return. When you lose big, it is mathematically difficult to recoup. Suppose you bought a tech stock at 100 and it falls in a year to 50. So you're down 50 percent. What percentage move will the stock have to make within the following two years to give you an annualized return of just zero over three years? Answer: 100 percent. A 50 percent rally from that low would only get you back to 75. Yet, during the strong Nasdaq rally off the 9/11 lows, when stocks that had fallen 80 percent briefly doubled, the Shills & Mountebanks trumpeted about the fabulous returns investors were getting, proving, they screamed, that the sell-off had been just a mirage.

2. *Compounding.* Remember Einstein's principle: "The most powerful force in the universe is the law of compound interest."

The easiest way to compound your investment is to have an automatic reinvestment of dividends or interest in the asset class you own. Mutual funds do that for you. So do zero coupon bonds, which pay no interest but rise toward maturity with time: You do nothing but live and watch. If you withdraw money from your retirement portfolio for personal needs, you prevent compounding from working for you. In particular, if you borrow against your 401(k), the compound interest on the loan may well be as high or higher than the compound internal interest in the fund, and you will be getting no closer to the Promised Land. In nature, egg robbers are despised creatures such as crows. Protect your nest egg.

3. *Maintenance of an acceptable level.* There are two aspects to acceptability. First, "acceptable" means that if you keep earning at that rate, you will reach your goal with the savings you can afford to commit over the time available to you. Second, "acceptable" means that over each market cycle you have earned close to, at, or above what the market delivered.

If stocks and bonds both earned double-digit returns for three years, then even if you earned 8 percent a year, that would probably be unacceptably low. Why? Because, like Joseph, you have to make hay while the sun shines and the water remains high. Those double-digit returns cannot last.

Investors who kept their money in bank accounts from 1996 to 2000 earned unacceptably low rates of return, because stocks were delivering 20 percent a year and bonds were delivering 7 percent. However, those investors looked smart two years later compared to their friends who made the big returns and threw more money into their funds at the top. A few of them would still be ahead of the cautious depositor, but most would not.

4. *Risk-adjusted returns*. Those high fliers who made big gains in the late 1990s and stayed in the game, only to lose their stake—and then some—should have calculated their annual rates of return after adjusting for the risk they were assuming.

Example: Suppose Patricia earns 11 percent per year over the three years ended July 2000 in her 401(k), which she has fully invested in a High Yield Bond mutual fund. Angela, meanwhile, earns 7 percent per year in that time in her 401(k) invested in a Government Bond Mutual Fund.

Their risk-adjusted returns are almost identical. The yield differential between the two kinds of bonds reflects the differing risk levels in those bonds, yet Patricia is feeling fat and sassy about her fund, and Angela is feeling resentful.

Now we review their performance two years later. Patricia has only managed to break even, because her fund had big exposure to WorldCom, Adelphia, Vivendi, and Enron bonds. Meanwhile, Angela kept on earning 7 percent compounded. So their stakes as of July 2002: Patricia's $100,000 is now $136,760, whereas Angela's is $140,255.

As of the bottom in the bear market, Angela's conservative style had substantially outperformed Patricia's style on a risk-adjusted basis, and had also outperformed in absolute, unadjusted terms.

If each woman sticks to her style through this decade, and they retire in 2010, I have little doubt that Patricia will have more money in her 401(k). Nevertheless, I would not recommend that any would-be-happy camper have all her 401(k) invested in junk bonds.

What each woman should do is decide how much risk she is willing to assume in order to earn, over a decade, the extra money she thinks she'll need for retirement. She should then construct a portfolio that has roughly that level of risk, and she should measure her annual returns on a risk-adjusted basis. No single-asset class portfolio can meet those requirements for long.

5. *Real rate of return.* The real rate of return is the return earned after deducting from your *nominal* return (which is the interest and dividends received plus the net of capital gains minus losses and investment expenses) from the *actual* inflation experienced (when reviewing past

results) or the *anticipated* inflation (the number used in forecasting). In Japan it is the rate of return *after adding back the year's deflation or the anticipated deflation.*

For example, if your mutual funds increased in value by 7 percent over two years and the total inflation experienced in that time was 4.2 percent, your real rate of return was 2.8 percent, or 1.4 percent per year. For a Japanese investor, that 7 percent nominal return would have been boosted by 2 percent to cover actual deflation, giving 9 percent returns, or 4.5 percent per year.

Back in the 1970s, there were times you could be earning 11 percent a year and your real rate of return was zero. Now that inflation has been tamed from tiger to tabby status, should an investor bother calculating it all? (See Charts 9-1 and 9-2.)

The answer is certainly yes. Baby Boomers lived through the worst inflation since the Civil War. Few Boomers I meet show concern about deflation—they remember inflation too vividly, and many of them think it will come back.

They're not the only ones who worry about a return of inflation. Many wise, experienced investors believe in the inevitability of inflation. They

CHART 9-1   U.S. Consumer Price Index—Year-over-Year Rate of Change Monthly (January 1970 to August 2002)

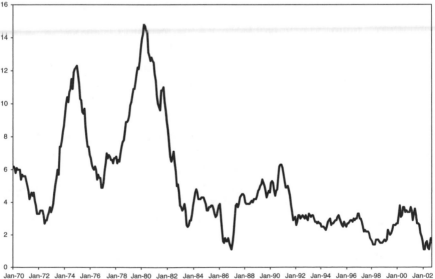

Data courtesy of Bloomberg Associates.

CHART 9-2   U.S. Producer Price Index—Year-over-Year Rate of Change Monthly (January 1, 1979–December 31, 2002)

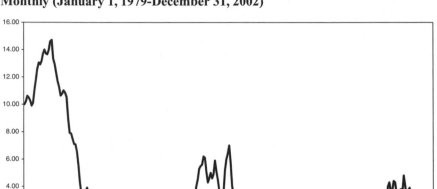

Data courtesy of Bloomberg Associates.

admit to surprise that recent data have been so benign, but they point to the rapid growth of some monetary aggregates and say, "The Fed is printing money, so inflation is coming back."

The long-term investor must assume that in a democracy that issues paper money not backed by gold, long-term inflation will be the norm. It is a melancholy truth that every paper currency ever devised by man has been devalued—and most have been devalued to the point of worthlessness.

What protects us now?

First, the Federal Reserve and other major central banks. The men who run those organizations got their jobs by their perceived ability to fight inflation, and that is what they're happiest doing.

Second, we are not in a major war. David Hackett Fischer's interesting book about inflation (*The Great Wave,* Oxford University Press, 1996) shows that inflation has, for a millennium, been largely a phenomenon of war (see "Peace at Reasonable Price," in Chapter 4). The sustained inflation from 1939 through 1995 was, by far, the longest in recorded history. It occurred because the West went almost without pause from World War II to the Cold War. The War on Terror and the "regime change" in Iraq will probably not be enough to tip us back into the kind of war-related inflationary pressures that prevent the economy from functioning effectively.

Third, we are the beneficiaries of a bonanza of technological development. Yes, many—or even most—of the gizmos and technology that captivated the public during the 1990s are not true productivity enhancers. The Internet has certainly helped improve business productivity, particularly in supply chains, and in price recognition generally. The national productivity statistics for recent years show 2 percent productivity gains per year, up from just 1.4 percent in the two decades from 1974. That is an improvement, but it is hardly a number to send one dancing in the streets.

Besides, much Internet usage is trivial and time wasting, and much of it can be deemed productive only by a twisted definition of productivity. Spam is a new curse and time waster, and some of the "exciting breakthroughs" may cost us as much in loss of privacy and thinking time as they deliver in instant messaging. (Do people really need to be reachable at all times on their cell phones and BlackBerries?) The Shills & Mountebanks exulted in statistics such as 100 percent gains in Internet usage every six months, arguing that this seemingly cancerous growth betokened exploding productivity.

Well, maybe.

Against that contrived ebullience, consider a study reported two years ago in the *Wall Street Journal*. The report covered the glowing success of the woman they identified as the true Queen of the Internet—Pamela Anderson Lee (not Mary Meeker, Morgan Stanley's famed Internet analyst). Ms. Lee, we were informed, recorded on video some "very naughty" activities she enjoyed with her then husband, which ended up on the Internet. The *Journal* noted, of the great success of pornography on the Web: Fully 22 percent of all Internet usage is for pornography.

In June 2002, I was returning from Atlanta. My seatmate was the senior marketing officer for a small, Nasdaq-traded fiberoptics company. He had been attending a major technology convention in Atlanta. We talked all the way to Chicago about the outlook for his industry. I kept expressing my reservations, and he kept expressing his optimism that "things would soon turn around." At one point I asked him, "Which of your customers are making money these days?"

He pondered that question for a moment, then brightened and said, "The pornographers."

"Anybody else?" I smiled.

He admitted that he doubted that any of his firm's nonporn customers were profitable.

So much for massive productivity gains.

Although I never did believe the Shills & Mountebanks about this being the greatest productivity revolution since the discovery of the wheel, and though I always felt that Alan Greenspan was overenthusiastic about the economic impact of technology, I concede that the Internet, wireless, advanced microprocessors, and fiberoptics technology are major economic events. As the years unfold, they will deliver more productivity gains, even if the rate of delivery of the "Next New Thing" slows to a walk and Silicon Valley at times seems more like Death Valley.

Finally, as discussed in the previous chapter, the continuing impact on global pricing from the relentless growth in China, Taiwan, and Korea, will prove to be a formidable restraint on price increases for globally traded goods.

A cautious planner will assume that global free trade powered by deflation out of Asia will continue to deliver deflation in the price of goods, but service inflation—such as health care, professional fees, electricity, day care, garden and lawn care, and restaurant dining—will continue, albeit at reduced rates during economic slowdowns. In particular, you should worry about long-range costs for electricity and natural gas. As a result of the implosion of the energy transmission industry after the supposed California crisis, the aggressive new firms that were going to meet the nation's energy needs have been driven to the edge of collapse. Proposed capital investments have been slashed. Nobody seems to know who will build the power plants, power lines, and pipelines we will need in coming decades. You should plan on the assumption that the next time you hear about a "national energy crisis" it will be the real thing—and it will cost you plenty.

As you age, you'll spend an increasing proportion of your money on services, so you should assume that those national statistics could become less and less relevant to your actual spending experience.

TIMING: WHERE YOU START INFLUENCES WHERE YOU FINISH

The most obvious reason for investing in U.S. stocks in 2003 is that they are far cheaper than they have been since 1997.

That does not mean they cannot remain cheap for years, but it does mean you have a chance for that Law of Compound Interest to begin working in your favor.

Numerous studies of long-term rates of return on equities confirm that the cheaper one buys stocks—that is, the lower their p/es at acquisition or book cost—the greater the returns over the long term. If you entered the market with the p/e at 35 times earnings, based on 100 years of market records you had almost no chance of getting a positive return on your investment for many years, let alone an acceptable risk-adjusted real rate of return.

Some asset allocators argue about adjusting one's exposure to stocks, bonds, and cash in a balanced account primarily by the market's multiple: When the multiple is 25 or above, one should cut equity allocations to the minimum and await a market correction—or crash. When it gets down to the low teens, one should go to maximum equity exposure and wait for the enthusiasm to return. It always does.

Since mid-2002, the stock market's multiple has been in a range consistent with reasonable but not ebullient growth in corporate profits, and reasonable but not ebullient foreign interest in American stocks. That multiple is certainly not enticing.

But it isn't flashing a big "Abandon all hope, ye who enter here," either.

After you've thought through the factors that will influence your future plans so powerfully, you're ready to begin accumulating the resources for your own personalized Survival Pak—the stuff that will, in considerable measure, determine the financial health you'll have to get you through the rest of life's journey.

HOW TO MANAGE RISK IN YOUR PORTFOLIO

Campers setting out on a long canoe trip carefully estimate how long it will take the party to reach the destination, planning overnights at favored campsites along the route. They build in extra time to allow for foul weather, or side trips to beauty spots.
—R. Graves

How do you adjust for the risk in your portfolio as you aim for an acceptable risk-adjusted real rate of return?

The two kinds of portfolio risks are *endogenous* and *exogenous*. These sound like highly technical terms, but they are easily understood.

What Kind of Risk?
Here are outdoors examples of the three kinds of risks:

1. *Endogenous risk.* Two personal examples will illustrate this kind of risk.

First, in our family we have the expression—"Earthquakes in Alaska"—for unforeseeable bad news. Back in the 1960s my wife and I invested in a small oil and gas exploration company that was drilling for gas in northern Canada. Just as the drill bit was approaching the horizon (where, we were told, there could be a major gas deposit), it was shattered. Shockwaves from an earthquake in neighboring Alaska had broken the drill, which then blocked the hole. The weakly financed company lacked the funds to rescue the well, and abandoned it. The stock was blasted.

Second, as I began to write this book I was hit by an autoimmune response that triggered massive internal bleeding. It turned out that I'd developed sensitivity to the doctor-recommended aspirin I had been taking daily for years. It interacted with a normally harmless bacteria that many people carry in their systems. The E.R. doctor who set up my transfusions told me that if I had waited another hour to get to E.R. then . . . well, you certainly would not be reading this book. I had two endogenous risks— internal, and specific to me.

2. *Exogenous risk.* One of the most accomplished outdoorsmen I have ever known was killed by lightning when climbing to the Great Divide in Colorado. His death came from exogenous risk—entirely external to himself.

3. *Endo-exo-risk.* The wife of a college friend of mine accompanied him on a lepidoptery trip to northern Ontario. She stepped on a ground wasp nest. She was dead within a few minutes from wasp bites.

She had endogenous risk, in that she must have been allergic to wasp bites. But that risk only became a catastrophe when exposed to the exogenous risk of a wasp nest.

Analyzing Your Portfolio Risks

Endogenous Risk
A portfolio with a 50/50 weighting in stocks and bonds as of March 2000 might seem to have been well balanced and able to ride out market travails. Suppose, however, that 75 percent of both the stock and the bond exposures were in technology and telecom issues. That portfolio would have lost more than half its value had the investor held on to it through the Triple Waterfall collapse. All those positions were exposed to what were, in essence, the same or quite similar risks, and those risks materialized almost simultaneously.

Contrast that disastrous outcome with a 50/50 portfolio with equities indexed according to the S&P 500 and bonds indexed according to the Lehman Aggregate Index. This second portfolio would have lost approximately 12 percent of its value from the market top to mid-July 2002—and those losses would have been primarily driven by the endogenous risks associated with its holdings of technology and telecom stocks and bonds, and Enron stock and bonds. *Because of the diversification of the portfolio, those endogenous risks were well contained through a major bear market.* (The rest of the losses would have come from the exogenous risks to stocks arising from a recession that unleashed a Papa Bear market.)

As the investigations into Wall Street's abuses and conflicts of interest proceeded, investors in major stocks such as Citigroup and J.P. Morgan sustained heavy losses, whereas holders of other leading financial stocks did relatively well. The losers had specific risks internal to their situation—particularly their exposure to Enron, and perceived conflicts of interest between research and investment banking. Those were endogenous risks. Had those been the only financial stocks an investor held, he or she might have thought the market was a disaster for big banking institutions, but in fact the market distinguished between companies that had major problems and those having some tough times with the economic cycle.

Biotech stocks had a grim time of it in 2002. But ImClone plunged from 73 to 7. As readers may know, its new drug, Erbitux, was supposedly a major breakthrough in fighting colon cancer, but the FDA rejected it on the basis of inadequate clinical trial evidence. According to prosecutors' allegations, the CEO and his family knew of that rejection and sold some of their shareholdings. Investigators probed stock sales of some of their friends, including Martha Stewart, whose broker sold what was for her a trivial position, a sale that led to a barrage of negative publicity that was hugely out of proportion to the transaction and its impact on the stock market. IMCL shared the exogenous risk of stocks in an overall bear market, but what trashed the stock were its massive—but secret—endogenous risks.

Exogenous Risk

Everyone who owned stocks on the morning of 9/11 got an unforgettable lesson in exogenous risk. Hardest hit economically and in the ensuing stock market panic were airlines. No reasonable summary of "what ifs" that could affect airline valuations would have included that event. That a substantial proportion of the population would simultaneously develop fear of flying, thereby devastating the airline industry, was an exogenous shock. The other major losers from exogenous risk were casualty insurance companies, particularly reinsurers. Yes, risk is their business, but this act of war was so far outside the foreseeable range of risks insurers evaluate that it could be classed an exogenous risk.

The holder of a 30-year Treasury bond has the month-to-month endogenous risk of price changes associated with bond market fluctuations. But the holder has one overriding, exogenous risk: inflation. If inflation rises above anticipated levels, the holder will lose heavily. Alternatively, if inflation were to turn negative—as in Japan—the holder would win big from an exogenous risk that worked out well (for bondholders, but badly for just about everybody else, particularly holders of money market funds).

For most long-term investors, inflation is the biggest exogenous financial risk they face. The problem is greatest for those who plan to retire early. If they have fixed pensions and heavy bond investments, then even a 2.5 percent annual inflation rate starts to hurt after a dozen or so years of retirement. But if inflation were to climb back to 5 percent or so, then the consequences for such investors would be serious indeed. Dividend-paying stocks are an excellent vehicle for protecting a retiree against inflation but in today's era of low overall dividend yields, only a very sizable stake will produce enough dividend income to live on.

When you have identified the risks in your portfolio, how do you manage them?

Most exogenous risks are, by their nature, unmanageable. Risks arising from overall bear markets are the easiest to control, because any competent asset allocator would adjust exposure when a portfolio became greatly imbalanced in favor of equities, particularly long-duration high-multiple stocks (see "Duration and Risk in Bonds and Stocks," Chapter 10).

Endogenous risks can be managed, once you have identified them.

- Diversification is the classic technique for managing endogenous and market-based exogenous risk in portfolios. If you own differing asset classes, differing bond maturities, stocks denominated in differing currencies, and mutual funds managed in differing investment styles, it's likely that you've reduced overall risk. (You can never eliminate it; risk is always present.)

- Within your self-managed equity portfolios, you can build your own internal insurance by owning stock groups that tend to trade in contrary fashion. This is called *inverse correlation* and is a useful concept in portfolio construction. Some kinds of assets trade like teeter-totters with other kinds of assets. Oil-producing companies, for example, tend to trade inversely to chemical companies, because so many chemicals are derived from petroleum or natural gas; oil-producing stocks also trade inversely to telecom stocks, because oil is the preeminent hard asset and the telecom group is on the high, risky side of the knowledge-based technology industries. Gold stocks tend to trade inversely to both the U.S. dollar and to U.S. stocks. Philip Morris (now renamed Altria) tends to trade inversely to growth stocks because it pays big dividends, which are most attractive to investors when the stock market is weak or falling.

RULES FOR DIVERSIFICATION

On army rations by Dr. Woods Hutchison: "Nobody but a Scotchman can live on oatmeal as his sole breadstuff; and it has taken generations of training and gallons of whiskey on the side to enable him to do it."

—H. KEPHART

After the tech Triple Waterfall, the Street began to praise diversification with the ardor of the newly converted. The same organizations that had spent prodigiously to convince Boomers that stock market gains from technology stocks and aggressive growth funds would let them retire at—or maybe even before—50 now oozed oleaginous assurances about the values of diversifying with bonds and money market funds. (The Street's enthusiasm for convincing clients of the investment merits of bonds and money market funds during the mania had ranged from the barely observable to the too tepid.)

If it took a Triple Waterfall crash to get the Street to argue the virtues of diversification, then something good came out of that disaster. But what kind of diversification?

I regularly meet people who tell me they *are* well diversified and cannot understand why they lose so much money in this bear market. They thought that holding several mutual funds and a couple dozen stocks meant they had spread their risks.

Achieving Diversification in Your Survival Pak

Survival strategy diversification means investing across asset classes, and it means you always hold significant exposure to some asset class—or asset classes—that you do not really like at that point.

If you expect good returns in the next year from everything in your portfolio, you are not diversified. Think of diversification the way you think of nutrition. You do not confine your diet to the foods you love most, because you want balance in your consumption. When your mother told you, "Eat your broccoli!" she was insisting you diversify your food intake to include something that would be good for you, even if you felt that it tasted yucky.

(No, that doesn't mean having half your portfolio in dot coms and half in government bonds. Each asset class should have intrinsic investment merits. If you choose to buy lottery tickets, don't include them in your Survival Pak.)

A Survival Pak should include, through a market cycle, varying levels of exposure to:

1.   *U.S. Large Cap Equities.* They are the foundation of America's economic performance globally. It makes sense to own big companies that make big waves.

2.   *U.S. REITs.* These are short-duration assets (see "Duration and Risk in Bonds and Stocks," Chapter 10), and you will need expert advice to choose which ones you should own—and when you should sell.

3.   *U.S. Small Cap Equities.* Yes, small can be better, and Small Caps trade differently than Large Caps, so owning some of them reduces portfolio volatility.

4.   *Foreign Equities.* You achieve several kinds of diversification at once—and there are many great companies abroad.

5.   *Emerging Market Equities.* People—both young and middle-age— are going to be the most precious resource in this century. Most of these countries have great demographic profiles, and most established economies have poor demographic profiles.

6.   *U.S. short- and medium-term tax-exempt bonds.*

7.   *U.S. short- and medium-term taxable bonds* (10 years and less).

8.   *U.S. long-term tax-exempt bonds* (11 to 30 years, and long zero-coupon bonds).

9.   *U.S. long-term taxable bonds* (11 to 30 years, and long zero-coupon bonds).

10. *Gold mining shares and/or bullion.* Either directly or through a resource-oriented mutual fund.

When you own an investment-grade bond mutual fund, you automatically get exposure to these differing durations of bonds. If you choose to accumulate them yourself, prepare for higher costs—except for new Treasury offerings, which you can buy direct with an account at your regional Federal Reserve Bank. Yes, you can have an account at the Fed just like big banks and big dealers.

The next stage is to use mutual funds, with their large portfolios, to increase your diversification because of the wide range of securities held, and to take advantage of the special skills of managers within an asset class.

What properly managed diversification does for you is reduce portfolio volatility. You cannot expect to get returns as high as some of your friends brag about when stocks are roaring upward, but you will come close to—or even exceed—break-even levels in bear market years. That means your long-term returns will be good, and it also means that if you experience misfortune and cannot contribute further, or if you have to cash out some of your retirement funds, the money will be there.

Shills & Mountebanks, academic and otherwise, who tout great long-term returns from stocks have the luxury of using the mathematics of dividend-reinvested compound growth over 30-, 40-, and 50-year periods. U.S. stocks solidly outperform bonds in any such long comparison. Their forecasts of sure-as-certain wealth accumulations make no allowances for such personal inconveniences as unemployment, disability, and death. I endorse those feel-good forecasts only for readers who consider themselves immune to the first two of those risks and have very large life insurance coverage for the third.

Otherwise, use caution in implementing their recommendations.

Some shills use very long-term data misleadingly: One such cites a survey that covers nearly two centuries, and it shows stocks outperforming Treasury bonds, which, according to his figures, averaged 2 percent per year. What relevance are those comparative data when Treasurys yield nearly 5 percent?

A dubious diversification strategy that is, regrettably, very widespread, is to keep adding new U.S. equity funds to one's portfolio. In part, this is psychological: The ones you hold have disappointed, so why not try something else? In part, it represents buying the latest "hot" fund based on recent performance numbers. In part, it represents inertia and laziness, the investment equivalent of the pack rat who adds more clothes and shoes to a cluttered closet without sending some of the old stuff to the Salvation Army.

In one of its regular columns on mutual funds last year, the *Wall Street Journal* called the practice of owning numerous equity funds "di-worsification," a splendid term coined by the legendary Peter Lynch. The writer noted that owning a large number of funds of varying investment styles— growth, momentum, deep value, relative value, analytics-driven, and core—meant the holder, in effect, owned the S&P Index, but at much higher fees than by buying an Index Fund. (Fees charged by fully managed funds tend to be roughly double those charged by Index Funds.)

If you have substantial resources and can obtain professional advice in managing your exposure to a range of U.S. funds, then having several funds works well, because of continual rebalancing as stock markets wax and wane. Bad diversification or di-worsification comes when you just clutter up the portfolio, pay too much for investment management, and misman-age the allocation, which is the worst possible outcome.

If you shouldn't overdiversify by managerial style, which style should you choose as your own personal "core" U.S. investment management tech-nique?

Investment managers can be compared to health care professionals. You have a primary care physician who looks after your basic require-ments, sending you to specialists as needs arise. In addition, you may choose to consult other kinds of advisers on such topics as organic foods, acupuncture, macrobiotics, and "healing hands," depending on your opin-ion about nontraditional health care advisers.

If you look at a mutual fund family, you'll see a wide range of choice. Your financial planner might recommend a "core" fund for you. You need to think about the design characteristics of that basic building block. Man-agers not only invest in different kinds of asset classes and in different kinds of stocks, they also have different ways of deciding which stocks to buy and sell. There is no "right" way to invest in stocks that will outperform under all kinds of stock markets. What is on offer is a smorgasbord of equity management styles, including deep value, relative value, growth, aggressive growth, GARP (Growth at a Reasonable Price), sector rotation, blends of all or some of these, and other approaches. Furthermore, man-agers use different research and portfolio construction styles as they appraise valuations within the style they have chosen.

Perhaps you are confused at this point.

Different kinds of stocks, different ways of valuing the stocks: Which is best for you?

In the interests (and the SEC's requirements) of full disclosure, let me preface these remarks by disclosing my financial bias. My company uses computer analytics as the basic building technique for *all* its U.S. funds. Indeed, our organization, in conjunction with the University of Chicago Department of Finance, was a pioneer in developing computer-based sys-tems that were designed to take the human emotion out of stock analysis. (That the Nobel committee chose to give the 2002 prizes for economics to behavioral economists is, to us, confirmation that emotions, biases, and fads continue to be big influences in the market, giving great opportunities for managers who use impersonal valuation techniques.) Since we started, hundreds of firms have adopted analytics techniques, and most others use computers extensively to assist their analysts.

We did learn, over the years, not to rely exclusively on "black box" worship, the kind of technofaith that led Long Term Capital Management to and over the abyss. The maxim "Garbage in, garbage out" applies in spades to financial analysis, so, like most other analytics firms, we use fundamental analysis as an overlay to the computer-driven process. Financial data are so prone to error, massaging, and retrospective revisions that any computer-based stock valuation process needs some human intervention.

Is analytics-based portfolio management superior to other techniques? After long involvement in that style of investment management process, I believe it can be, given the right staffing, with Ph.D.'s to create and manage the mathematical models, and the right staffing of fundamental analysts and portfolio managers to overlay the process with creativity, caution, and consistency. But, yes, I could certainly be biased.

Our competitors offer a bewildering array of products. Some organizations are renowned for their consistent styles: Bernstein and Neuberger Berman, for example, have produced excellent results using various kinds of "Value" investing. Neuberger's Genesis Fund, run by Judy Vale, is an example of long-term success sticking to a style. Chicago's Ralph Wanger has achieved great results over the years by sticking to a Value approach that includes a hearty component of skepticism about Street research.

Other organizations are famed for their growth products. Industry leader Fidelity offers virtually any kind of equity fund you could imagine, and backs up that offering with an array of investment tools to help clients maximize their choices.

Momentum investing was in vogue during the mania, because it worked—better by far than any fundamental or analytics-driven technique. Fast-stepping portfolio managers who bought the stocks moving up fastest had the highest returns in 1998–1999, and they attracted the most money to manage, which meant they kept backing their favorites with more money, which made the process self-reinforcing. Momentum investing is the favored mode of hedge fund managers. It doesn't work so well now that the market isn't going straight up. (It has worked well for hedge funds with bear strategies, because they have had the luxury of continually selling short tech stocks, as they kept going down in their Triple Waterfall collapse.)

Momentum investing works best when it is driven by what is known as the Greater Fool Theory. This is a well-known investing technique. The investor buys stocks that are soaring, suspecting that they are overvalued but relying on being able to sell them at higher prices to an even greater fool. From 1998 onward, the Greater Fool Theory was the *only* justification for investing in Nasdaq stocks, based on established investment knowledge, once the index crossed 2500. The great problem with investing via the Greater Fool Theory is that eventually the greatest fools run out of money and there is no one to support the market. Then you, the presumed lesser fool, are "up dancing when the music stops."

Growth investing is the term used for a range of management techniques that emphasize capital gains rather than dividend income. Growth investors' portfolios are heavy with high-multiple stocks.

When a bull market becomes established, long-duration growth stocks outperform short-duration Value Stocks (see "Duration and Risk in Bonds and Stocks," in Chapter 10). When the stock market is delivering double-digit capital gains, dividends become a diminishing component of total returns. In that kind of market, you want your equity portfolio to have good exposure to growth managers.

Yes, it has been tough on growth funds since March 2002. Most of them made a fatal error in technology and telecom investing: They assumed those stocks were true growth stocks, but they were really capital spending cyclical stocks. True growth stocks—such as Walgreens, Microsoft, and Johnson & Johnson—grow their earnings almost regardless of economic cycles.

Once upon a time, we thought there were many true growth stocks. One of the more disagreeable recent discoveries is that many more companies called themselves growth companies than could actually meet that acid test.

We have learned that sustained growth is much tougher to achieve than a spate of big earnings gains, followed by a stumble—or a series of stumbles. Baseball fans can understand that. It has been 62 years since Ted Williams hit .406, and nobody has managed to hit .400 since then (and no one has come close to Joe DiMaggio's record of hitting safely in 56 straight games). The record that has been blown to smithereens is Babe Ruth's 60 home runs. Power is obviously easier to produce than consistency.

Result: These have been grim years for holders of growth funds.

There have been bad spots for growth funds in the past, and they have always rebounded. *It will happen again.*

A good time to think about growth funds is when they have suffered for a few years, dumped their managers, and issued a string of apologies and affirmations. As long as those funds are managed by great organizations, they will rebound when the stock market's duration once again expands.

Finally, you must consider the implications of the dollar bear market and put a little gold into your portfolio.

Getting Started on Your Investment Survival Pak

As discussed earlier in this chapter, building your Survival Pak starts with an analysis of *your* liabilities. There is no such thing as a single ideal investment program, any more than there is a single ideal automobile, or a single ideal house. You must invest to meet *your* family's long-run needs, which usually include retirement, education for the children, rainy-day funds, and wealth to give you more options about how long you work full-time and where you take vacations.

Draw up your balance sheet—with the help of your spouse and some professionals, such as your broker, financial planner, accountant, and lawyer.

You then start calculating how you're going to fund those liabilities—which asset classes you will be buying and what the makeup of your diversified Survival Pak should look like. You will have plugged in a few basic numbers:

- How much you should be able to set aside.

- What retirement date is expected.

- The average intervening rate of inflation before and after retirement.

- How much money would be needed at retirement to finance the kind of lifestyle desired.

The difference between the contributions and the money needed must come from investment returns after taxes—the average after-tax risk-adjusted real rate of return.

Perhaps you recoil at making those forecasts.

We all resist putting something down on paper in the presence of witnesses in which we make flat-out predictions about the future. After all, many of Wall Street's biggest names in forecasting have been as wrong about what this millennium would bring as those 1970s forecasters who predicted a new Ice Age—just before global warming became the prevalent fear. Why should we be any smarter?

Unlike the Mayan calendar, your forecast isn't set in stone. You make it, get working on it, and keep updating your balance sheet as you get new statements about your assets, and as you rethink those long-term liabilities.

Your personal balance sheet is on paper and hard drive—so you can update it easily and often.

Asset classes go in and out of favor. Your needs will change in response to the good and bad things that will happen in your life and in the economy. *Just make a start.*

Portfolio Strategists' and Economists' Asset Mix Advice

As you contemplate building a diversified Survival Pak, you'll want advice from experts. Start by consulting some people you do business with, such as a broker, financial planner, life insurance salesman, or the investment advisory person at your bank or credit union.

But you will be curious about the kinds of experts you encounter through the media. In particular, you'll hear a lot from portfolio strategists and economists. Are they useful?

Predicting the stock and bond markets and telling clients how to invest their money is the task for portfolio strategists. Predicting the economy, inflation, Federal Reserve actions, and interest rates is the task for economists. Many investors are confused about these specialties. That confusion is understandable, because some economists make comprehensive stock market forecasts, and some strategists make comprehensive economic forecasts.

I have been a strategist for decades, and I do my best to confine my detailed forecasts to the behavior of capital markets—bonds, stocks, commodities, and currencies. Those variables are more than enough to keep me busy.

Because I have also doubled as a portfolio manager for most of that time, managing balanced funds and pure equity funds, I consider myself a practitioner, not a theorist. I use the work of economists I admire in preparing my forecasts, but distrust their stock market calls. The two disciplines are different, both in the education and background needed to perform them and in day-to-day research time allocations.

How should investors treat stock market advice from economists and predictions on retail sales, durable goods orders, or real GDP from strategists?

The cover of a golf magazine a few years ago showed a picture of Michael Jordan, who was at the time not only the greatest basketball player in the world, but had been voted the Most Admired Person in the World. The cover trumpeted an article by Mr. Jordan giving tips on better golfing, golf being another game he loves.

As a nongolfer, I was unequipped to evaluate his advice. I recalled how he had quit basketball for a while to try to become a major league baseball player, and how Chicago Bulls fans mourned that decision. To his chagrin, and his fans' relief, he found that he could not hit a curve ball, so he came back to the Bulls, and a new Bull market was born, as they then won the NBA championship three years in a row. I could not help thinking that his golf advice might be worth roughly what his hitting advice might be. If I were a golfer, I would rather read what Tiger Woods recommended.

So it goes with portfolio strategy and economic advice. As an investor, you need both kinds of help. Why not listen to specialists dissecting the complexities of their own discipline, rather than bloviating about someone else's, even though there is much overlap in the material covered? (That said, there are a few economists who are such splendid communicators that I'm willing to listen to them talking about anything they choose.)

I read economists far more than I read strategists, and I make that suggestion to readers. Some Wall Street strategists are shills or mountebanks, and others just find it too hard to ever say no to stocks. Economists help me to understand the macro and micro trends that affect valuations of stock sectors. (I have the help of a colleague, Sherry Cooper, who was recently ranked by Bloomberg as the most accurate forecaster of U.S. GDP numbers of the economists they monitor.)

All the Wall Street houses have strategists who tell clients how to diversify their investments, usually among just three options: stocks, bonds, and cash. (Goldman Sachs's star, Abby Joseph Cohen, also includes commodities as a class in her reports.)

Even the most casual watcher of CNBC will have seen interviews with some strategists. They tend to be smart, articulate, and persuasive. And, if you're heavily into stocks, the shills among them can make you feel good, because it seems they've never seen a stock market they didn't like. Taken straight, they are splendid nonalcoholic tonics for blowing away the blahs of a bear market. If you're down 50 percent, it's oh-so-reassuring to have someone much smarter and better known than you explain that over the long term you're bound to win big. Like good scotch, they can help you forget—including their past stock market forecasts, which were ridiculous.

It is an arresting fact that the star Wall Street economists as a group have never predicted a recession in advance, and the star strategists as a group have never predicted a bear market. The advice of both groups of experts should therefore be taken with caution.

Economists and strategists collectively have disappointing records for predicting when you will lose money. You should look to them primarily to help you make money, and build in your own risk controls, not expecting them to warn you of coming bearish times.

That is a generalization, of course. Richard Bernstein, Merrill Lynch's quantitative strategist, stands out from the group. He has been either bearish or cautious about stocks in recent years, and one reason for his skepticism is the data he personally accumulates about the recommendations of his competitors. According to his work, which he updates monthly, the strategists of the leading Wall Street firms have been bullish throughout the long bear market, as evidenced by their recommendations on what percentage of clients' assets should be invested in stocks. Collectively, they never got as low as 50 percent, and they were at a record high of more than 70 percent commitment to equities just before the market's brutal sell-off in July 2002. (It is a melancholy fact that the only prominent strategist other than Bernstein who warned of the bear market and stayed bearish even during the post-9/11 rally was Douglas Cliggott of J.P. Morgan, and he ceased to be their strategist in 2002, joining a small firm.)

The reader is entitled to ask: Well, if you're a strategist and you don't work for the Street, did you predict this bear market?

Although I did predict—over and over and over—Nasdaq's Triple Waterfall, I did not predict the onset of the Papa Bear market. I recommended more than 50 percent exposure to bonds in balanced accounts from 1998, moving stocks up to 55 percent in July 2002, two weeks before the market dove to its low. (I do not consider myself a market timer.)

However, though I failed to see the Papa Bear coming until it was obvious a recession had arrived, I had consistently told clients to hedge their equity exposure with long Treasury zeros and with gold stocks, thereby sharply reducing portfolio risk. My favored equity groups since the market peaked in 2000—Canadian oil and gas producers, golds, defense, and medical devices—have risen through almost the entire bear market.

A checkered record.

10

Constructing a Survival Pak Portfolio

It will be allowed that Admiral Peary knows something about food values. Here is what he says in The North Pole: *"The essentials, and the only essentials, needed in a serious arctic sledge journey, no matter what the season, the temperature, or the duration of the journey—whether one month or six—are four: pemmican, tea, ship's biscuit, condensed milk. . . ."*

—H. KEPHART

YOUR INVESTOR SURVIVAL PAK should be a diversified collection of asset classes designed to deal with the kinds of issues discussed in Chapter 9. Survivors are the kind of people who meet the test that Wall Street legend Ben Graham long ago formulated: There are two kinds of investors—those who make money in the market and those who keep it.

Survivors plan to live well up to and right through retirement. They accumulate wealth to give them more freedom throughout their lives.

So what kinds of assets should be included in your Pak?

The culture of the 1990s was so addicted to equities as an asset class—and to technology and telecom stocks as the heavy-overweight group within that class—that it was difficult to make the case for diversification. Stocks were all you really needed, and the inclusion of bonds of various kinds merely meant you made less money.

That was then.

Now, because of Nasdaq's Triple Waterfall and the Dow Jones Papa Bear, so many investors have experienced such disappointing equity returns that revulsion against equities is currently fashionable.

That is exactly what happened after the Triple Waterfalls of the Great Crash and the Nifty Fifty (and in Japan's case, after the Triple Waterfall there). Many investors who now understand they were betrayed by Shills & Mountebanks and the CEOcracy have begun deserting stocks in favor of bonds, bank deposits, money market funds, and cash.

Lyme disease is not in itself reason to give up hiking and camping in the Berkshires. You check for ticks, and you see your doctor fast when you spot one of those red doughnut marks on some exposed skin. You'll do more for your health by hiking than staying in bed or, for that matter, in a bar where the only lime comes in drinks.

So it must be with equities. A Survival Pak that included no equities would force you to set far more money aside during your working years than the Pak of a fellow camper who maintained judicious exposure to stocks during his or her working years.

That said, this is a tough time to make the case for long-term equity investment. Those shills who were most shrill about the inevitability of great gains from stocks have poisoned the streams. In the long overdue reaction against their meretricious merchandising—and to the powerful bear market—many thoughtful critiques have emerged.

Two years ago this kind of analysis could not get a hearing. Now, it threatens to become received wisdom. Contrarians will instinctively begin to look for alternative viewpoints whenever one market view has become suddenly fashionable, at a time when the market, in a major move, makes that viewpoint look like gospel truth.

Therefore, our discussion of asset mix must, in fairness, begin with consideration of today's arguments against U.S. equities.

ARGUMENTS OF THE NAYSAYERS

The knocks against stocks can be summarized in 10 points:

1. They have been bad investments since 1999. Why should they be any better now?
2. Even with a long and painful bear market, U.S. equity valuations are nowhere near the bargain levels seen after past crashes. They

may seem inexpensive compared to their former valuation levels, but they are not cheap.

3.   It will take many years of mediocre to poor equity returns to get the long-term average returns on stocks back to historic norms. Those years of excessive returns during the bubble years have to be worked off. An investor who bought into the overvalued equity markets of the 1960s at their peak would have waited nearly two decades before making a sustained profit. If you're under 40, you can expect to live long enough that today's prices will look attractive. If you're over 60, and seek justification for buying stocks heavily now, then your parents should still be living, and showing no signs of heart disease, cancer, or diabetes.

4.   The U.S. stock market was *the* place to be in the 1990s; it is the *last* place to be in this decade.

5.   Dividend yields are near historic lows. Moreover, some of the most conspicuous dividend payers are having serious financial and/or litigation problems that call those generous payouts into question. Those charts showing long-term returns on stocks in the 9 to 10 percent range were based on reinvestment of dividends, which provided roughly two-thirds of compounded long-term returns. With these unattractive yields, reinvesting dividends is hardly worthwhile.

6.   Corporate America is shot through with sleazebags and overpriced so called superstars who have drained corporate coffers to enrich themselves at stockholders' expense—primarily through stock options. Why help to provide the financing that will be used to make the unjustly rich even richer?

7.   The problems for the American economy of the long debt binge are finally coming home to roost. Consumers are in hock to their eyeballs, corporations have levered their balance sheets so they need fast economic growth to survive, and now Washington is going back into deficit because of the War on Terror and the big spenders in Congress. With the nation's economy paying the price for all that folly, there will be no room for corporate profit growth.

8.   Yes, a few of the crooks who got caught are going to get punished, but what about the hundreds of other CEOs of companies with dubious and misleading accounting? They are still there, collecting huge salaries and perks, in possession of millions of share options that could become valuable once stock prices climb, even though

those beaten-down stocks will never climb back to break-even for most investors. Those pampered insiders who made such a hash of running their companies are going to be the only winners in the next market recovery, just as they were the only real winners from the boom.

9. The U.S. trade deficit continues at more than $36 billion a month, with the pulse of the U.S. economy barely observable. So much for those economists who told us that the reason we kept running red ink on trade was that our economy was so strong and the rest of the world was so weak. The United States cannot compete anymore. Eventually, this monthly hemorrhaging will lead to another dollar crisis like in 1987. Why invest in a manufacturing base sliding toward oblivion?

10. We're in the early stages of a long decline, and we might as well face the inevitable. No nation stays on top forever. Britain was the world economic and military leader for most of the 19th century. Then we overtook the Brits as the global trade powerhouse, and eventually became number one militarily. We've had a good run, but it's time for someone else to move up. China is the next global economic leader. Last century was America's century; this one will be China's.

11. The tech mania was the biggest in history, making the excesses of the Roaring Twenties and the Nifty Fifty years look like periods of prolonged Puritanical probity by comparison. Those previous financial follies produced, respectively, a Depression and a deep recession, whereas this one has so far produced only a mild downturn. We can't expect to get over the biggest binge of all time with just a brief headache. Since 1980, total U.S. debt has risen far faster than GDP, which means we've been living on borrowing, mostly from abroad. Result: Debt loads are far worse now than in those earlier eras, and the United States is nowhere near as competitive globally now as it was then. When prices of homes, factories, office buildings, and shopping plazas finally reach bottom, then the long period of rebuilding can begin. And just as we will be getting ready to emerge from it, the nation will be hit with the horrendous costs of social security and Medicare for the retiring Boomers.

That sums up most of what I hear about the problems for U.S. equities, although the reader has doubtless encountered a few more. In boom times, a considerable proportion of the nation's intellectual energy is expended in devising new theories and evidence to prove that things will only get better. In bum times, a considerable proportion of the nation's intellectual energy is expended in devising new theories and evidence to prove that things will only get worse.

Frankly, those arguments are well based and persuasive. But they really boil down to an attack on equity investing *now*. They do not necessarily undermine the basic thesis about the intrinsic *long-term* investment merits of stocks. Making a case for a vacation trip to Alaska is a tough sell in January.

So let's go back to basics.

THE EQUITY RISK PREMIUM

Why do smart people invest in stocks, and what has historically made stocks good investments?

The answer experts give is based on a mathematical appraisal of returns on stocks as against returns on other assets. Stocks do better than other assets over time, and the difference between their returns and those on government bonds is called the Equity Risk Premium—what you get paid for taking on the extra level of risk over long Treasury bonds. That premium is, by the way, the basis of market capitalism: If stocks do not earn more than bonds over the long haul, capitalism is dead.

Although the Equity Risk Premium concept has been around for a long time, it did not become properly documented until the advent of what is now known as Modern Portfolio Theory. This approach looks at long-term rates of return on asset classes, and measures them against the volatility of annual returns in those classes, which is the accepted way of measuring riskiness. It can also be derived by examining changes in credit spreads within fixed income instruments. Investors then use those comparative data to produce the "optimal" asset mix—the percentage allotments that give the best trade-off between expected returns and expected risks.

When you take long-term return numbers for differing asset classes and compare them to the riskiness of those classes, they tend to fit very well: no pain, no gain. Cash has no volatility, and gives the lowest returns; short Treasurys are next, long Treasurys next, and so on. Stocks are risky (as the reader is by now well aware), but over the long term, you get paid to assume that risk.

Another way of thinking about this is to consider insurance premiums, which are set according to the company's assessment of the risk. A teenage boy pays far higher automobile insurance rates than a 50-year-old woman with an accident-free record who has not been convicted of speeding in 10 years. Well-managed insurance companies set their premium rates so they're paid adequately for assuming risk; badly managed insurance companies fail to charge high enough premiums for the risk they assume.

So it is with investors: Wise investors earn an adequate Equity Risk Premium, or they move money into less risky asset classes; foolish investors look only at the potential rewards, and ignore the risks. The wise prosper; the foolish blame their brokers. (In my experience, not even the wisest and most professional stockbroker can hold out against client pressure for long once irrationality grips the market and many "investors" are reaping outsize rewards. Among the many victims of the Nasdaq Triple Waterfall collapse are experienced brokers who counseled caution, then were forced by peer pressure to let clients load up on techs and telecoms to keep their business. To be blamed by clients now merely makes a bad experience worse.)

What numerous studies of long-term equity risk premiums have shown is that stocks deliver roughly 2.5 percent more per year, on average, than long Treasury bonds (issues that have 10 to 30 years to maturity).

If you think 2.5 percent per year is hardly worth the muss and fuss of equity investing, then think again.

It means that, if bonds are delivering roughly 5 percent real returns, you double your money in roughly 14 years. If stocks are delivering 7.5 percent returns, you double your money in 9.6 years. Over 42 years, the bond portfolio would grow to roughly eight times its original value— assuming no taxes, as is the case in a 401(k)—whereas the stock portfolio would grow to roughly 16.5 times its original value.

Those are the kinds of numbers actuaries use when advising pension funds on long-term asset allocations. Pension funds should be able to ride out swings in the equity markets, seeking the best returns over the long term. That is why most pension funds invest most of their money in equities.

That's the theoretical way of looking at the Equity Risk Premium. The practical way is to calculate the Risk Premium implied by what you pay for assets today. If long Treasurys are yielding 5 percent today and the S&P 500 is trading at 800, what is the Risk Premium?

To answer that question, you take the published price-earnings ratio for the S&P and convert it to a bond yield. If the S&P is expected to earn $50 this year, then the price-earnings ratio on the market is 16 times, which implies an earnings yield of 6.6 percent—which means the Equity Risk Premium appears to be just 1.6 percent. But if you assume earnings (and dividends) will rise at roughly 3 percent in real (inflation-adjusted) terms over the long run, and assume 2 percent long-term inflation (which the distinguished Dr. Jeremy Siegel, author of *Stocks for the Long Run,* McGraw-Hill, 2002, shows is the case), the implied Equity Risk Premium on the stock market today is roughly 4.6 percent (depending on the interest rate discount factors you use on earnings in future years). That means the market should be attractive to investors with a long-term time horizon.

Why bother going through the numbers?

Well, at the advent of the millennium, when all the Shills & Mountebanks were shouting Allelulia!, the S&P 500 had an earnings multiple of 42 times actual earnings after deducting the costs of stock options and adding in the true costs of corporate pension plans. This meant that the implied return to someone investing then—in terms of earnings and dividends— was just 2.38 percent. Adding the 3 percent for long-term real earnings growth, you could expect just 5.38 percent returns—at a time when long Treasurys were yielding 5.8 percent. That meant you had an implied negative Equity Risk Premium of 0.42 percent at your acquisition cost. The only way that could be a good investment would be if you assumed real earnings of the S&P would rise at 6 percent for the next two decades, something that has never happened. Yes, the Shills & Mountebanks threw around numbers like 7 percent real earnings growth, but those figures were no more honest or objective than the rest of their sales pitches.

An investor should consider the following points:

- You need a 2.5 percent Equity Risk Premium over the yields available on long Treasurys to make stocks worth the volatility that comes with investing in assets whose price changes are driven by the vagaries of the economy, productivity, wars, investor sentiment, and other real and emotional factors.

- You get that premium over the long run (30 years and more) if you dollar-average into the stock market. You do not get that premium if you bet your wad at a market top.

- What you earn on any one year's contribution is obviously driven by how much you paid to buy a dollar's worth of earnings: If you bought a group of stocks whose combined earnings multiple is 80 times earnings at a time of a strong economy, then unless those stocks have compounded earnings growth of 20 percent a year or more—for decades—you are investing at the rate of a negative Equity Risk Premium. The mathematics of the market say you're going to be a big loser.

- After all Triple Waterfall collapses, price-earnings ratios pull back to lower ranges, because the fevers that drove the manias have subsided. For long-term investors, the years immediately after a Triple Waterfall tend to be years that deliver the highest Equity Risk Premiums over ensuing decades. (They are also the times when the fewest number of people are excited about the outlook for the stock market.)

Before leaving this brief discussion of the Equity Risk Premium, it's worth reporting on a recent debate in print between Dr. Jeremy Siegel and Bill Gross, the head honcho at Pimco, and the world's most famous bond investor, sometimes called the "Warren Buffett of Bonds." This discussion may seem too technical for some readers, but it's worth the effort.

Gross published a provocative analysis of the stock market's Equity Risk Premium on his Web page in September 2002.

- According to his calculations, the Dow Jones Industrials would have to fall to 5000 before stocks would be cheap. (At the time, the Dow was in the 8300 range, so Gross was arguing for a renewed bear market that would make the total plunge since March 2000 a crash reminiscent of the Great Crash.)

- He began by pointing out that 2 percent of the *real* 6.7 percent stocks have earned over the long run came from increased p/e ratios, and that cannot continue.

  To understand this point, think of a stock that's earning $1 a share in 1990 with the market's p/e ratio in the 14 range: It sells at $14 a share. Then assume that a decade later it is earning $1.50 a share (after stock option and pension accounting adjustments) and is trading at the market multiple of 42 times earnings, or $63. Of the implied $350 percent return, only 50 percent came from increased earnings. (If the market multiple were still 14, the stock would be selling at $21 a share.)

- Gross asserts that the real (inflation-adjusted) dividend growth has been just .6 percent annually over the past century. For stocks to be worth more than Treasury Inflation-Protected Bonds (special bonds that increase in par value along with inflation, called TIPS, currently yielding 3 percent), the dividend yield on the Dow would have to be 3.5 percent, growing at 2 percent in real terms going forward, which is roughly twice today's yield. So the market is clearly overvalued unless you assume an almost immediate surge in earnings and dividends.

Dr. Siegel refutes Mr. Gross as follows:

- Gross ignores taxes, which are brutal on TIPS: The holder is not only taxed on the interest, but on the upward inflation adjustment in the principal value of the bond, even though that will not be paid out for many years.

- Stocks have much better tax treatment, because so much of the return comes in the form of capital gains taxed eventually at 20 percent.

- Long-term dividend growth statistics are misleading; Siegel believes that dividend growth from today's levels will be well above 2 percent. (Critics may note that Dr. Siegel is probably the best-known and most persuasive advocate of using long-run return rates on equities as proof that they are, by far, better investments than bonds.)

- The current dividend yield on the market is 1.7 percent, and with a p/e ratio of 20; that means the "earnings yield" is 5 percent, so total implied returns to an investor buying now are 6.7 percent. They will rise at least as fast as inflation, which amounts to a real rate over the long term. With TIPS yielding 3 percent real returns, equities have a 3.7 percent Risk Premium. If measured against the fixed returns of 5 percent on long Treasury bonds, they still have a Risk Premium of more than 2.5 percent because of the long-term increases in earnings and dividends.

Dr. Siegel's mathematics are superficially persuasive. A critic would argue that the actual earnings of corporate America were far less than he was using in his calculation, because of stock option and pension and other accounting overstatements routinely used by corporations. I never believed those published numbers, and have always adjusted for them. By my calculation, the stock market was still overvalued, but by nowhere near as much as it had been for at least four years. Rationality and reason were returning.

To me, the stock market—except for techs and telecoms—at the 800 range for the S&P was mildly attractive. The people at S&P who manage the S&P 500 Index were at that time doing the work on a new way of reporting the earnings of the companies in their index, called "core earnings," which adjust what companies report for stock options, as well as pension fund losses and asset write-downs. By their numbers, the S&P was actually earning less than $19 on a trailing 12-month basis, compared with the Street's numbers in the $45 range.

If you find this debate confusing, join the crowd.

Few investors understand the complexities of the Equity Risk Premium concept. Nevertheless, because it represents the attempt to quantify what distinguishes capitalism from other economic systems, it may be the most important concept in all investment theory. If you put a fair price tag on the long-term rewards for well-directed "animal spirits," you have revealed a powerful truth.

Think of the Equity Risk Premium the way the doomed George Leigh Mallory explained why he needed to climb Everest: "Because it's there."

It's there because it prices the force that has made capitalist nations rich compared with those who use other management and reward systems.

That Equity Risk Premium tells you when you have a decent chance of earning good returns on stocks, and when you have almost no chance. Shills & Mountebanks were most vociferous in urging investors to buy stocks precisely when the very data they were using to seduce the unwary—long-term Equity Risk Premium numbers—showed that stocks were terrible investments.

The long-term daily water temperature average for Chicago's beaches show that swimmers face modest hypothermia risk. Those averages shouldn't be used to schedule a swimming party in January.

INVESTMENT ALTERNATIVES TO EQUITIES

The knack of finding what we want in the woods lies a good deal in knowing what we don't want, and passing it by at a glance.
—H. KEPHART

Treasury Bonds

If you buy a 20-year Treasury bond today, you will be locking in a return of less than 5 percent a year. That is not a very attractive rate for building your retirement wealth. Moreover, that rate is close to the lowest on long Treasurys in 30 years, so it will probably look too cheap sometime during the next economic cycle, which means the face value of your bond will fall. The only way you can ensure you won't lose money on a Treasury bond is to hold it to maturity. If you are already nearing retirement age, you might not feel 100 percent certain that you'll live long enough to get paid back by Washington—although the actuaries say that is your probability.

Treasurys have one attribute that makes them worthy of your consideration: In bear markets for stocks, they trade inversely to equities. They are a low cost form of put option.

A put option gives the holder the right to sell a stock to the other party at a fixed price. It is the equivalent of selling short. If an investor believes S & M Technology is about to plummet, he can buy a put. Supposing S & M is selling at $80 on June 1 and the publicly traded September $80 put is trading at $9. The investor can buy 1000 of those puts for $9000. If S & M is trading at $71 on the day the option is due to expire and is sold, the investor broke even (apart from brokerage). If, however, it fell to $55, he cashed $25,000 before commissions.

What long Treasury bonds do is hardly as dramatic, but since hedge funds trade the highly volatile futures and options contracts on those bonds, the results would be similar. A day the S&P falls 1.5 percent would typically be a day the 10-year note would rise at least 1 percent. Returns on the highly leveraged futures and options contracts would be roughly equal to what the investor would have earned by shorting the S&P, but at less risk—and at much less trading cost.

Long Treasury zeros are useful in your Survival Pak because they trade opposite to stocks, reducing the overall volatility of your portfolio. If the economic recovery falters and the United States falls into a Japanese-style deflationary recession, long zeros will be the top-performing asset class—by far. Any Japanese investor who bought long government zeros as the Nikkei peaked in 1989 and held them to the Nasdaq peak got better returns over the next decade than if he had put all his money into U.S. tech stocks.

So, Treasurys have their place in your Pak, but primarily as low-cost insurance against loss in your equity portfolio at a time of frothy stock markets. Over the long term, their low yields hamper your returns. Other bonds do better.

Corporate Bonds

In late 2002 the buyer of the bond of a highly ranked corporation was offered a yield of 6.5 percent today, roughly a 1.75 percent premium over the yields available on long Treasurys.

The buyer of bonds ranked as junk—in Street talk, "non-investment-grade" or "High Yield"—was offered interest rates as high as 20 percent or even more—if the company meets its obligations. Naturally, those sky-high apparent yields were fair warning that the market considered those bonds very risky.

High-quality corporate bonds are wiser *long-term* investments than Treasurys when Treasurys are trading primarily as put options on stocks. It is my belief that, because of the fast-proliferating hedge funds, much of the trading in the "benchmark" long Treasury bond futures and options is by hedge funds that are switching their asset mix from day to day—and even within the day—by trading in Treasury derivatives. Such trades are cheaper than trading stocks, and a speculator can "sell short" without facing the "uptick" rule. Because they are so cheap and convenient, hedge funds can trade the stock market's ups and downs more easily than if they stuck to going long and short stocks. In my view, this accounts for much of the record levels of volatility the stock market is seeing day to day. Vanilla Treasury bonds are the cocktail du jour on Wall Street.

(When you sell a stock short, it must be declared at the time of the sale, and can only be sold for a price higher than the previous trade; that is designed to prevent the old-style "bear raids" in which speculators just hammered down stocks by continuously shorting them. Treasury futures and options are the low-cost, legal, and genteel way to do something on a big scale that would be illegal on a small scale.)

Although high-quality corporate bonds are the logical bond investment for your Survival Pak at today's spread over speculatively driven Treasurys, it's difficult for small investors to acquire quality corporate bonds at reasonable trading costs. Brokers are not interested in orders for $20,000 face value of corporate bonds, so they'll charge you a big commission to do the deal. If you decide to switch the bond into another investment later, you'll be punished by the commission costs once again.

The best way to acquire corporate bonds is through an investment-quality bond mutual fund.

Real Estate

Some prominent economists have been worrying about the possibility of a U.S. real estate bubble. Although home price changes cannot be documented and analyzed with the precision of stock price changes, and although rates of price change vary by region and by neighborhoods within regions, no one doubts the vigor of the housing market in the past three years. There's also no doubt that housing heated up as stocks cooled off.

One economist who disagreed with those who said the United States was experiencing a bubble was Prudential's Ed Yardeni, who noted that the U.S. housing boom paled in comparison to the UK's, where house prices soared 19 percent year over year—and that definitely was a bubble.

Over the long term, homes have proved excellent investments. However, house prices can fall sharply from lofty levels when mortgage rates rise, because most homes must sell at prices buyers can afford. The Affordability Index matches buyers' incomes with the monthly carrying costs on listed homes. When mortgage interest rates fall to their lowest levels in 40 years, house prices can go up and still be "affordable" to a wide range of buyers.

If you're investing in residential properties as part of your retirement planning, you would be wise to do your shopping when mortgage rates are very high, forcing house prices down so the homes remain affordable to most buyers.

Buying a home or second home at a time of record-low mortgage rates is likely to be a losing investment for most of the rest of an economic cycle. As the economy strengthens and mortgage rates rise, fewer home buyers will be able to pay up to buy homes. Stocks will be outperforming residential real estate at that point.

Of course, if you plan to live in it yourself, then it can be valued differently from portfolio investments.

For retirement planning, own your home or condo, and maybe a vacation property, but rely on financial assets to provide your retirement income. Aim toward having those residences mortgage-free by the time you cash your last paycheck.

The surest saving you ever achieve is the principal repayment component of your monthly mortgage check. In good markets and bad, paying extra to your mortgage company makes good sense. It's your most obvious and certain savings vehicle, which may be why the Street never tells you to sock away more in paying off your own debts.

Bank Deposits and Guaranteed Investment Certificates
The (mostly) unsophisticated savers who ignored the hype from the Shills & Mountebanks and simply searched for the best interest rates on bank deposit instruments have been among the most successful investors in recent years. But this has been one of those unusual times when people who put their money under their mattresses outperformed those who invested in equity mutual funds.

Bank instruments and savings products are now available across a wide range of maturities and vehicles—from five-year CDs to money market funds—both taxable and nontaxable. Even savings accounts have their place, offering interest, checking privileges, Federal Deposit Insurance Corporation guarantees, and 100 percent payout on minimal notice.

They make sense in a Survival Pak because of their safety, liquidity, and up-front investment returns. However, you don't get all those advantages for nothing. Never forget Milton Friedman's dictum that the basis of economics is that there is no such thing as a free lunch.

If these bank vehicles continue to deliver great performance compared to stocks, then it means the economy will have failed to revive from its long torpor.

Low-interest, low-risk bank deposits have sharply outperformed stocks over the past three years. If that happens over the next two years, then the United States will have endured its worst economic crisis since the Depression, even worse than the brutal stagflationary recession of 1973–1975.

Why? Because it's not possible under any respectable economic or financial theory for that to happen without a Japanese or 1930s-style deflationary depression.

In that event, long Treasury bonds will remain the best-performing major asset class, as they did in 2000, 2001, and 2002.

THE IMPROVING OUTLOOK FOR NONTECH EQUITIES

For many investors I meet, the biggest argument against stocks is their own portfolio statements. They do not require any thoughtful analysis of why stocks will remain dismal investments. They think they know the answers.

Having set out the arguments against stocks and stated the basic intellectual argument for stocks, it is time to consider those negative arguments.

Interest rate forecasts are a good place to start. After two decades of falling interest rates, falling inflation, and rising price-earnings ratios, what can we expect in the future?

In last year's election campaign, Democrats told us that the nation's troubles were largely caused by the "Bush Deficits," which were the result of "tax cuts for the rich."

They were, let it be quickly observed, consistent. They had explained the fiscal surpluses of the 1990s by the Clinton tax increase (not the Cold War fiscal dividend), and told us that his fiscal surpluses were paving the way to a bright future of falling inflation and falling interest rates. Now, because of Bush's tax cuts, deficits were paving the way to a future of rising inflation, rising interest rates, and rising unemployment.

Their case seems unshakable until one notes that the lowest short-term and long-term interest rates in four decades have coincided with the nation's rapidly deteriorating fiscal situation since 9/11. It is also worth observing that the most powerful bond rally in history began in 1981, just as President Reagan was cranking up defense spending and deficits. The Reagan era was also, let it be remembered, a time of falling inflation.

In the 1990s many of the best and brightest told us that a New Era based on new technology would mean continued economic growth that would guarantee continued rising stock prices. Now, many of them tell us that investors should expect, at best, 6 or 7 percent compounded returns on equities in the future—roughly the returns available on investment-quality corporate bonds.

The critics' case against U.S. stocks is persuasive.

Indeed, it is the most persuasive argument against equities as an asset class since 1974, when the Club of Rome and other great minds were outlining a grim long-term future for stocks other than shares of companies producing oil, precious metals, and basic materials. A world in which governments would have to assume ever greater control over the economy to (1) allocate the forever scarce supplies of raw materials, (2) to control prices, wages, and markets against seemingly intolerable inflationary pressures, and (3) to create jobs for the endless oversupply of young people was hardly a world in which the corporate sector could expect to prosper.

That was one of the greatest buying opportunities in the history of stock markets (see Chart 10-1).

Consider the elements in the outlook for this decade that should make investors consider stocks a cornerstone of their retirement wealth planning:

- Benign inflation
- Low interest rates
- B-minus prospects for world trade
- Cheap technology
- The Latino advantage

Benign Inflation

Inflation is the great destroyer of wealth. One of the more pernicious come-ons peddled by the 1960s generation of Shills & Mountebanks was the claim that equities were a hedge against inflation. That Shared Mistake was a crucial component of the run-up to the Nifty Fifty Triple Waterfall.

Equities are a good hedge against low-to-moderate, *anticipated* inflation, which we've experienced since the end of the Cold War. Equities are no hedge against double-digit *unanticipated* inflation, because few companies can grow their earnings fast enough to keep up with the price increases. A portfolio of dividend-paying blue chip stocks can be an excel-

CHART 10-1   Dow Jones Industrials (January 1, 1974 to December 31, 2000)

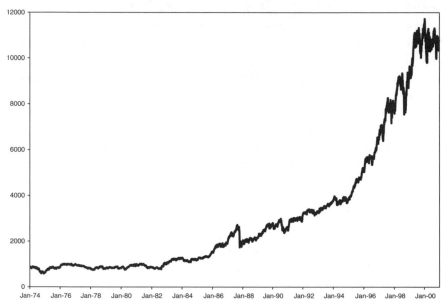

Data courtesy of Bloomberg Associates.

lent hedge against moderate inflation (at least in terms of income), because companies with top-notch dividend records—such as Exxon Mobil, Procter & Gamble, and Kellogg—will tend to increase their payout faster than the rate of inflation. Indeed, part of a sound retirement plan comes from owning dividend-paying stocks, either on their own or through income-oriented mutual funds, because the retiree then has two income sources that rise at least as fast as inflation: social security and the stock portfolio.

As noted previously, the primary challenge to price stability now comes from deflation. It is unlikely to prove devastating for U.S. stocks generally, because central bankers can expand money supplies to offset it, and because so many services in a knowledge-based economy come from professionals who are relatively immune to pressures to control prices.

Likeliest outlook: inflation at a level so low that it would have seemed to investors in the 1970s attainable—if at all—only in Utopia or Heaven (whichever came first).

Low Interest Rates
Low inflation means low interest rates. Low interest rates make stocks attractive in three ways:

1. Compared to bonds, on the kind of comparison used by the Federal Reserve and by asset allocators generally. (Asset allocators are people and organizations that manage balanced funds—or make recommendations to clients who manage balanced funds—on the appropriate exposure levels to stocks, bonds, and cash.)

    The Federal Reserve's model uses the forward price-earnings ratio of stocks compared to the actual yield on the 10-year Treasury note. Yes, it is an imprecise comparison, because the note's yield is known, whereas the forward earnings on the S&P 500 are subject to broad disagreements, depending on the forecaster's view of the economy and on the accounting techniques used. Nevertheless, history has shown that when the "earnings yield" of the S&P 500 was below the yield on the note, stocks proved to be overpriced, and history tends to support the reverse proposition as well. By that test, stocks are good value.

2. Low interest rates lower the carrying cost of corporate debt, making stocks safer investments. U.S. corporations debased, degraded, and, in all too many cases, debauched their balance sheets during the mania, borrowing to buy back stock to cover millions of shares issued to insiders under options, and borrowing to buy other corporations at what in all too many cases turned out to be absurdly high prices. Low interest rates mean that, for investment-quality corporations, carrying that debt burden is eased. For individuals, as the saying goes, the only sure things are death and taxes; for corporations, the only sure things are *debt* and taxes: Once the debt is assumed, it tends to acquire a life of its own. For most companies, low interest rates will make the punishment of past sins less painful.

3. Low interest rates make it much easier for corporations to finance sales to consumers. What may have saved the United States in 2001 from falling into a recession deeper than the 1973–1974 slough of despond was the cheap money available to the automobile companies to allow them to offer zero percent financing, and the cheap money available to mortgage lenders that let them slash mortgage rates to the lowest levels seen in 40 years. Those enthusiasts who predicted a roaring U.S. economic recovery because the nation seemed awash in cheap money were mistaken: Cheap money alone does not guarantee economic progress. However, the converse *is* true: When money is tight and expensive, the economy can go into free fall, and stock prices get savaged.

B-Minus Prospects for World Trade

It may seem odd to suggest a mildly favorable outlook for global trade, given the Bush administration's seeming embrace of old-style protectionism and the intransigence of countries such as France toward any progress toward freer trade in agricultural products.

However, Bush probably learned a salutary lesson from the reactions to his steel tariffs, and he could well be a defender of free trade for the remaining years of his term.

He allowed himself to be convinced that the Democrats would grant him "fast track" negotiating authority for new trading agreements if he acquiesced in major new protectionist ventures, including punitive tariffs on steel and textiles and massive subsidy increases for agriculture. *Fast track* is the term for authorizing trade deals negotiated by an administration. Trade deals have to be approved by Congress; without "fast track," every clause of every treaty is open to multitudinous amendments from every vested interest, a process reminiscent of the torture in which a victim was covered in honey, then tied to pegs sunk in the desert and left to the attention of millions of ants. "Fast track" means that Congress can only vote the deal up or down—it cannot amend it.

Well, "fast track" did squeak through Congress, but the protectionists festooned it with so many trade-blocking provisions that it bears about as much resemblance to the principles enunciated by Adam Smith as do the manifestos of al Qaeda to the principles enunciated by Muhammad.

With that sorry record, why do I include freer trade as a reason for investing in stocks?

Because most global production still crosses most boundaries relatively freely and at low tariffs.

In retrospect, it was fanciful to think that the Doha Round of World Trade Organization reform could have brought down the barriers to agricultural trade. Almost everywhere except in Australia and New Zealand, farm policies are costly, retrograde, and protectionist.

Why are the products that have been trading internationally for centuries those most resistant to free trade initiatives? Milton Friedman cites agricultural policies in modern democracies as evidence of a perverse political principle: The fewer the farmers in the electorate, the greater their political clout.

To understand how this counterintuitive law of politics operates, consider what could be called the bookends of agricultural protectionism: repeal of the Corn Laws in Britain in 1846 and the twin triumphs of old-style protectionism—the U.S. farm bill in 2002 and its cousin, the European Union's Common Agricultural Policy (CAP).

Sir Robert Peel launched Britain on the road to free trade in 1846 by abolishing the Corn Laws that had protected British farmers from cheap foreign-produced grains. That repeal smashed the power of the British landed gentry, impoverished small farmers—driving them into the cities—and set the stage for the development of the American Midwest after the Civil War, which in considerable measure was based on supplying grain to the British Empire. At the time Sir Robert pushed that revolutionary law through Parliament, roughly half the voters in Parliamentary elections derived their incomes from farming.

Contrast that farm policy conceived and executed in the days of aristocratic democracy with the ways modern democracies respond to their farmers' wishes. Today, with farmers protected by tariffs and quotas, and cossetted with subsidies and handouts—to the extent, for example, of nearly half the entire budget of the European Union—less than 5 percent of the electorate in the industrial nations makes its living from farming. In the United States, where the 2002 farm bill raises largesse to previously undreamed-of levels, less than 2 percent of the electorate can be considered full-time farmers. Among the largest recipients of farm handouts are urban millionaires with country estates.

In other words, *pace* Friedman, half the electorate was powerless to stop Peel from achieving free trade even though it meant catastrophe for that group's interests, whereas less than 2 percent of the electorate gets Congress to do what it wants, at vast cost to U.S. taxpayers, large cost to U.S. consumers, and devastating cost to would-be food exporters in the Third World. (Pakistan, which stood with the United States in the War on Terror, was one of the biggest losers from the farm bill.)

Despite the administration's sorry record on agriculture, steel, and textiles, the United States runs a trade deficit of approximately $36 billion each month. In other words, U.S. consumers are getting the benefits of free trade in most goods, and U.S. corporations are benefiting from free trade by outsourcing much of their production abroad.

The end of the Cold War was a boon to free trade. Buyers and sellers could search each other out without having to deal with the red tape and restrictions of wartime. The World Trade Organization and NAFTA came quickly thereafter, and multinational corporations were quick to build international supply chains. At the Ambassador Bridge in Detroit, for example, more trade flows on wheels each day than at any other point in the world. Trucks line up on each side of the border, carrying parts and finished automobiles. If the flow is cut off for even a few minutes, assembly lines may shut down. The beleaguered auto industry learned in the 1980s from the Japanese the benefits of just-in-time inventories.

Although the world is still far from a free trade zone, it is closer to free trade than at any time since World War I. Because of the collapse of communism, more people live and work in economies that are market-driven or, at least, market-oriented than at any time in human history. That means more opportunities for the ingenuity and aggressiveness of multinational corporations—a category in which the United States is preeminent—to trade and prosper.

Because of those *global* opportunities, U.S. stocks and the shares of major foreign multinationals such as Toyota, Sony, and Unilever could well be worth more than in previous economic eras. Great global brands are more valuable under free trade than under protectionism. Given the B-minus rating for the current global trading environment, all one can say is that it's the best of our lifetimes—and just might get better.

Cheap Technology

The technology/telecom Triple Waterfall was a two-edged sword for the global economy and the stock market. On the one hand, that long mania inflicted enormous damage—on the economy and financial markets—and the destruction has not ended. On the other, it led to the development and delivery of an array of technology and software, much of which will help businesses and economies to grow during this decade. Yes, as noted in earlier chapters, the enthusiasts, academics, economists, Shills & Mountebanks, and Alan Greenspan overstated the economic gains from gizmos, but there is no gainsaying that much of the new technology contributes to productivity gains. Although U.S. productivity growth is not back to the lofty levels of the post–World War II era, it's better than it was in the stagflationary 1970s.

Because the tech and telecom industries are so overbuilt, they have no choice but to engage in cutthroat competition for what business is out there. As this is written, there are still far too many suppliers of just about everything technological a consumer may desire. For tech and telecom buyers, this is a dream market. The exception, of course, is Windows application software; this manuscript is written on Microsoft Word, an aggravating word processing system that consumers would not allow to exist were it not for the monopoly position of its supplier, the almighty Microsoft. The worldwide drive for free markets stops at the Gates of Redmond.

Yes, modern man and woman cannot live by technology alone.

But they can sure do it cheaply.

On the assumption that a significant proportion of all the gizmos and systems invented and marketed in the 1990s actually fulfill useful and needed functions, then the continued oversupply of such gizmos and systems from companies that should not exist but are managing to stave off bankruptcy means that businesses and consumers will continue to get real bargains. Mark down cheap tech along with cheap money as reasons to believe that many smart managers will be able to use those resources effectively, thereby increasing earnings and competitiveness.

The Latino Advantage

Primarily because of Latinos, the United States has the best demographic outlook in the industrial world. According to the U.S. Census Bureau, Latinos are now America's most populous minority, having edged ahead of African Americans—an epochal development. Not only is the influx of Latino immigrants—legal and illegal—offsetting the deterioration of American demography, but the access, on favorable terms worked out deal by deal, to the huge, youthful labor force of Mexico gives the United States a manpower advantage no other industrial nation can equal.

The demographic problems unfolding across the industrial world (as outlined in Chapter 8) are on a scale that makes the use of statistics on past economic growth rates look irrelevant. The United States is unique—and primarily because of its Latino immigrants and its free-trade agreement with Mexico.

A report in *The Chicago Tribune,* citing the Selig Center for Economic Growth, notes:

- From 1990 to 2002, the U.S. Latino population rose 74 percent, to nearly 39 million.

- Latino buying power (income after taxes) is $581 billion.

- Latino buying power is increasing at nearly twice the rates of the rest of the U.S. population.

- In 2007, the U.S. Hispanic population is expected to reach 50.2 million, with a buying power of $926 billion—roughly 9 percent of total expected buying power for that year.

When the Cold War ended, Henry Kissinger announced that, for the future, Mexico would be the most important foreign policy challenge for the United States. He noted Mexico's population explosion, and America's population stabilization. He commented on the War on Drugs, a war that was already failing, and on the problem of defending the U.S. border.

What happened was a combination of good management and good luck.

Good management came in the form of NAFTA, a treaty negotiated by George H.W. Bush and enacted by Bill Clinton—against the wishes of a strong majority of congressional Democrats. (Newt Gingrich delivered an overwhelming majority among Republican House members, and William Daley, called in from Chicago by Clinton to round up enough Democrats to put it over the top, put on a masterly performance against the largest union and NGO lobbying operation Washington had ever seen.) NAFTA swiftly transformed substantial sections of the Mexican economy and integrated the supply lines of North American industry in a way that made Mexico a junior partner in U.S. progress.

Good luck came in the form of the booming U.S. economy and a recognition by a wide range of American businesses of the advantages of hiring Latinos. That has been good fortune for many U.S. industries, but in the long run the greatest beneficiary could be real estate and housing.

At the moment, the United States may be in a form of housing bubble (see "Real Estate," in this chapter), and the nation is overbuilt in office buildings and shopping plazas. That happens at the end of every economic cycle.

What matters is the outlook in the next cycle and in the cycles after that. The Latino population is growing rapidly, and is more than replacing itself. Doubtless, the rapid growth of the Latino population will be accompanied by new social challenges, but like each of the successive waves of immigrants in our history—Germans, Irish, Jews, and Italians, etc.—the Latinos are revitalizing our society. Each group's success enriched the nation culturally and economically; the Latinos are the latest chapter in a great story. No other industrial nation has benefited so greatly from immigration as the United States.

I traveled to the Albuquerque area last spring, during the campaign season for local elections. Everywhere I went I saw signs for the competing candidates. Nowhere I went were there signs with non-Latino names. Latinos have already taken over the first rung of the political ladder, and they'll move higher in each successive election. You can't help but be impressed by that, and you can't help feeling that U.S. politics and the U.S. economy will be big beneficiaries of this demographic force.

As the rest of the industrial world faces the uncertainty of a future in which the only certainty is demographic decline, the United States can look with optimism to its demographic future.

SPECIAL KINDS OF EQUITY INVESTMENTS

Small-Cap U.S. Stocks

The heavyweight stocks that drive indices such as the Dow Jones Industrials, S&P 500, and Nasdaq, and the performance of most mutual funds, are large-capitalization stocks.

You should routinely consider diversifying out of reliance on "large-caps" by investing in "small-caps," companies whose stock market capitalization is generally ranked as less than $1 billion. The premier index of such investments is the Russell 2000. (It is made up of the next 2000 stocks after Russell has compiled the Russell 1000 of large-cap stocks.)

If you were an enthusiastic technology speculator, and you've hung on to most of what you bought, you already own many shares listed in the Russell 2000. Triple Waterfall crashes turn large-cap stocks into small-cap stocks—those that continue to be stocks at all. It's doubtful that a portfolio of small-caps acquired when they were large-caps is going to do much for your survival. Bad big ideas rarely become good small ideas. I never cease to be surprised at the number of people I meet who console themselves with a touching belief in what can be best characterized as the financial equivalent of retroactive virginity. They refuse to believe that the tech stocks they hold have been deflowered. They keep trusting that something will happen to restore their stocks' virtue and validity. But, then, surveys show that many Americans believe Elvis lives, and that more than one-quarter of U.S. high school students do not know which half of the 19th century included the Civil War.

A sound way to invest in small-cap stocks is through mutual funds. It is very difficult for part-time investors to get adequate information to make good investment decisions on small-cap stocks. Good brokers can be very helpful, but small-cap stocks are less likely to be long-term buy-and-hold situations than quality big-cap stocks, and history suggests that waiting for sell recommendations from the Street is as productive as waiting for Godot.

Small-caps are part of diversification, but they are both something more and something less than a basic portfolio component. Your Survival Pak should include good exposure to a small-cap mutual fund during periods when small-caps are outperforming large caps, but you should scale back that investment when large caps reassert their leadership.

How do you know when this has occurred?

Once small-cap outperformance has ended for nine months, it is unlikely to come back for at least two years. No one knows the moment when the roles reverse, but anyone who eyes the returns for mutual fund classes as reported in the financial press will know that a new trend is in place within a relatively short time after the market has changed its characteristics.

One problem you'll face in buying small-cap funds: Those managed by top performers, like Judy Vale at Neuberger Berman, can be closed against new contributions. This does not happen to large-cap funds, which are always eager to take on new money. Small-cap managers can quite literally be embarrassed by riches, because it forces them to buy excessively large positions in their companies—positions they may have great trouble liquidating when the market goes sour. When small-caps are hot, you may find that the funds most eager to accept your money are precisely those that, in the interests of your financial health, you should avoid, whereas the ones with the best record are only slightly easier to get into than Fort Knox.

Foreign Stocks

Most Americans confine their equity investing to U.S. stocks.

As one who has been interested in global markets throughout my career, I am familiar with the reasons—and excuses—for this stay-at-home attitude. The usual arguments against investing abroad include:

- They are hard to follow on a day-to-day basis.

- By the time I watch CNBC, read the *Wall Street Journal, Investor's Business Daily,* and all the Wall Street research I get on U.S. stocks, I have no time for boning up on companies abroad.

- Most foreign CEOs avoid talking to the press or to stockholders.

- Their accounting practices are not up to American standards.

- Getting dividends in foreign currencies is a nuisance, and besides, most of those currencies seem to be falling against the dollar most of the time.

- Crony capitalism is the norm in Asia, which means you will not get a fair shake.

- Europeans are so bogged down in regulations, red tape, and socialistic practices that their companies cannot function effectively.

- I can get all the diversification I need here, so why go through all the nuisance of investing abroad?

- It seems that every time I pick up the paper, I read of some disaster somewhere—either natural or manmade. Why should I invest globally when it means that wherever there's trouble, my money is on the line?

■ Returns abroad have been terrible: EAFE (Europe, Australia, Far East), the major international index, has delivered zero returns for the last nine years.

When I hear objections like these, I usually counter with questions like these:

■ Do you restrict your major purchases, such as TVs, stereos, and automobiles, to products made in the United States?

■ Do you reject foreign products in department stores and supermarkets unless no domestic product is available, or do you shop on the basis of comparable price and quality?

■ Do you restrict your vacations to the United States?

■ Do you restrict your leisure reading to books by American authors?

■ With all the recent revelations of dubious accounting and outright sleaze, why do you believe that American companies are more virtuous than foreign firms?

The U.S. trade and services deficit testifies to American willingness to shop for the best deals and to vacation where they expect the most enjoyment.

So why, in what could be the most important expenditures they will ever make—the investments that will determine the scope and options of their retirement—should they buy American to the exclusion of everything else the world has to offer?

The most important objection—nine years of EAFE returns that add up to zero—demands comment. First, that index's heaviest weighting is in Japanese stocks, which means that the index has been distorted by Japan's Triple Waterfall. Second, the bear markets of 2000–2002 have wiped out all the gains of preceding years for major markets abroad; but to be fair, returns on U.S. stocks for that same period are roughly equal to those earned on EAFE, *once you delete the 35 percent rise in the value of the U.S. dollar against the euro.* The sad truth is that a typical institutional buy-and-hold investor globally for the past nine years got virtually all its returns from currency changes. Despite the widespread perception that this was a golden age for stocks, most investors would have done better in Treasury bills—and much, much better in long Treasury bonds.

If I thought it probable that the next nine years would be as poor for equity investors as 1993–2002, I would not be writing a book on investor survival.

Since 1960, leadership among national stock indices has moved around. The country that in each decade was the best performer falls far down in the ranks in the ensuing decade. For the 10 years ending December 1999, the United States was the best major country to investors—both for its stock performance and currency performance. The odds on a repeat of that performance are very long indeed. Some other country or region will become the global investors' favored destination, and that will produce the kind of overvaluation that the S&P 500 had as the millennium dawned.

Most of the objections against investing abroad boil down to convenience, not to informed decisions based on careful weighing of alternatives. Trading foreign stocks that do not have NYSE-listed American Depositor Receipts—ADRs, which trade as easily as U.S. stocks—is indeed more complicated than trading U.S. stocks. *But buying a mutual fund that invests abroad is not.*

Single Country Foreign Funds
Consider the closed-end foreign funds traded on the Big Board. You have a wide range of choice. These resemble mutual funds, in that you pay a management—but not a sales—fee. Unlike mutual funds, you cannot redeem them at net asset value, and the company does not issue new shares at net asset value. They can—and frequently do—trade at big discounts to net asset value, because the Americans who trade them can change their views dramatically about having money in a particular foreign country at any time. The stocks held in the fund are chosen by a global investment management firm.

In my experience, these funds are excellent ways to participate in economies abroad.

Here are three that I have used at various times, when I was interested in those markets. *I do not suggest that they are the best ADRs you will find the day you happen to read this book,* but they are representative.

France Growth Fund
The French economy has been the strongest of the major Eurozone economies in recent years. You automatically get exposure to the euro with this fund, even though it trades on the Big Board in dollars. (See Chart 10-2.)

The Korea Fund
This has been a splendid performer at times in recent years, reflecting the performance of the Korean economy. South Korea is a unique story within

CHART 10-2   France Growth Fund (May 11, 1990 to December 31, 2002)

Data courtesy of Bloomberg Associates.

CHART 10-3   Korea Fund (September 1, 1984 to December 31, 2002)

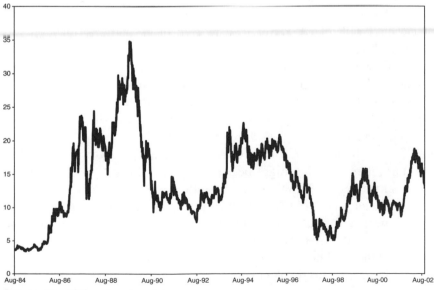

Data courtesy of Bloomberg Associates.

CHART 10-4   Japanese Smaller Capitalization Fund (March 15, 1990 to December 31, 2002)

Data courtesy of Bloomberg Associates.

the "Asian Tiger" group. Under the leadership of Kim Dae Jung, recently retired, that nation has come back from financial crises, survived near-war experiences with North Korea, and reveled in its outperformance of its major rival, Japan.

Kim's story is worth telling, because it illustrates how a great leader can have a decisive impact on an emerging economy.

Kim, a left-wing opponent of the military junta during the 1970s, was imprisoned and sentenced to death in 1980. Shortly after his election, incoming President Reagan's foreign policy advisers told Reagan that they did not believe the junta's claim that Kim was a Communist; furthermore, they said, he might be just the kind of charismatic leader to bring democracy to South Korea. It would be a tragedy, they said, if he were executed. They told Reagan that if he called up the junta leader and made a personal request for Kim's safety—though Reagan was not yet officially president—it might work. Reagan did just that. The junta was angry, but they did not want to infuriate the president-to-be over one nuisance. They agreed to revoke the execution order and eventually freed the prisoner.

Kim came to the United States briefly, then returned to South Korea, where he eventually was elected. He became the major force in transforming the sclerotic Korean economy and its incestuous decision-making structure based on the giant conglomerates, called *chaebols*. South Korea went from economic underachiever to star overachiever, a force for stability and progress in the region.

As you can see in Chart 10-3, it became a rewarding place for investors—until the threats of war from North Korea scared investors.

The Japanese Smaller Capitalization Fund
This is very different from most closed-end country funds. It doesn't invest in the big companies that are included in the Nikkei Index. Its roster of companies come from the equivalent of the Russell 2000—the leading index of smaller U.S. companies.

To me, the fund's performance is a useful gauge of the extent of reform in Japan. If small, entrepreneurial companies I have never heard of and could never get annual reports on are doing well, then things are getting better there, which means I should be taking a look at Sony, Matsushita, Toyota, Honda, Toshiba, and the other major Japanese global companies. Warning: As you see in Chart 10-4, this fund is very volatile; it can be up or down 40 to 60 percent in any year.

The next way to invest abroad is to buy an international mutual fund. Note that global mutual funds invest in the whole world, which means they may have 60 percent or more of their assets in U.S. stocks. International mutual funds buy only non-U.S. stocks. I do not recommend that you consider global funds, because their fee structures are much higher than U.S. equity funds, so you would be paying more on the U.S. equities in your fund than you should. Besides, why pay a manager based in London or Zurich to buy U.S. stocks for you?

Benchmarks for Foreign Funds
Before you buy a foreign mutual fund, find out what index the fund manager uses.

The term for understanding the investment program of a mutual fund is the "benchmark" used by the manager. The benchmark is the specific stock index by which the manager's results are measured. A country-specific fund, for example, will be benchmarked against an index in that country alone: Most American equity funds are benchmarked to the S&P 500. The manager is entitled to take a bow when he or she outperforms the benchmark, and can be expected to offer detailed explanations when bested by that benchmark.

The reason you want to buy a foreign equity fund is to move money abroad. So you need to know how the manager constructs your portfolio.

Morgan Stanley is the leader in constructing global indices, and your manager will benchmark the fund against one of the Morgan Stanley indices. The biggest and best-known international index, as noted earlier, is called EAFE, an acronym for Europe, Australia, and Far East. You should certainly consider having an EAFE-based fund in your portfolio, because you automatically diversify your savings internationally, without having to decide whether Europe, Latin America, or Asia are particularly good values at the time you invest.

At the risk of sounding repetitious, a major reason why Americans should be putting foreign stocks in their Survival Paks is the dollar's bear market. You protect your share of total global wealth better by owning foreign stocks (and bonds) than by keeping all your funds in greenbacks. The German investor who stayed loyally at home during the 1990s, for example, lost heavily in terms of share of global wealth because of the deep devaluation of the deutschemark and the euro.

Emerging Markets Funds

Finally, there's my special favorite in international investing, *Emerging Markets*. I say "special favorite" with a wink, because this is the wildest and wooliest international equities category. To own an Emerging Markets fund means that you can never read a good newspaper without reading some bad news about a country in which you have some exposure. Emerging Markets, as an asset class, tend to include the best-performing international stocks and the worst. When they are good, they are very, very good, but when they are bad . . .

The 1990s were not a good time to invest in Emerging Markets stocks.

Major, gut-wrenching crises hit emerging markets frequently from 1992 to 1999. A wag coined a definition: "An emerging market is one you cannot emerge from in an emergency."

With that background, why do I suggest that Emerging Markets funds could well be in the smart investor's Survival Pak? Here's why:

1. Collectively, the countries included in the list of Emerging Markets have splendid demographic profiles. Ultimately, people build economies, companies, and markets. The industrial world faces permanently deteriorating demography, so an investor should seek true diversification by acquiring exposure to parts of the world with growing, youthful work forces that are large in relation to the middle-aged and elderly.

2. Emerging Markets tend to be more commodity-oriented than mature markets. As of August 2002, the Morgan Stanley Capital Index for Emerging Markets showed that industry weightings were 9.24 percent for Energy, 10.5 percent for Mining, Paper, and Steel, and 4.9 percent for Chemicals, meaning that virtually one-quarter of the companies were in primary and commodity industries—far above the comparative weightings of those industries in the industrial countries. Although the Club of Rome had it wrong that commodity supplies would forever dwindle, the world has gone through a 22-year period in which commodities have been plentiful and cheap. All it would take to get commodity prices rising would be a sustained, synchronized global economic recovery. We have not had one for decades, and we're overdue. The powerful performance of commodities in late 2002 indicated that their bear market had ended and that they had entered a new bull market.

3. The dynamic economies of Asia are heavyweights in the Emerging Markets indices. South Korea emerged last year from the emerging category and is ranked as an industrial society. It is higher risk than other industrial societies because of the growing threat from its northern neighbor. Still in the Emerging category are such fascinating economies as China, Thailand, Malaysia, and India. Some global investment experts think that Thailand is now the most interesting of the established Emerging Markets, with stocks selling well below book value, and with p/es in the four to five times range. Thailand, you will recall, was the country that started the whole string of Asian financial crises in 1997, when it devalued the baht. It has suffered years of misery, but is now coming back. Russia is a special case: an industrial society that is classed—for very good reasons—as an Emerging Market. It was Russia's default that triggered the great global crisis of 1998. Russian stocks have been among the world's few big winners since 2001, and Russia has begun to prepay some of its foreign debts out of its rapidly rising foreign exchange reserves.

4. Those economies that have become indispensable parts of the supply chains of the global multinationals have local publicly traded companies whose price-earnings ratios are cheap compared to those of the multinationals they serve. The West is on its way to becoming a postindustrial region. Health care is already more than

three times the size of the automobile industry in the United
States, in terms of GDP contribution. The fast-growing industrial
companies of coming decades will be heavily concentrated in the
Emerging Markets.

5.   Only by investing in Emerging Markets funds that concentrate on
      Asia will you be able to get exposure to the world's most important
      economic revolution: China. (Yes, you could acquire shares in
      some of the Chinese companies who have listed their stock abroad,
      but for a variety of reasons, these are bad bets for nonprofession-
      als; get a foreign-based fund manager to select a range of Chinese
      companies for you—do not try to outguess the accounting wiles of
      the newly inscrutable. Many well-known Chinese companies have
      even worse accounting than many well-known U.S. technology and
      telecom companies—as hard as that may be to imagine.)

6.   Emerging Markets bonds were, remarkably enough, a great asset
      class in the past decade. According to the *Wall Street Journal,* the
      J.P. Morgan Index of EM Bonds rose 340 percent from 1991
      through August 2002, far ahead of returns on U.S. junk and invest-
      ment-grade bonds (up less than 200 percent) and the S&P 500 (up
      249 percent). That could well mean that those high-risk markets
      are gradually building in the kind of internal asset choices that
      could be the foundation of higher-return, lower-volatility perform-
      ance for their equities in coming years.

Hedge Funds

In recent years, there has been spectacular growth in the number of victims
of West Nile virus and the number of hedge funds. According to the *Wall
Street Journal,* since 1993 the number of U.S. hedge funds on the industry-
leading TASS database (not, I note, the most felicitous name for an organization reporting information that people rely on, given the record of the
Russian news organization) has increased from 805 to 2068, with assets
increasing from just under $50 billion to $278 billion. TASS estimates a
roughly equal number of funds exist outside its database.

Though few readers of this book presumably will have the financial
resources to be eligible to participate in a hedge fund, most will be curious
to know how they fit into the current financial system.

Hedge funds are of all stripes and sizes, so it's impossible to gener-
alize about them. Many of them claim to virtually eliminate stock market risk by using long/short investment strategies. Many others
concentrate on small price differentials within sections of the debt mar-

kets. Others focus on risk arbitrage, which attempts to profit from mergers by buying the shares of one of the proposed partners and selling short the other, or, in outright purchase situations, buying the shares of the company to be acquired at a price below what is offered in the takeover bid. Others go for anything that moves—stocks, bonds, commodities, or currencies.

Because hedge funds use leverage (debt) in their capital structures, they win bigger—and lose bigger—than standard funds. Successful hedge funds tend to be expert users of financial derivatives—futures, options, and swaps. Use of these instruments allows a manager to get completely out of stocks and completely into bonds by selling his position in, say, the S&P and Nasdaq Futures, and buying the Treasury Bond Futures—a trade that can be executed in less than a minute, for face values ranging to hundreds of millions of dollars.

Hedge funds charge healthy investment management fees, and then add on a 20 percent—or occasionally even higher—share in the profits to the manager. It was that fee structure that made George Soros a billionaire.

Many hedge funds—such as Omega Advisors, run by the brilliant Leon Cooperman—are doubtless excellent investments. Many others are doubtless on their way to bankruptcy as these words are written. That so many have appeared in such a short space of time raises an obvious question: Has there been a sudden exponential growth in investment brain power, and if so, what mutation in cerebral DNA occasioned such extra-Darwinian environmental adaptations? If not, has there been a sudden growth in the number of rich fools who believe they can find brilliant people under 35 who can make them even richer?

Most people in portfolio positions in most of the new hedge funds lack long histories in portfolio management. Many had never seen a true bear market until now. That lack of experience creates special risks.

Even in the National Football League, which places such a premium on speed and durability, teams overloaded with rookies and sophomores never win titles. Although, given my long years in this business, I can fairly be accused of some bias in the matter, I believe experience is an important factor in serious institutional investing. Yes, there are times when the biggest rewards go to the most inexperienced. In 1999, when the mania was at its maddest, young fools rushed in where aged angels feared to tread, and those fools were, briefly, huge winners. (Perhaps you ask, what about the saying, "There's no fool like an old fool?" Answer: Not all old portfolio managers are wise, but few young foolish portfolio managers get to be old portfolio managers, just as few foolish little fish get to be big fish.)

If the current rate of growth in hedge funds were to continue for 10 years, hedge funds would collectively own the majority of the world's financially tradable assets, and there would be hundreds of hedge fund billionaires. But then, it's been estimated that if the offspring of one pair of mating house flies were all to live until they had reproduced, and if all their offspring also lived to reproduction, North America would be covered by house flies to a depth of several feet within a year. That has not yet happened.

Neither, I suspect, will that other case of sustained exponential growth.

DURATION AND RISK IN BONDS AND STOCKS

It's one thing for investors to know they're living in the era of a Triple Waterfall crash. But how does that crash influence the performance of investment assets?

Answer: It changes the duration of the stock market. The stocks with the duration characteristic of the crashing group are hit hardest; the stocks with the duration least resembling the crashing group outperform.

That change in the internal mathematics of the stock market evolves as the mania unfolds. During the Optimism and Faith stages in the run-up to the market peak, investors become more willing to assume greater risk because of their growing confidence in the probability of high rewards. In the final, orgiastic phase—the Fanaticism period—public discussion of risk virtually disappears, as the Shills & Mountebanks and elites speak only of the inevitability and durability of rewards.

Then comes the denouement and the three-stage collapse. The Shills & Mountebanks tensely refer to "the bubble" in the past tense, hoping to avert attention from their roles in creating the disaster. "Bubble" is, for them, a useful term, because it connotes something that is gone: Poof! It's over without leaving a trace!

The reality, of course, is that "bubble" is a euphemism for a catastrophic process for which the Shills & Mountebanks and the elites are heavily responsible. "Bubble reputation" comes from the "soldier" stage in the famous "Seven Ages of Man" speech in *As You Like It,* referring to heroism that will soon be forgotten. (That may be why the term was applied in 1720 to the South Sea scandal that was soon a mere memory, thanks to Walpole's shrewd management of the crisis.)

Those who made fortunes from the Nasdaq mania would rather be thought of as dreamy bubble-blowers than as co-conspirators in a $7 trillion stock market collapse and recession. The behavior of a diseased Triple

Waterfall asset class is not like a sudden stroke, from which the victim emerges healthy, but rather like a slowly progressing cancer that disfigures and disables for years before it finally destroys.

Although equity Triple Waterfalls are seemingly diverse, they share one aspect: Their duration gets stretched to absurd length in the run-up, and their duration shrinks back, accordionlike, on the way down.

What is the meaning of duration applied to equities?

Most investors know that the generally used measurement for interest-rate sensitivity in bonds is called duration. It measures the differing responses of bonds of differing maturities and interest rates to changes in rates along the yield curve. (The yield curve is an imaginary line drawn between money market items, such as Treasury bills—at the lower left—ranging up to the very longest-term bonds.)

Years ago, bonds were compared according to their maturities, and bond portfolios were compared according to their average terms. In recent decades, thanks to the widespread availability of computer power to perform the calculations, sophisticated investors have come to compare bonds according to their durations.

Duration is a more accurate measurement of interest rate risk, because it measures the interaction of the coupon rate of each bond issue and the bond's maturity in response to interest rate changes. A 30-year zero-coupon bond, for example, obviously jumps higher in response to a drop in interest rates than a bond with 8 percent coupons attached, because the only return you get on a zero is the payment at maturity, and it always trades at the present value—in terms of existing interest rates—of that maturity payment.

A bond's duration is calculated by adding together all the cashflows—coupons and principal repayments—an investor will receive, up to and including the full principal repayment at maturity, then assuming reinvestment and discounting that total back to the present at prevailing rates of interest.

Assume a $1000 6 percent bond maturing in 20 years. The investor will receive 40 coupon payments of $30 and one payment of $1000. All those future payments are discounted using current interest rates, and the resulting calculation gives the bond's duration. Although it has a 20-year term, its duration would be only about eight years, because the present value of all those payments, reinvested and then discounted back at current rates, would repay your investment in eight years.

Note that the bond's duration changes through time in three ways: as it gets closer to maturity, as interest rates generally rise and fall, and as the shape of the yield curve changes. (When the Fed is tightening, for example, short rates rise, but long rates may hang tough because investors are reassured that the Fed is fighting inflation, which means interest rates are bound to fall. That produces a flat yield curve—the same rate on very short instruments as on very long bonds. If the tightening continues, as in 1994, the yield curve *inverts,* which means short rates are actually higher than very long rates. This, by the way, usually leads to a recession, and a Papa Bear is drawn from hibernation when the curve inverts.)

If the bond had been stripped of its coupons and was trading as a zero, its duration would be exactly 20 years, because that would be when all the cashflow would be received: The zero coupon's purchase price assumes compound interest throughout the term of the bond, but you never actually receive that interest—you get it in one fell swoop at the moment the bond matures.

Long-duration bonds have been the best investments during the 21-year period of declining interest rates. Indeed, the returns realized by investors have been almost exactly in response to how long their bonds' durations have been—the longer, the better (apart from credit risks assumed by investing in corporate bonds).

Zero-coupon 30-year Treasury bonds hugely outperformed all major investment asset classes from 1981 to 1993, sharply underperformed during the brief bond bear market of 1994, then moved back to the head of the fixed income asset class for the period from 1994 through 2002. They also outperformed stocks by a wide margin over the long haul and in the period from 1994 through 2002.

It was easy money. The holders didn't even have to bother thinking about reinvesting the income each year—it was done automatically in the calculation of the purchase price. They beat everybody who invested in mutual funds without having to pay a dime in fees and expenses, and at all times they had the security of knowing that their security was a full faith and credit obligation of the United States.

Conversely, when the next bear market in bonds comes, the worst-performing major asset class will be 30-year Treasury zeros, and cash or Treasury bills will outperform all longer-duration bonds. As the Bible says, "So the last shall be first and the first last." (But it doesn't say precisely when.)

So how does duration apply to stocks?

A share of stock is worth the present value of all future free cashflows earned by the company, because the stockholder is entitled to all distributions—dividends, rights, or proceeds on windup or takeover.

The stock's price-earnings ratio is the valuation of all those potential and actual future distributions. So, in theory, a stock is worth all the future after-tax income it will earn, plus the current value of its stockholders' equity: paid-in capital, plus retained earnings, or, when you look at the balance sheet, all the company's assets less all the company's debts and liabilities; what's left belongs to the stockholders.

The discounted value of future profits makes it sound pretty much like a bond. However, with a bond you know exactly how much the interest payments and ultimate principal repayment will be (barring default or bankruptcy). With a stock you do not know with any certainty what future profits will be.

Furthermore, even if you calculated the profits correctly years in advance (which would be very lucky), you wouldn't necessarily get those rewards. As we saw during the 1990s, management may not use the profits in your behalf. They may feed their egos and justify even more generous stock options by buying other companies at excessive prices. They may buy up your company's shares in the market at excessive prices, thereby boosting their personal stock profits when they exercise their options, while draining the treasury and weakening the company. They may lavish funds on corporate jets and large donations to prestigious charities that hold big galas where executives and their wives can attend and be lionized for their generosity—with your money.

The only profit you can really count on comes in dividends. Milton Friedman argued decades ago that companies should pay out all their earnings in dividends, but have dividend-reinvestment plans so stockholders could reinvest in the company—if they chose. He said leaving funds in company treasuries encouraged CEOs to think they had "honey pots" to spend to boost their egos.

President Bush proposed, in January 2003, precisely the Friedman ideal, asking Congress to end double taxation. Unfortunately for logic and fairness, he made this plea at a time of soaring deficits and a rapidly deteriorating geopolitical outlook. Investors should assume that he will get, at best, a Canadian-style compromise (see "Wisdom from Canada," in Chapter 11).

He argued that the income tax code should be amended to eliminate the double taxation of dividends—because they are paid out of after-tax profits and are fully taxable in the hands of the recipients—meaning an effective tax rate in the 75 percent range. (That comes because the maximum effective corporate tax rate in recent years has been in the 35 percent range and the average maximum personal tax rate, including state income taxes, has been in the 40 percent range.)

So, in theory, the rock-bottom method of calculating the duration of a stock would be the present value of all future dividends. A stock yielding 2 percent would therefore have what amounts to an almost infinite duration—its nominal duration would be 50 years, but when you discount those future payments by current rates of interest, the duration becomes infinite.

But most companies in the habit of paying dividends are also in the habit of increasing them faster than the rate of inflation. So you actually have an offset to the interest-rate discount to recognize present value. That offset comes through growth in earnings over the long term. The stock market continually appraises those earnings prospects by assigning the company a price-earnings ratio. Companies presumed to have fast growth get high p/es; slower growers get low p/es.

Because the likely long-term growth in dividends and in stockholders' equity—which is the true value at any given time behind your share of stock—is appraised by the p/e ratio, the way to assign a duration is to add the p/e ratio (expressed as earnings yield) and the dividend yield ratio.

Suppose a company sells at 20 times earnings of $1 a share—or $20. Its earnings yield (the equivalent of bond yield) is therefore 5 percent. It pay 40 cents in dividends. Its dividend yield is therefore 2 percent. Add those two yields together—getting 7 percent—and divide that sum into 100. The stock has a duration of 14.28 years.

To illustrate that concept with real companies, let's start at the top by comparing the durations of two of the biggest names in the S&P 500, as they stood in October 2002. Think of Microsoft (MSFT) as the preeminent super large-cap long-duration stock and Exxon Mobil (XOM) as the preeminent super large-cap short-duration stock.

At that time, Microsoft had never paid a dividend. In contrast, Exxon has paid dividends throughout its history (and the histories of its predecessor companies, Standard Oil of New Jersey and Mobil Oil). Exxon has increased its dividends every year in recent decades, ensuring that stockholders' incomes at least stay ahead of inflation. (In January 2003, Microsoft announced it would begin paying small dividends. I am leaving this 2002 analysis intact because it shows the differences in duration so starkly, and because there is no other growth stock with the power of Microsoft. Its dividend yield is a mere 0.34 percent, so its character and duration have barely changed.)

As of October 2002, Microsoft was selling at $51.40, and its current fiscal year consensus earnings estimate is $1.92, so the price-earnings ratio was 26.77, which meant the earnings yield was 3.74 percent, and the stock's duration was 26.7 years.

Exxon Mobil was selling at $34.76, with the consensus earnings estimate being 1.62, making its price-earnings ratio 21.5, its earnings yield

4.65 percent, and its dividend yield on its 92 cents current dividend 2.65 percent. Add that yield to its earnings yield and you get 7.3 percent, which divided into 100 gives a duration of 13.7 years—almost exactly half Microsoft's duration.

At its all-time peak of $120, MSFT was selling at 70.6 times earnings, with an earnings yield of 1.42 percent and a duration of 70.6 years. At its all-time peak of $48, XOM was selling at 19.9 times earnings, and had a dividend yield of 1.8 percent, for a duration of 14.65 years.

Then came the bear market. In bear markets, long-duration stocks obviously get hit harder than short-duration stocks, because investors lose faith in the future as stocks plunge.

Microsoft is down 68.6 percent from its high and Exxon Mobil is down 27.6 percent from its high. But the Exxon holder has also been earning the dividend yield, so XOM has been a hugely better investment. If the XOM holder had been continuously reinvesting the dividends during this bear market, then by the time the next bull market gets going, average cost per share should look pretty attractive.

That's exactly how things have worked out over history: Long-term studies of equity returns show that, over the very long term, roughly two-thirds of returns on the S&P and the Dow Industrials have come from reinvesting dividends.

As the XOM and MSFT illustration shows, stocks paying reliable, growing dividends are shorter-duration stocks than those that pay no dividends, just as a 30-year Treasury bond with its coupons attached has a duration that is roughly one-third the duration of a 30-year Treasury zero.

From March 2000 through October 2002, the dividend-paying stocks in the S&P 500 Index were actually up modestly. The entire S&P bear market was accomplished by the plunge in the non-dividend-paying stocks. (One calculation reported in the press said the differential in performance was more than 100 percent in that time period.)

The differential was also vast from 1998 to 2000—but it was the other way around: Non-dividend-paying stocks outperformed dividend payers. (Few tech stocks ever pay dividends; some telecom stocks that used to pay dividends have cut or eliminated them.)

The shorter the duration of a stock, the more up front the returns, and in general the lower the risk. The longer the duration of the stock, the more you rely on returns in the distant future. A stock with a high dividend that is well covered by the company's earnings is much less volatile than a stock that pays no dividends and sells at a very high price-earnings ratio.

When everyone is wildly bullish about the future, long-duration stocks outperform, because the market is enveloped in a gauzy greediness about the size of the pie in the sky.

When the future is cloudy—or scary—short-duration stocks outperform, because investors collectively say, "Show me the money!" Classic example: In the run-up to the 1929 Triple Waterfall, long-duration stocks—particularly technology stocks—led the market to its peak. In the subsequent rallies that occurred in the Third Cascade of the 1929 Triple Waterfall collapse, stocks traded primarily on their dividend yields.

Prominent investment advisers in the 1940s and early 1950s summed it up: Since stocks are riskier than bonds (as proved by the Great Crash), the investor must have a higher income yield on stocks than on bonds to make them attractive investments. There was no assumption about long-term earnings growth, and no assumption about long-term capital gains. Instead of an Equity Risk Premium, stocks were valued at an Income Risk Discount, as if they were mere corporate bonds.

The crash had slashed the stock market's duration. The future was too risky to use in valuing equities; all you could use was the current dividend yield.

When short-term interest rates are high, a dividend yield of 2 percent might seem like a mere bagatelle, but when short-term interest rates are 1.7 percent, then the dividend is at least mildly meaningful.

Most value stocks are short-duration, and most growth stocks are long-duration. However, the duration depends not just on price-earnings ratios, but on dividends—and on the reliability of those dividends.

Just because a stock has a high dividend yield doesn't mean it isn't risky. There is an adage that "in bull markets, investors look at the income statements, and in bear markets, they look at the balance sheet."

When the economy is in trouble, banks get tough on borrowers, and it's difficult for all but the most credit-worthy companies to issue new bonds or commercial paper. The balance sheet becomes the primary tool used in valuation of equities, particularly dividend-paying stocks. Ford's highly publicized financial problems drove the yield on its common stock last year to astonishing levels, as investors concluded there was little chance the beleaguered company could maintain the dividend rate.

After an emotional binge of the proportions we have experienced, chastened investors are more inclined to appreciate the down-to-earth qualities of good short-duration stocks with strong balance sheets and reliable up-front returns.

For the rest of this decade, short-duration stocks should be the cornerstones of a Survivor Pak.

Why not bonds?

With long-term interest rates at record lows, long-duration government bonds have their highest level of endogenous risk in two decades. That risk arises because those bonds have been trading as put options against the stock market (discussed in "Treasury Bonds" in this chapter).

That rather remarkable relationship between long Treasurys and the stock market suggested to me in September 2002 that there was less endogenous risk in a portfolio of high-quality, short-duration, dividend-paying stocks than in long Treasury bonds. The primary locus of endogenous risk had been migrating from stocks to long Treasurys because of hedge funds' use of the futures and options on those Treasurys as a cheap way to sell the stock market short.

Mama and Papa Bear markets end when (1) the primary locus of endogenous risk is migrating to an inversely correlated asset class (bonds or cash), and (2) the market has completed the downside correction in short-duration stocks, which will be the stock market leaders in the next rally. As of October 9, 2002, those characteristics were clear, so I went on CNBC and Bloomberg TV and, for the first time since 9/11, suggested that the bottoming process was now well under way and that investors should begin positioning themselves with the stocks they would want to own for the next cycle.

At some point in the next cycle, animal spirits will not only revive, but they will be seen to revive. That will be a fateful time for investors. Animal spirits are, by their chemistry, long-duration hormonal stimulators. That will be the time when wise investors will be reducing their exposure to short-duration stocks in favor of long-duration stocks (other than technology stocks, which will still face many years in the Purgatory of the Third Cascade of their Triple Waterfall). The wise will maintain their diversification, but they will begin to emphasize the future—not the present—in their portfolio.

The most quoted American of our generation has three classic bits of advice that are relevant for duration analysts:

"It's tough to make predictions, especially about the future."

"When you come to a fork in the road, take it."

His third was the response to a sportswriter's question, "What will be the effect on baseball of the upcoming marriage of Joe DiMaggio to Marilyn Monroe?"

Yogi Berra pondered for a moment, then replied, "I don't know if it's good for baseball, but it sure beats the hell out of rooming with Phil Rizzuto!"

What he deftly did was evade the direct answer about all the unknow-able dynamics of a hazy future, but stated a very obvious up-front result.

That is a sound approach when the economy is in trouble, the bear mar-ket has been grinding on, investors are losing their faith in equities as an asset class, and deflationary forces sap the economy.

As the old commercial for a filtered cigarette used to put it: "It's what's up front that counts." A cigarette is a short-duration investment in pleasure, with long-duration risks.

EXAMPLES OF SURVIVAL PAKS

> *A ration list showing how much food of each kind is required, per man and per week, cannot be figured out satisfactorily unless one knows where the party is going, at what season of the year, how the stuff is to be carried, whether there is to be good chance of game or fish, and something about the men's personal tastes.*
>
> —H. KEPHART

Example One

Assume that Rick is 40 and he plans to retire at 65. He has $180,000 in his 401(k) and $120,000 in his brokerage account and mutual funds. He thinks he'll need $40,000 a year above social security to live his lifestyle, and he expects inflation to average 2.75 percent until and after he retires, which would mean he would need $80,000 a year at that date, and $160,000 at age 91. Allowing for a reduction in his lifestyle through aging, he rounds off his average needs to $100,000. (His grandfather still lives at 95, so Rick assumes he'll be a nonagenarian.)

He assumes a 5 percent nominal return on his stake after retirement, which implies that he would need approximately $2 million at age 65.

He figures he can save $15,000 a year now, rising to $30,000 at age 64, for an average of $22,500 annually, for a total of $562,500.

His starting stake is $400,000, and his average stake would be $681,250. If he earns just 5 percent a year in nominal terms (after-tax) between now and age 65, he will have met his goal.

Example Two

Here is how I set up a trust for a young handicapped person. One objective was to emphasize mutual funds, so the family members acting as trustees would not have to make numerous investment transactions. The diversification was achieved through the group of no-load mutual funds managed by my firm, Harris Investment Management Inc., and distributed as Harris Insight Funds. (In case the reader assumes bias, our family of mutual funds was ranked number eight out of all U.S. mutual fund families for overall quality of investment performance in *Barron's* annual mutual fund survey for 2001, a ranking it exactly maintained in 2002, a consistency in which we take pride.)

The objective was truly long-term, because the beneficiary of the trust was 33 years old, and despite varying disabilities and continuous, extensive medical care, should live a normal lifespan. We wanted a relatively tax-efficient approach.

As the U.S. Large-Cap Equity Fund, I chose the Harris Insight Equity Fund that I manage. It has a relative value style, which means it is neither a pure value fund nor a growth fund, and it is benchmarked to the S&P 500, which it has outperformed over time (except during the mania).

I added our Small-Cap Value and Small-Cap Growth funds, so that their combined weighting roughly equaled that of the large-cap fund.

I completed the equity portions with our International and Emerging Markets funds, with roughly equal weightings. I planned to gradually reduce the Emerging Markets weighting in favor of the International Fund as the next economic cycle matures, on the assumption that the Emerging Markets would outperform the established market in the early phases (which has happened in spades).

I added the three closed-end foreign equity funds (see "Single Country Foreign Funds" earlier in this chapter), believing that it makes sense to diversify investment management styles in international markets.

Finally, I completed the portfolio with our Tax-Exempt Bond Fund, which has ranked number one in the nation for all such funds over the past three years.

That mutual fund portfolio was supplemented with high-quality dividend-paying equities. In many cases, I chose companies that she related to, such as Walgreens, Disney, Church & Dwight (the well-run company that makes Arm & Hammer products, specifically the sensitive skin detergent she always uses), her phone company, Sony, and shares of her father's employer, the Bank of Montreal.

When her equity funds and stockholdings are added together, she has more exposure to foreign than to U.S. stocks. This reflected my view of relative valuations at the time the trust was funded in 2001. As the donors add more assets to the trust, it will be rebalanced, and new purchases will be made reflecting relative valuations at the time.

The overall equity weighting is very high—90 percent—because she currently has no income needs. Her parents support her and will be able to continue that support during their lifetimes. Had long-term interest rates been more attractive at the time the trust was funded, and had the stock market been near its peak, the bond rating would have been much higher. The objective was to build her wealth during her parents' lifetime, moving the growth in value of those stocks from her parents' estate, reducing capital gains and estate taxes. Most of the securities chosen were already held in her parents' portfolios, and they were transferred to her without incurring brokerage charges. (The tax position is that she takes the donors' book costs—mostly below market prices at the time of transfer—on the shares, and she will be responsible for the capital gains when they are sold.)

She has a portfolio that is very well diversified by asset class, number of securities held, investment management style, and currency.

Why diversify so broadly?

What's important is to reduce the portfolio's risk. Diversification by quality is a much less desirable attribute. Apart from many of the more volatile small-cap and Emerging Markets shares, the stocks and bonds she acquired are of good to very high quality. Yes, there's room for speculative positions in Survival Paks, but the investor, understanding that such positions have high-risk characteristics, should ensure that the total portfolio is not overexposed to such securities.

I excluded high yield bonds from the initial portfolio because of the portfolio's very high equity weighting. High yield (the euphemism for "junk") should be viewed as an alternative to equities, because most of the bonds in that universe are of companies where stockholders' tangible equity is minimal, nonexistent, or negative. At the time of funding the trust, I was particularly worried about what I expected would be an endless flood of bad news on the telecom companies, which collectively are a big weighting in typical junk bond funds. On the endogenous risk scale, telecom bonds as a group were top of the mast.

Note that the only diversification I included within the same asset class was in the international equity category, where I included closed-end American Deposit Receipts along with the Harris International and Emerging Markets funds.

Example Three: My Portfolio

As a final example of portfolio construction, it may be of some interest to readers to know how I divide assets among my 401(k), my personal brokerage account, and the mutual funds held in my personal deferred compensation accounts. My 401(k) is 90 percent in the Harris Marketable Bond Fund, and the rest in the International Fund. The only bonds I hold in my brokerage account are tax-exempt municipal bonds—both zero coupons and our Harris Tax-Exempt Fund, and a small position in a Korea Electric Bond that I purchased when it was trading to yield 14 percent because of irrational fears about Korea. The rest of my account is in equities, heavily weighted toward Canadian oil and gas producers, gold miners, financials, and defense contractors, and with sizable percentage commitments to international mutual funds, American Deposit Receipts, and Emerging Markets. My tax-deferred account is diversified across our family of equity funds and the Marketable Bond Fund, with special emphasis on the small-cap, international, and Emerging Markets funds.

As of December 2002, I had gradually built my equity weighting across my portfolios over the previous nine months to its highest overall equity percentage exposure in four years—65 percent (up from 35 percent in 2000).

11

Course Corrections and Tips for Staying on the Trail

The arts of fire-building are not so simple as they look. . . . In wet weather it takes a practiced woodsman to find tinder and dry wood, and to select a natural shelter where fire can be kept going during a storm of rain or snow, when a fire is most needed.

—H. KEPHART

WHEN TO REBALANCE YOUR PORTFOLIO

You rebalance your canoe when it tilts too far to one side.

You should also rebalance your portfolio when it is tilted too far away from your desired asset mix.

So you have a Survival Pak with what you (and your adviser) believe is the right mix of assets: different kinds of equities and bonds, plus a small short-term fund.

Then the stock market soared. Your portfolio now has a radically different makeup. What should you do?

Suppose that Harry aims for an asset mix of 50 percent U.S. stocks, 15 percent foreign stocks, 25 percent short and medium-term bonds and/or bond mutual funds, 5 percent long bonds, and 5 percent cash.

By mid-1999 he finds that U.S. stocks are now 70 percent of his portfolio. What should he do? His broker, heavily influenced by the firm's Shills & Mountebanks, says, "Let your profits ride; sell your losers" (which are overwhelmingly European and Asian stocks).

He should remind his broker that it's his money, not the broker's, and that he took a lot of time researching what asset mix was right for him. He should then rebalance his portfolio to get it back closer to his long-term goal:

1. He should sell some U.S. stocks, emphasizing long-duration stocks that have moved up sharply, and he should buy some medium and longer-term bonds.

2. Or if Harry is truly uncomfortable with the tax consequences of large-scale selling, it could mean writing covered call options on the riskiest stocks in his portfolio. (If you don't know what this involves, don't worry too much. Rebalance your portfolio by lightening up on your riskiest stocks. In my experience, many investors who lie awake worrying about paying capital gains taxes and who decide to use elaborate strategies to avoid paying them end up having few capital gains to worry about.)

Example: Suppose that one big reason for the portfolio's imbalance has been the sensational performance of its tech stocks, led by an absolutely amazing IPO—Shills & Mountebanks Technology—he got into that has gone to the moon.

Harry owns 2000 shares of S&M that he bought at $12 a share, and it now trades for $125 a share. He should sell all or a substantial part of his position so (1) he doesn't have such an overweighting in equities and so (2) he isn't carrying so much endogenous risk. (He obviously has enormous endogenous risk on a stock that has made that kind of move, and he also should realize that with the market up that high, he also has high exogenous risk, even if it turns out that S&M's transasteral deframinator gets pitched by George Gilder and even if its CEO gets on the cover of *Time*.)

Suppose that two years later, after the Triple Waterfall collapse, Harry has only 39 percent in U.S. stocks and 11 percent in foreign stocks, with 10 percent in long bonds, 33 percent in medium-term bonds, and 7 percent in cash. What should he do?

He should begin to rebalance his portfolio back toward his long-term goal by:

1.   Reducing his long bond position
2.   Reducing his short- and medium-term bond position
3.   Beginning to rebuild his equity exposure with regular purchases of high quality, short-duration, dividend-paying stocks

This kind of bear market rebalancing should never be done in a hurry just because Harry has seen one of the leading Shills & Mountebanks on TV proclaiming the birth of a new bull market. They were so wrong for so long, why should he believe them now? (What he should be asking himself is: Why do they still have jobs and why does any self-respecting TV channel let such shameless shills talk on their tube?)

WHEN SHOULD I HAND THE RESPONSIBILITY TO SOMEONE ELSE?

An old campaigner . . . has learned by hard experience how steep are the mountain trails and how tangled the undergrowth and downwood in the primitive forest.

—H. KEPHART

- Maybe you think you can manage all your finances by yourself.
- Maybe you think you would rather trade totally online.
- Maybe you think you would like some help while still keeping the decision-making power.
- Maybe you think that your own investment performance is an overwhelming argument for handing the portfolio over to full-time management by professionals.

Each of those strategies is right for some investors. The only certainty is that you won't be able to manage your portfolio after you're dead, and you might want to factor that into your planning.

The financial world has an array of products and services to help you manage your wealth. Insurance agents, mutual fund distributors, financial planners, and stockbrokers offer the resources of large financial institutions through individuals, partnerships, and local offices.

One major help these professionals can provide is assistance with your tax planning. U.S. inheritance taxes are among the world's highest, and one would have to be an incurable optimist to believe that the total repeal scheduled for 2010 will actually happen.

You can run your portfolio by yourself most cheaply by trading your stocks online, for a pittance, with a discount broker. You can get help in running it by using a full-service broker backed with a good research department for somewhat larger costs. You can leave the securities selection to trained investment managers and buy mutual funds through a bank, broker, or an investment planner. (Unless you really have the experience, patience, and time to manage your portfolio effectively yourself, what you spend on a *good* broker or financial planner could well be the best investment you'll make.)

I believe that each of those products or services has its merits. But there may come a time when you want—or need—to hand over actual management of some or even all of your financial assets to an organization dedicated to looking out for your interests—now, later, and after you die.

These are the trust departments of banks that offer full investment services, with which they can fold in their expertise on trusts, wills, taxes, and estate planning. I strongly recommend that you use an organization that specializes in this kind of service, has been in it for decades, and is well capitalized. Get references from existing clients, particularly from heirs who are the beneficiaries of arrangements made by their parents with that institution, and ask a few questions:

- How well were the estates planned?

- How tax-effective were they?

- How well have the investments been managed?

- How complete are the reports?

- Are the trust officers now handling your parents' file competent and caring, and do they relate to the beneficiaries as the true objects for which the account was created, or as locked-in clients who should be glad to be partaking in the earlier generation's largesse?

In the last decade, I have spent a lot of time with my counterparts at the Harris, the private bank of the Bank of Montreal–Harris Bank organization. They have taught me a lot about the sophistication of services available through the top-line U.S. private banking organizations. Part of their expertise comes from experience in dealing with the consequences of marriage breakups and family strife as the generations change, particularly in family-owned businesses. If you're fortunate enough to accumulate meaningful resources that you hope to leave to your children and/or grandchildren, then in a real sense a part of you will be at risk for generations to

come. The ultimate outcome will depend on how well the financial consequences of interpersonal relationships of people are handled. Family fights
are the worst fights.

Helping you construct sound long-range investment policies is only a
part of what private banking organizations can do for you. If you involve
them in your estate planning, and maintain them as your trustees and managers after you die, you improve your chances that the wealth you accumulated will be a blessing—not a curse—to your heirs. No, you can neither
rule from the grave nor achieve immortality. What you can do is offer guidance and protection, so that at least some of the values that helped you to
accumulate those resources are influential in their longer-range disposition.

HOW SHOULD I MONITOR MY MANAGERS?

If you do not manage all your money yourself, then you need to monitor the
managers you are using—whether they're stockbrokers, mutual fund managers, or bank trust departments.

This may sound so simple that it doesn't warrant special comment. Just
get the investment return numbers and compare them to the market and to
the listings in the papers of the top-performing funds.

Following this approach led many investors to dump their broker,
mutual fund manager, or trust department during the mania years. Too
often, listening to friends bragging at the golf course or at cocktail parties
induced the suddenly greedy into switching their funds to hotshots and
aggressive growth funds, where they thought they would get much richer
much quicker. Instead they got much poorer much quicker.

Here are a few rules for investment survival:

1. Information and pitches about investment returns received along
   with alcohol should be considered cautiously, applying the same
   rules as those for driving while under the influence.

2. When salespeople quote impressive performance numbers on
   managed accounts, ensure that you're given full details on the
   manager's style and to which index he or she is benchmarked.

3. When reading mutual fund results in the financial pages, check
   into which style category the manager is included, and how many
   years the current manager has been in that post.

4. "Past performance is no guarantee of future results" is the SEC-
   required line on all sales information. It is also a 100 percent accu-

rate statement. If a manager's results last year were truly astounding, odds are the results this year will be ordinary—or worse.

5. Do not let your ego get in the way of your wealth accumulation. That may mean being willing to let somebody who is in the business full-time look after your money; it also means that if there is something in a report you do not understand, ask.

WISDOM FROM CANADA

Canadian investors had a rough time of it during the early to mid-1990s. They were forced to invest 80 percent of their tax-deferred RRSPs—the Canadian equivalent of 401(k)s—in Canada at a time the Canadian stock market was an underachiever compared to the U.S. and most European markets. Their personal income taxes were among the highest in the G-7, and their economy underperformed the United States'. These were the consequences of decades of tax and spend policies. Foreign investors, knowing as much, tended to shy away from Canadian equities.

As if those weren't enough reasons for Canadians to look south in envy, their currency responded to political mismanagement by sliding south. The Canadian one-dollar coin has a loon on the obverse. The loon is a diving bird, and that's just what "the loonie," as Canadians call it, did.

The good news is that the Canadian attitude toward taxation and spending is changing. The federal Liberals were first elected on a platform of rejecting the key economy-opening policies of the previous Conservatives. Once in office, they reconsidered. Canada also became a participant in NAFTA, and, arguably, a far bigger beneficiary from that treaty than the United States. Canada consistently runs trade surpluses with the United States, the destination for 82 percent of Canadian exports, and exports are now more than 43 percent of Canadian GDP, among the highest in the world.

Canada has also benefited in recent years from having an independent central bank that has a flinty attitude to inflation. Governor David Dodge is on his way to being a global star in the rarefied world of central banking.

Ultimately, those positive factors will pay off. The Canadian dollar is no longer diving, and I believe it will strengthen against the U.S. dollar when the greenback enters the next phase of its long-term bear market. Canadian stocks have solidly outperformed U.S. stocks in this millennium, and I believe they will continue to do so. Canada has a wide range of fine short-duration stocks, including its big banks and insurance companies and its leading oil and gas and mining companies.

Meanwhile, Canada is way ahead of the United States in two very important kinds of taxation that affect investors.

What many investors—including many Canadian investors—do not realize is that Canada has two tax advantages for investors that outweigh almost all the nation's perceived disadvantages: It has a dividend tax credit that goes a long way to eliminating the double taxation of dividends, and the nation has no inheritance taxes.

Double taxation was used by the technology and other go-go U.S. companies to justify their refusal to pay dividends. They argued that stockholders did far better when the corporation bought back its own stock in the open market, which drove up the stock price, giving shareowners capital gains at the low rate. This proved to be another example of a principle I learned years ago: "To almost every question there is an answer that is clear, concise, coherent, and *wrong*."

Why are tech stockholders worse off when management buys in stock?

Because the really big winners from those large-scale stock buybacks are not the public owners of the company's shares, but the owners of tens of millions of stock options. The share buybacks are needed to prevent massive flooding of the market by the insiders when they exercise their options, and to support the stock price as the insiders sell. Look at the most conspicuous losers of recent years, such as Nortel and Lucent. If they still had the money they spent buying in their shares at prices 20, 30, or 60 times current levels, they would not be on the deathwatch list.

Canadian tax law mitigates the double taxation effect by granting a tax credit for 20 percent of the dividend. The effect is that Canadians should have greater interest in reliable dividend-paying companies than do Americans. It means that Canadian retirees should be emphasizing quality dividend payers, such as the banks, rather than bonds.

On inheritance, Canadians are not liable for estate taxes, but their estates are liable for capital gains taxes, since the deceased was deemed to have sold the stocks held at the time of death (subject to the spousal rollover provisions, which are similar to the U.S. tax treatment). From a tax standpoint, compared to the United States, Canada is an expensive place to work but a cheap place to die.

Many Canadians die in residences they own in the southern United States, having retired to sunnier climes. That can create estate tax problems. If the reader is in this category, he or she would be wise to get advice from U.S. tax professionals. (This is another example of the ways in which having private bank trust services from a bank that offers such services on both sides of the border can work to your advantage.)

One other aspect of Canadian investments is worth special mention: The Canadian equity market offers a wide range of income trusts, including oil and gas, energy, mining, and other income streams. The best of these are splendid short-duration investments (see "Duration and Risk in Bonds and Stocks," in Chapter 10) that have very attractive tax treatment. The U.S. market also offers tax-advantaged trusts, but not to the extent that they're available in Canada.

CHAPTER 12

Conclusion

FREEDOM IS THE RIGHT TO CHOOSE.
The power to exercise that right in its fullest dimensions comes from three kinds of health—physical, financial, and mental.

Wilderness survival depends on health and wisdom—wisdom based on personal experience, knowledge of wood lore, and the ability to analyze risks, both during planning periods and in real time.

So does financial survival.

From 1993 to 1999, the yield from the financial environment, in outdoor terms, was Blueberry Hill with unlimited fish and game. Even careless novices lived sumptuously without stress. The financial environment then changed from inviting to hostile.

In nature, the bountiful harvest years do not last. Those seven fat years will be followed by a string—not necessarily seven—of lean years. Cycles are the norm. When the lemming population explodes, so does the population of snowy owls. When the lemming population shrinks, the snowy owls that survive are those that fly south, diversifying their food supply to include other small mammals.

Historians may well conclude that the Triple Waterfall collapse of technology and telecom constitutes the greatest ever blot on the escutcheon of capitalism. Not only did it unleash a bear market that wiped out $7 trillion of wealth, it caused an utterly unnecessary recession. Those who abused the capital markets to enrich themselves on a grand scale, while inflicting damage to the economy on a grand scale, are the most disappointing exemplars of capitalist morality in the history of capitalism. They professed the virtues of risk taking and gutsy entrepreneurship, but they designed their compensation programs to enrich themselves in the way big city machine politicians used to ensure their personal wealth from the perquisites of office. In many cases what they did—and are still doing—is legal, but it belies their rhetoric about identifying their interests with the stockholders'. Contrast that to Warren Buffett, who has never received a share option, earns $100,000 a year running Berkshire Hathaway, and assures his stockholders that they'll do as well as he will from the company's fortunes.

Never before had so many entrepreneurs become cultural heroes. That process of deification was part of the process that drew millions into equity investing. They wanted to share in the wondrous profits produced by the wondrous products produced by these wondrous people. When investors learned how these supposed paragons became so rich so fast while the companies they led were heading into serious troubles or outright destruction, the disillusionment was profound.

Some of them, it appears, were outright crooks, and one hopes they will be severely punished. What's most appalling is that the great majority of them apparently violated no laws or statutes and continue to enjoy their prestige and perquisites, along with their ill-got billions. In the history of capitalism, never have so many given so much wealth to so few for such short-lived performance.

In the coming years of fallout from the endless investigations, recriminations, lawsuits, and bankruptcies, we will hear continued assaults on capitalism itself. We will be told that CEOs as a class are dishonest—not just a passel of New Economy CEOs—and that some new economic system is needed to protect us from the evils of capitalism. In fact, what's needed is accounting reform—and that has begun. What's needed more is investor skepticism about Wall Street research that chooses to overlook spurious accounting—and that is emerging. What's needed most is investor rage against those who cashed fortunes in stock option profits on companies whose share prices were on the verge of collapse—a collapse that came not from a depression or even a deep recession, but from the most modest economic downturn in 50 years.

The stock plunges did not come from exogenous economic risk. They came from the endogenous risks of management expertise in producing earnings through creative accounting, managerial expertise in ensuring that top insiders got rich regardless of what happened to stockholders, and managerial incompetence in dealing with a slowdown in demand at a time when overinvestment had created excess supplies of technology gear.

The great new breakthrough that accounted for most of those lustrous profits reported for most of the New Economy companies was the audacity of the accounting: No Silicon Valley companies were willing to account for the cost of the stock options that were making senior officers astoundingly rich. Silicon Valley companies relied on "pro forma" accounting statements that had the effect of including all the good news while excluding most of the bad.

In too many cases, the CFOs proved more important than the engineers and techies in terms of producing results that drove investors mad with desire to buy the stocks. The engineers and techies produced new gizmos and new software, but with the exception of monopolist Microsoft, few companies were able to produce sustained profit growth on their breakthroughs, because the barriers to entry into that ebullient marketplace were so minimal.

Microsoft apart, the marketplace is probably as close to perfectly competitive as modern capitalism has seen. And the accounting was probably equally as close to sustained imperfection.

The law of compound interest is the greatest force in the universe; the law of compounding profit overstatements is the greatest force in that small part of the universe known as Silicon Valley. (There is precedent for that kind of geographic exceptionalism. Woody Allen once rejected an accusation that he did not believe in God by replying, "I believe that there is an intelligence to the universe, with the exception of certain parts of New Jersey.")

Wall Street was part of this process of degradation of accounting principles, and some of its big names should be held in low esteem by true capitalists, along with many of the big names in Silicon Valley. Some of those who have committed crimes have done far less harm to the economy and the financial markets than some of those who violated no laws.

Fortunately, there are attractive investment alternatives to placing one's savings with companies whose senior officers have displayed such minimal concern for stockholder returns (while displaying such maximal concern for their personal returns). Looking forward, investors will have a wide range of quality stocks that use scrupulous stock option accounting. Reform is progressing, albeit less quickly than the market would wish.

Until Nasdaq's collapse, the issue of stock option accounting concerned only a minority of financial analysts, accountants, and students of corporate governance. Why were people of the stature of Paul Volcker and Warren Buffett so upset about them, and why did Silicon Valley and Wall Street fight so bitterly to prevent their publication? We learned the answers to those questions when we heard about the new class of insiders who had suddenly made billions in profits on options of shares from companies whose stockholders—and, in many cases, bondholders—had experienced financial losses of trillions.

That relationship between the unseemly rewards to the powerful few and the losses of the powerless many was at the root of the Triple Waterfall—the defining financial and economic event of our era.

In the arid investment landscape after the floodwaters of the Triple Waterfall have receded, investors need to concentrate on returns that are both visible and reliable.

In the 1990s, an American had no obvious reason for investing abroad. To most observers, the U.S. currency, the economy, and accounting and governance practices were the foremost in the industrial world.

Investors have now learned they were somewhat wrong about the underlying strength of the U.S. economy and the dollar, and terribly wrong about the quality of U.S. accounting and governance practices. They will, presumably, be more willing to investigate opportunities abroad.

In the 1990s, almost all asset classes except cash gave good nominal and real returns, both in absolute and risk-adjusted terms. Long-term interest rates kept falling most of the time, even though the economy continued to strengthen. That meant investors made effortless capital gains in both bonds and stocks. Capital gains in tomorrow's investment landscape will not be effortless, and they will not accrue simultaneously to bonds and stocks.

When the economy revives, the Federal Reserve will have no choice but to raise short-term rates, and, at the very least, that will prevent further capital gains from bonds. It will also tend to put a cap on any tendency toward euphoria in the stock market.

When interest rates are as good as they can get, can house prices be far behind? The winning asset class of this millennium has been housing. Plunging mortgage rates and plunging stock prices have produced a boom in house prices that many fear is another bubble.

We have learned from the Fed's 12 interest rate cuts that cheap money could not save the stock market from collapsing under the pounding of the Triple Waterfall. But when mortgage rates plummet, "the house always wins." Cheap mortgages have produced costlier homes. Those who have consoled themselves that even though they lost heavily on tech stocks, they can make it back on their home, are in for a shock when the economy comes back.

At some point the economy will revive, and so will interest rates.

When the Fed tightens again, the housing boom will slow. If the economy is so strong that the Fed has to tighten more than 75 basis points, then mortgage rates will rise significantly and housing prices will sag. If the economy continues to strengthen and the Fed gets short rates back up to 3.5 percent, housing prices will fall sharply. If the economy booms again, and the Fed gets short rates back up to 5 percent, well, just hope you don't have to put your house on the market. House prices—unlike Triple Waterfall stock prices—always eventually come back and go to new highs, so if you keep up those bargain basement mortgage payments, you will eventually profit, even if you bought one day before house prices peaked.

Water far downstream from a waterfall can collect in stagnant pools when there is no further descent in the riverbed. Today's low interest rates and slow economy are the downstream consequences of the technology/telecom collapses. What will get the water moving briskly again in coming months?

At some point, the U.S. economy will surprise the doubters by moving back to the path of sustained growth. That will help faltering economies in the rest of the industrial world. Asia is already in its strongest economic and financial shape since 1996. A global economic recovery should unfold by the end of 2003.

The War on Terror will take many twists and turns. If the United States is seen to have achieved an overwhelming victory against terror groups and terror-sponsoring states, insurance rates will pull back from their onerous levels, and so will oil prices. Those are two big costs on global economic activity imposed by al Qaeda and other terrorist organizations. The global economy would be a big beneficiary from a U.S. victory in Iraq and a prolonged period in which Islamic terrorist activity was sporadic and small-scale.

If, on the other hand, the terrorists acquire weapons of mass destruction and murder hundreds of thousands or millions, then the consequences for financial markets and the global economy would be catastrophic. Is it moral and ethical to raise the question in public? Is there any real hedge for investors against the financial and economic consequences of a suicide bomber detonating a nuclear explosion in New York or Chicago? Should investors think about the unthinkable?

Successful investing is about trying to discern future reality and then deciding how much to pay for it. We may have entered a period in human history where the risks are unquantifiable.

One reality is that no major asset class is likely to perform in this decade as it did in the 1990s. Yet, long-established investment principles will continue to drive returns. How can that paradox exist?

Answer: because the 1990s were an aberration. Perhaps they were America's reward from the Fates for the virtue of persevering and winning the Cold War. If so, then the nation's current discontents could be the punishment for how the nation frittered away those blessings.

Chances are, few of us will see such a beneficent confluence of sustained peace, falling inflation, falling interest rates, strong economy, and strong stock prices again in our lifetimes. But we do need to invest in our lifetimes, even if there are terrorists and terrorist states out there, and even if they are acquiring access to weapons of mass destruction.

When Frodo learns of the threat of the Ring, he says to Gandalf: "I wish it need not have happened in my time."

"So do I," Gandalf replies, "and so do all who live in such times. But that is not for them to decide. All we have to decide is what to do with the time that is given us."

Use your time with wisdom.

Index

About the Author

Donald Coxe's three-decade investment career has been almost equally divided between the United States and Canada. He has been CEO of successful investment management firms in both countries, and has been a respected portfolio strategist and research director on both sides of the border. His personally managed portfolios have routinely outperformed bond and stock market indices, and institutional investors have frequently voted him a top-ranked strategist. He is a sought-after speaker at investment and public policy conferences across North America and abroad.

Since 1993, he has resided in Chicago, where he serves as Chairman of Harris Investment Management. He is also Chairman of its sister company in Toronto, Jones Heward Investments. Together, these firms manage $35 billion in pension and mutual funds.

A prolific writer, he got his start in New York as an Associate Editor with *National Review*. His work has appeared in leading publications in the United States, and he currently contributes a weekly column on financial markets to *Maclean's*, Canada's leading current affairs and news magazine.

Because of his knowledge of pension funds and capital markets, he has been an adviser to governments on social security and benefits programs in Canada and the United States, and has addressed actuarial conferences across North America.

His academic career includes a degree in Modern History from the University of Toronto and a degree in law from Osgoode Hall Law School. His background includes practicing law, playing piano in dance and jazz bands, acting as a public school trustee for a large school district, serving on boards of charitable foundations, and conducting music and drama programs for handicapped children.

He is married, with two children.